The Definitive Guide to Taxes for Indie Game Developers

Indie developers and other people who work on games for a living face all kinds of interesting income tax and small business formation issues that more traditional businesses simply don't: not being geographically bound, relying on alternative funding, long periods of time with no income, and having multiple options for tax treatment of game development costs. *The Definitive Guide to Taxes for Indie Game Developers* addresses the income tax issues that the average indie game developer is most likely to encounter, in the context of the American Internal Revenue Code and types of taxes.

Written by a former tax law practitioner turned game developer and industry consultant with a decade of tax and accounting experience, this newly revised *Second Edition* includes key provisions of the 2018 tax reform, such as the new qualified business income deduction, R&D credit expansion, and permanent reduction to corporate income taxes. In-depth explanations and examples are provided along with references to Tax Court and Supreme Court cases relevant to each tax benefit.

Key Features:

- Includes authoritative sources with relevant IRS publications, Revenue Rulings, and Tax Court cases

- Features easy to read, accessible, and humorous language: No legalese!

- Approaches how business decisions as an indie developer affect personal finances

Readers will gain a thorough understanding of taxation's role in managing a game studio of any size and going indie with any lifestyle. The accompanying companion website is a valuable resource that is annually updated to keep current on any tax reforms.

The Definitive Guide to Taxes for Indie Game Developers

Second Edition

Rachel Presser

CRC Press
Taylor & Francis Group
Boca Raton London New York

CRC Press is an imprint of the
Taylor & Francis Group, an **informa** business

Second edition published 2023
by CRC Press
6000 Broken Sound Parkway NW, Suite 300, Boca Raton, FL 33487-2742

and by CRC Press
4 Park Square, Milton Park, Abingdon, Oxon, OX14 4RN

CRC Press is an imprint of Taylor & Francis Group, LLC

First edition published by Sonic Toad Media 2015

ISBN: 978-1-032-37185-6 (hbk)
ISBN: 978-1-032-37180-1 (pbk)
ISBN: 978-1-003-33573-3 (ebk)

DOI: 10.1201/9781003335733

Typeset in Minion
by codeMantra

Access the companion website: https://www.routledge.com/9781032371801

Contents

Acknowledgments, vii

Author, ix

LEVEL 0 ▪ Introduction and Why Game Developers
Need Their Own Tax Guide   1

LEVEL 1 ▪ Types of Taxes   9

LEVEL 2 ▪ Chaotic Neutral Married: Filing Statuses   19

LEVEL 3 ▪ Deductions, Credits, and Exclusions   23

LEVEL 4 ▪ Solid Recordkeeping as an Important
Framework   31

LEVEL 5 ▪ Tax Impacts of How Your Game Gets Funded   45

LEVEL 6 ▪ Is Game Development Your Livelihood
or Just a Hobby?   53

LEVEL 7 ▪ Business Entities: Formalities and Setting Up   71

LEVEL 8 ▪ The Load Screen: Startup and Organizational
Costs   93

LEVEL 9 ▪ The Main Event: Business Expenses   101

LEVEL 10 ■ The Lost Levels: Nondeductible Items and Net
Operating Losses   117

LEVEL 11 ■ The Bonus Round of Travel, Meals, and
Entertainment Expenses   125

LEVEL 12 ■ Turn-Based Strategy: Depreciation of
Big-Ticket Items   163

LEVEL 13 ■ Gone Home: The Deal with Home Office
Deductions   181

LEVEL 14 ■ Late Game Content: Minding Your QBI   197

LEVEL 15 ■ Why Your Fiscal Year Is Like Dinosaurs Living
with Humans   207

LEVEL 16 ■ How You Treat Development Costs and All the
Gamasutra Content That Filled You with False
Hope about the R&D Credit   221

LEVEL 17 ■ Rubber Chickens with Pulleys in the
Middle (Inventory)   235

LEVEL 18 ■ Sales Tax: Torment   241

LEVEL 19 ■ Classification Quest: Do I Issue a W-2 or 1099? 249

LEVEL 20 ■ Where in the World Are Your International
Dev Team Members?   261

LEVEL 21 ■ How to Choose and Work with a Tax
Professional   271

INDEX OF CITATIONS, 285

INDEX, 305

Acknowledgments

I'D LIKE TO THANK the incredible indie developer communities who have been behind me ever since I made the career change I always dreamt of, especially frequent hosts like the Powell Group, East Coast Game Developers Conference, and Playcrafting: the Taxes for Indie Developers class is what led to the first edition of this book that was originally self-published on Kindle. I'd like to extend a thank you if you bought the first edition as well!

Other thank-yous: My long-time right-hand man Danny Flexner of Flex Pixel Design, Zach Strebeck, Sean Connelly and Danielle Zarfati at Taylor and Francis, Wolters Klouwer CCH, Cornell Law School and Legal Information Institute, Don Mikrut and Marc Goldman, my wily monitor lizard Liora, and may Yael the original Sonic Toad's memory be a blessing, and my family and close friends for putting up with me barely answering texts, as I feverishly expanded and updated the original manuscript into an even clearer and more comprehensive version that took several major legislative shifts into account.

No pixels were harmed in the writing of this book.

Author

Rachel Presser is a former Enrolled Agent who retired from the tax profession just to use her years of taxation and business advisory experience to help other creatives go their own way with Sonic Toad Consulting. After co-running Himalaya Studios as CFO and Executive Producer for several years, Ms. Presser shifted her focus to Sonic Toad's business and creative projects. She has taught courses and spoken at various gaming industry events about business development and tax law issues for indie developers. She lives in Los Angeles with her monitor lizard, Liora.

Introduction and Why Game Developers Need Their Own Tax Guide

W HEN *THE DEFINITIVE GUIDE to Taxes for Indie Game Developers* was first published in 2015, both the media landscape and level of business-focused resources for game makers were drastically different than they were when this second edition was published.

Today, people still use Amazon as a search engine, and trillions of terabytes of information are still exchanged through the Kindle ecosystem daily. As my own career and business ventures evolved alongside the tax and legal landscapes that independent game developers must navigate, I recognized the value in working with a publisher when it comes to a topic that is subject to frequent updates such as tax law. While entrepreneurship concepts themselves may not experience as many dynamic and frequent updates, business practices still change with time, and the business of games is absolutely no exception. So many evolutions took place from the publication of the first edition to the updated version you're holding now!

The 2018 tax reform was the largest and most sweeping material change to the Internal Revenue Code since the Reagan administration, and the pandemic we didn't see coming resulted in numerous temporary and permanent changes. At the time of preparing this manuscript for publication, the Inflation Reduction Act of 2022 has also introduced several key and

DOI: 10.1201/9781003335733-1

1

lesser-known provisions, also both temporary and permanent, that will materially change tax filing on business and personal levels.

In turning over the keys to Taylor and Francis/CRC Press, annual updates will be provided every December so that owners of this book can access a webpage with an overview of key tax law changes most likely to affect indie game developers.

In spite of frequent law changes, however, there are business and recordkeeping principles that rarely or never change. Properly organizing your business and building recordkeeping infrastructure isn't as exciting as making a game and getting players hyped up about it: but it's direly important to ensure your continued success, especially if you aspire to game development becoming your primary income source.

Without further ado, I know that indie developers are busy and constantly absorbing information. The tone of this book is intended to be conversational, relatable, and as concise as possible. You want to read a book that's in accessible English, not material more appropriate for the annual National Society of Accountants meeting. I also tried to make the topics at hand fun, which is actually not as difficult as it sounds, given some of the absurd Tax Court cases you're going to read about.

Up ahead, there will be times I have to provide figures to explain certain rules and show examples, but otherwise tried to keep tables, figures, and legalese to a minimum.

But just like with programming and complex narrative design, many of the concepts covered are cumulative. Subsequently, I would recommend reading this book in order, rather jumping to specific topics, especially if you are unfamiliar with the language of tax administration. Many of the references in later chapters build upon material that was already covered.

If you are not a game developer reading this, there is a strong chance you are an accountant, tax professional, attorney, or other business and financial professional trying to gain an understanding of the gaming industry. You may be seeking new clients in the video games industry, particularly from the growing population of indie developers. You should be aware that this book is ultimately targeted toward game developers themselves. However, I've included citations from authoritative literature if you are an accounting professional seeking quality supplemental materials and guides to share with your clients.

So with all that said, the author deserves a proper introduction here. After all, why should you trust this Rachel Presser character with your tax questions, primarily the ones pertinent to making games for a living?

I hold both a B.S. and M.S. in accounting and until 2020, I held an Enrolled Agent or EA license. (Did you just ask yourself, "What's an Enrolled Agent?" Don't worry, you'll read about that later.) I let my license lapse when it was apparent I wasn't returning to the accounting field, having found success and fulfillment in the games-dominant but mixed media career I always dreamt of.

Between working on my degrees and license, I worked as an independent tax practitioner for most of my time in the field but also worked at retail tax outlets and boutique tax law firms. I've done tax returns for everyone from food stamp recipients to people requiring 2,000-page tomes to account for all their holdings. I wrote about tax law for trade publications like *Tax Pro Journal*, then thousands of pieces of content for small CPA firms and tax attorney practices, in addition to large brands such as eFile. com, Jackson Hewitt, TaxBuzz, and Rocket Lawyer.

I chose 1099 fraud and abuse as my master's thesis topic, as there is incredibly complicated case law regarding whether a worker is an employee or independent contractor, and this practice area has only grown more confusing with Trump-era Department of Labor rules and more narrowly-devised state laws with countless ensuing clean-up bills such as California's AB5. For three years running, I also worked with a large test development company and directors of the IRS' Return Preparer Office to write and assemble all three sections of the Enrolled Agent professional exam and determine what the basic minimum competency for Enrolled Agents should be.

Most of all though, I co-ran Himalaya Studios for seven years as CFO and Executive Producer, and oversaw raising six figures on Kickstarter for our point-and-click adventure/RPG hybrid *Mage's Initiation: Reign of the Elements* in addition to kicking my own Unity and Ren'Py projects around. My experience co-running an indie studio followed by a games-focused solo business, coupled with my tax law and accounting background, made me uniquely qualified to write the first and only tax law guide meant for indie developers.

I waited my entire life to write and design games. I tried to leave the tax field time and again, but didn't officially do so until mid-2014. After going through various teaching gigs and vagaries of the Craigslist economy, I started Sonic Toad when I realized there was a demand for experts who knew both the games industry, and more esoteric sides of business and accountancy. Not someone who analyzed Activision and EA sales numbers all day for management consulting firms: ground-level small business advisers who had been in the trenches of independent game development.

I decided to go one step beyond and not just provide flexible consulting services, but an ongoing resource to indie developers and digital creators. It was quite clear how developers badly needed and wanted resources for dealing with the tribulations of indie developer life, and how shifting to entrepreneurship actually affects our personal lives even more than our finances.

I was inspired to write the first edition of this book upon seeing that there was a real dearth of "brass tacks" type of business resources for indie developers, with taxation being one aspect of many that gets vastly overlooked.

Having taught a variety of business courses for Playcrafting NYC, a game development education collective that started as a humble Meetup. com group then became a massive industry hub on the East Coast, I was inundated with requests to show regulars how to do their taxes and explain how tax law affects business decisions.

With the success of *Basics of Business for Indie Developers* and *Best Practices for Crowdfunding*, a class on taxation was born. I was then spurred to write the book upon seeing numerous accountants' submissions to Gamasutra in a bid to get game developers as clients, but they were clearly eyeing AAA and III studios, as it was incredibly evident they did not know how "garage-level" game-making actually impacted one's personal and business finances. Ergo, I figured it was time for other indie developers to benefit from the years of my life that were spent in the tax and accounting fields.

Why do game developers need an industry-specific tax guide? Isn't it just "canned software" like my family accountant said?

Most general tax guides aren't tailored to a specific industry like this one is, and are also fairly dry and not engaging. While they may contain relatable real-world examples, the readers can tell they were written for a general audience. The writers also fell victim to familiarity blindness in marketing a tax guide to the average person on the street but it was really written for other tax professionals.

Every industry has its quirks and games are no exception: We need our own taxation guide. As the industry luminary Don Daglow often says in his annual GDC talks, "Games is a big business but a tiny industry." Because it's so tiny, it's incredibly misunderstood, and there's very little proper support from the professional sector as a whole.

Hence, I wrote the very first tax law book *by and for* indie developers, as one who has been in the trenches and remains there.

Many of the tax law areas and concepts outlined here could apply to any business type; but let's face it: the Internal Revenue Code is hundreds of thousands of pages long. Looking for just the right code sections if you lack background in tax law can take days. IRS publications and instructions are written in Tax: not English.

Throw in some of the complicated aspects of game developers' operations and personal finances that may also affect those decisions, and it's a recipe for your head feeling worse than waking up after you hit The Fig at E3 and wound up downing a bottle of Jaeger chased with trashcan punch. (As of the second edition, E3 is no more, so replace this reference with your event of choice.)

Obviously, not every single tax topic and situation imaginable can be covered. And as I frequently heard at continuing education sessions, every taxpayer is unique. But this book should give you a solid understanding of how your taxes will change as a result of working for yourself in some capacity, whether you're already a full-time indie developer, trying to transition to just that, or you make games strictly as supplemental income.

Game devs also aren't a monolith: some of you are artists first and entrepreneurs second. I've met devs who really want to grow their businesses and others who want to keep it simple. That's all fine and well, but the law applies to you all the same. Becoming familiar with it helps you make more informed choices regardless of which creative and career paths you embark on.

The world is forever changing and becoming more digitally-centered. We live, communicate, and create in a world of e-signatures on documents, powerful devices that fit in our pockets, and virtually never dealing with a human at the bank. In spite of this, America's legislative and business environments are unfortunately stuck in the era of file cabinets, offices being the only place you can possibly get work done, and fax machines that were built before the Eisenhower administration.

Subsequently, the IRS has painfully outdated infrastructure as do most state tax departments.

Game developers don't just have the concerns any other small business owner or freelancer would: We also have to worry about some of the more nebulous areas of tax and business law that apply to people who frequently relocate out of choice or necessity.

Some of us work alone. Others work in teams whether temporarily or for the long haul, and don't know how to structure them to achieve that sweet spot of both the least amount of hassles and taxes paid. Most indie developers also have to do something else to subsidize their pursuits such as a day job, participating in the gig economy like driving for Uber, renting out your couch on AirBNB, or if you're like me, yet even more self-employment via multiple sources like consulting work and passive royalty income from books or music.

Game developers and the numerous sub-professions within the games industry share many aspects of different fields: fine and digital art, technology, software, music, writing, digital media, and sometimes there are retail applications, given that many indie studios crowdfund and supplement their income with merchandising efforts. This is why indie developers require special attention in their tax planning considerations.

The original book, and this new update, pinpointed what I felt were the most important issues an indie developer is likely to run into, so you will be aware of what to discuss with your tax professional and the types of records you really need to hold onto. More often than not, there are benefits you probably weren't aware of. There are also pitfalls that are better hidden than all the Easter eggs in any given Daedalic adventure.

Just like how engines and operating systems upgrade, so do tax laws. Ever have Unity update their best practices and go to a new version, then all of a sudden your last build is completely inoperable? That's how tax code updates work sometimes.

Some items completely die (sunset) after a certain point, or you were previously eligible but no longer are. Other items are indexed for inflation, meaning that certain benefits remain and the amounts are apace with inflation. It's sort of like how processors generally get faster when new computers hit the market. You can still wind up buying one that runs like a snail on Valium waiting for the Second Avenue subway to be built, but chances are a laptop built in 2022 runs faster than one built in 2010.

This book is also predominantly about federal US tax law. International developers filing US tax returns may want to pay attention to Level 19, however, if you plan on working with any American studios for a significant timeframe or have US-sourced royalty income, as most of the major distributors like Steam are US-based.

State and local taxation is not covered at length, because otherwise this book would wind up being longer than the entire *Dreamfall* series. However, certain aspects of state tax differences will be covered.

THE FINAL NOTE BEFORE THE GAME BEGINS

I really hope you're working with a tax professional, unless you also come from a background of preparing complex tax returns. The last chapter is dedicated to finding one. Please swear upon your favorite swag right now that you're going to use this book with them: because there's also an entire index in the back with authoritative literature and Tax Court citations for harder-to-find topics and discussions of case law.

With that, this cutscene concludes.

Types of Taxes

THINK ABOUT HOW YOU don't start making a game the size of *Stardew Valley* in your first game design class: You start with the very basic foundations of getting a build functional, like a one-room maze or a short sidescroller using assets skinned from your favorite game. Maybe *Unity Asset Store: The Game* before you're ready for your first commercial release.

Similarly, becoming familiar with the terms used and types of taxes you have to pay in the course of business provides a solid foundation. Just like how you don't need to regularly watch three-hour video essays on ludonarrative dissonance to become a good game designer, you don't need to regularly watch the Tax Court docket and understand the contents. But knowing the basics is invaluable for making informed business decisions, especially in the crucial formation stage.

In short, income taxes aren't the only class of taxes. They're definitely not the only taxes that will affect you.

Subsequently, there are different types of **tax returns** that may require quarterly or annual filing. For instance, you must file your personal tax return annually. Your business may also have annual filing requirements, or there may also be quarterly or monthly filing obligations depending on the state or country of incorporation. I've frequently heard people use the term "tax return" when they receive a check from the IRS, but the correct term is **tax refund**. A tax refund is what results when you paid more than you were assessed for the year and chose to have it refunded (opposed to allocated to next year's tax bill). The "return" is the actual form you filled out.

DOI: 10.1201/9781003335733-2

Even right on your personal tax return that you have to file every year, there are other types of taxes aside from income taxes but it just doesn't seem like it because you're filing and/or paying them all on the same form.

Think about how you are likely to pay for your driver's license in a different place and file different forms compared to procuring a business license or a marriage license, with the filing process and payment collected through different offices or websites. It's all revenue to the government regardless. There are certain taxes you can pay in the same place as your personal income tax bill, as you're going to read about. But just like procuring those different licenses, the way you calculate and pay some of these taxes is going to be a bigger pain than others.

INCOME TAXES

If you're a *TV Tropes* fan, **income taxes** are *Exactly What It Says On the Tin*: These are the taxes based on how much income you earned during the year after applicable benefits and penalties. Income tax can be assessed on a salary you earn working for someone else or from working for yourself in some capacity. It can also be assessed on royalties, investment income, rental income, certain prizes, and numerous other sources.

But not so fast! If the notion of income taxes was THAT simple, why does the average American spend 40–80 hours every year trying to stay compliant with the tax code, 100–120 hours if an entrepreneur like yourself? Why do some people have income tax returns that are just a couple pages and can be completed in less than fifteen minutes, while other people have leviathans that outweigh dictionaries and take a team of accountants at least two weeks to prepare? (By the way, that statement isn't an exaggeration. The largest tax return I ever prepared exceeded 5,000 pages, and I had to collaborate with a tax lawyer and my office's junior partner.)

The tax code is highly complex, as previously stated. But income tax is the first and foremost tax that all taxpayers have to deal with, no matter what they do for a living: You'll pay income tax whether you work a regular salaried job and your employer takes taxes out of your paychecks for you, and you'll also pay income tax if you work for yourself.

Income from a job, your share of profit from a shared business, or solo self-employment is called **earned income**. Even if you don't have any earned income, you likely still have to pay income tax such as if you're subsidizing game-making by having rental properties or living off investment income like dividends from stocks. That kind of income is called

unearned income. Unearned income won't be discussed much in this book, but this distinction is important, because the law applies to earned and unearned income differently.

Much unearned income has **preferential rates** attached to it, such as the rates for dividends and capital gains, while other types have more stipulations attached. Most income, including earned income, is taxed at what's called the **ordinary rate**. Ordinary rate is simply the rate you will wind up being taxed at for most of your income, which is often higher than the preferential rates for investment income.

Federal income taxes are **progressive**. Generally, the more taxable income you have, the higher the rate you must pay. However, the **tax bracket** you fall into may not tell the whole story because we're going to discuss the different types of tax-reducing moves available to you and how your situation is different depending on how you formalize your game development pursuits.

Income taxes are paid at the federal level, but depending on where you live, it's likely you also pay a state income tax. Some cities and counties also collect local income tax, such as New York City and Philadelphia.

There are also personal income taxes and business income taxes. As this book deep-dives into the options you have for formalizing your business, it includes the pluses and minuses of each option as the rules for personal and business taxes are quite different. Your personal taxes will also be affected by what form your business takes: it may be for the better or worse, depending on what happens with both your business and personal life.

Regardless, **personal income taxes** and **business income taxes** have differing rules, even though it doesn't seem that way at first; think about how C++ and C# have similarities but execute differently. That's basically how business and personal income taxes can be, at a glance.

In short, income taxes are based on how much income was generated. We're going to spend plenty of time later exploring the numerous ways to strategize paying less income tax at both the top-down level and as situations arise during the tax year, but that's the basic gist.

PAYROLL TAXES

Payroll taxes, unlike income taxes, are conditional on employment, meaning that these taxes are paid as a result of *being* an employee or *having* employees.

If you work for an employer, there are taxes that you pay and taxes that your employer pays. The most common payroll tax that we all have to contend with is Social Security and Medicare, which are separate components but combined they are referred to as FICA taxes (for the Federal Insurance Contributions Act). These taxes have to come out of your paycheck at a total of 15.3%, but your employer pays half of this amount (7.65%) out of their own funds.

You'll see the sum of these amounts paid for the year on **Form W-2** after the year ends, and a new tax filing season begins. If you did not receive Form W-2 and have taxes properly withheld, you may be misclassified, which is covered in Level 18.

Payroll taxes are generally flat, or **regressive**, unlike progressive income taxes. If your employer pays you $60,000 per year, both you and the employer are paying at the same exact 7.65% rate as your supervisor who gets $100,000 per year.

However, while the sky's the limit on how much you can pay in income tax, that's not the case for the Social Security portion of FICA taxes. Of that 7.65% tax you and your employer have to pay, 1.45% is for Medicare and 6.2% is for Social Security. Medicare taxes have no limit, but there is a cap on Social Security.

At the time of writing, the Social Security cap was last indexed in 2020 with an annual maximum of $137,700. Let's say you now earn a $200,000 salary at your job: You're not paying 7.65% per year, you're actually paying in at 5.72% ($137,700 * 6.2% = $8,537, 1.45% of $200,000 is $2,900. $11,437 is 5.72% of $200,000). The employer also pays an identical $11,437 out of company funds.

Since this percentage decreases as income continues to increase well past the cap, this is why FICA is a regressive tax rather than progressive. Lower earners pay a higher share of their income despite the flattened rate.

This cap applies for the entire year, so if you switch employers or have a second W-2 job and you already hit the $137,700 cap, you will need to get the excess Social Security taxes refunded to you when you file your personal tax return.

Payroll taxes don't start and stop at Social Security and Medicare, though. Unemployment insurance is paid at the federal level (FUTA) and state level (SUTA).

FUTA is always paid by the employer, never the employees. FUTA entails complex calculations based on the wages paid and how many hours the employee is putting in that are out of this book's scope, but this employer-only payroll tax is typically 6% of the employee's gross pay.

SUTA can be even more arcane based on variegated state unemployment insurance laws. Some states, such as New Jersey, also mandate employees to pay into the state unemployment fund in addition to the employer contributions.

If you have employees, you will need to factor payroll taxes into tax and financial projections. If you're hiring a full-time programmer at a base salary of $80,000 per year, you'll need to account for your share of FICA and FUTA alone, plus SUTA and payroll administration costs. Just like how you definitely wouldn't receive a flat $80,000 if you were that employee, as an employer you would be paying at least 15% more than that $80,000, depending on administrative costs plus state and local payroll taxes.

Payroll taxes carry an onerous administrative burden in addition to their actual cost. Federal payroll tax returns must be filed quarterly, and diligent records concerning wages, salaries, hours, and employees' states of residence need to be kept (remote employment has become more of a hot-button issue in the COVID era since the publishing of the first edition). You may not be thinking about hiring employees just yet, or decide not to altogether, but becoming familiar with the concept of payroll taxes will shape your decisions, budgeting process, and tax obligations.

SELF-EMPLOYMENT TAX

Self-employment tax is likely the tax you will be the most concerned with as an indie developer, especially if you operate alone and want to keep it that way.

To sum it up, this is the 15.3% FICA tax just like what you'd have to pay if you were receiving a regular paycheck with taxes taken out, but it isn't calculated the same way, and you're also going to pay this 15.3% by yourself. After all, what would the phrase "self-employed" mean without you also being the employer in the eyes of the law?

The FICA cap applies to self-employment tax just as it would if you were an employee. But while your and your employer's shares of FICA are determined by your gross pay, self-employment tax is determined by your self-employment income after expenses.

This tax can be harder to beat down than income taxes, as you'll see in later chapters. However, the biggest determinants in how much self-employment tax you're obligated to pay will be how much revenue was generated and how much you spent. Then what you spent the money on and how those expenses appear on paper.

Self-employment tax will sneak up on you if you're not mindful of your income and expense fluctuations, so it's important to know which items must be reported as income and which expenses you are allowed to deduct, because this vastly complicates your tax situation more than having income reported on Form W-2.

CORPORATE INCOME TAX

We briefly touched upon the concept of personal versus business income taxes earlier. Corporate income taxes are a form of business income tax, but with specific nuances.

There are two types of corporations: S corporations and C corporations. When you hear about corporate income tax rates on the news when a Congressional proposal comes out or during election cycles, they are always referring to C corporations.

S corporations not only have many limitations with complicated rules and administrative burden, but also present several opportunities for major tax savings. C corporations offer greater separation of your business from personal finances and far more leeway with business formation compared to S corporations. Depending on your circumstances, however, choosing a C corporation can either result in astronomical dual-level taxes or save you more money and red tape than you could ever imagine.

Basically, S corporations don't pay taxes at the entity level like C corporations do; your personal tax rate will apply. Corporate income taxes have brackets like personal taxes do.

Both S and C corporations require their own tax returns in addition to your personal tax return. The concept of entity-level taxes will be discussed in Level 7, but regardless of whether taxation takes place at the entity level or personal level, they need their own business tax returns regardless of what your personal tax return will look like.

Sounds confusing? Level 7 has more in-depth information on the different corporations and how you treat income generated by them, in very easy to understand terms. In summary, corporate income taxes can be entity level or personal level.

FRANCHISE TAX

Franchise taxes are assessed on the state and/or local level. Typically, franchise taxes are based on your company's right to exist or the capital structure.

Capital structure may refer to how many owners of your business there are. In most cases, capital structure is in the context of forming corporations with respect to how many shares are issued regardless of the number of owners and who owns those shares.

If ownership stakes and the number of shares issued don't change year to year, you shouldn't face an exorbitant franchise tax increase. But if you issue more shares to accommodate incoming investors or experience other major shifts in ownership, the state or city can assess a higher franchise tax.

Then regardless of ownership and share issuance, some states and cities just charge an annual franchise tax for the business to exist, no matter what entity it is. California has one of the highest franchise taxes in the US, charging $800 per entity per year, even if it's a single-member LLC that brings in little income. New York has a biannual franchise tax system, charging LLCs just $9 every two years from the date of incorporation. Unlike California's annual bill, many New York business owners often forget that this franchise tax exists since it's so small and isn't charged every year.

Whether the franchise tax is annual or more esoteric like New York's system, pay careful attention that you file and pay your franchise tax bill on time and use the right forms for it. Many small business owners get lulled into a false sense of security that they are compliant and up to date on their tax obligations so long as they took care of federal income tax filings. If you forget to pay franchise taxes, the state can revoke your permission to do business. The world needs to play your games, so set reminders in a calendar or your phone or hire a service to put this obligation on autopilot.

SALES TAX

Sales taxes are the bane of customers and businesses alike. Another regressive tax, the burden is on the customer to pay the tax when they buy something, and lower-income earners pay higher shares of their income on these taxes compared to higher earners. Then the burden is on you—the business owner to ensure sales tax is correctly collected on taxable items, and then reported and remitted to the correct jurisdictions in a timely manner.

As game developers who primarily deal in the digital realm where corporate behemoths with their own accounting departments like Valve,

Apple, and Nintendo take care of obligations like sales tax and VAT since the sale is facilitated through them, most readers don't need to worry about sales tax right away.

This is not the case if you are a board game developer and would like to sell directly to players on your website, through third-party platforms such as Amazon and eBay, and in person at events. You're going to need a plan for sales tax infrastructure immediately.

Even if your income is primarily digital, but you plan on selling swag and physical versions of the game on your website or at events, you will also need to determine your sales tax requirements before you make that first sale.

You MUST be aware of the obligations to collect and remit sales tax, because revenue-starved state and local governments won't buy "I didn't know I had to charge sales tax" if they determine that you made too many sales to ignore (even if you actually didn't know).

There are over 9,600 sales tax jurisdictions throughout the United States. There is still no federal sales tax referendum, although the chapter on sales taxes has been updated to include the Wayfair case argued in the Supreme Court since the first edition was published. Subsequently, making sense of sales tax administration is like having a never-ending list of bugs you can't get out of the game even if you put hungry toads in the mainframe.

Poor handling of sales tax is also what frequently causes small businesses to shutter at worst and face heavy fines at best. While a brick-and-mortar business or one that relies more on the sale of physical goods is more apt to run into sales tax problems than primarily digital game developers, there still much rapid legal and administrative change taking effect. The Internet was a Wild West as far as dated administrative procedures go, lawmakers didn't predict how much the economy would soon run on digital product sales, and laws have yet to catch up with no universality on the horizon for the time being.

In summary, sales taxes are a transaction-based tax with collection and remittance procedures that vary based on location.

TRANSFER TAX

The most well-known transfer taxes are estate and gift taxes. Estate tax, or the death tax, is paid when you die. Federal gift taxes are paid if you gift someone more than $16,000 during the year. This is the per donee (recipient) exclusion for 2022, which is indexed every two to three years by the IRS while state gift tax rules vary.

If the donor doesn't file a gift tax return and pay the gift tax, the government will go after the recipient if they become aware of a large taxable gift. Gifts given for medical and educational expenses don't incur the gift tax, provided that the institutions are paid directly. Paying colleges and textbook vendors, doctors and hospitals, prescription drug suppliers, and so forth is treated as a tax-free gift. It wouldn't be the case if you gave the recipient cash to pay their medical bills or tuition.

The only exception to this is if you are married. Two spouses can make unlimited transfers to each other throughout the year provided you are still married, because they're treated as one taxpayer under the law of the land no matter how independent and couple goals you may be as individuals.

Transfer taxes are a topic that game developers should be aware of since it is common for indie developers to be wholly or partially supported by a spouse, non-spouse romantic partner, parent or other family member, or share ownership of their business with people they are related to. Subsequently, personal and business transfers may be mixed up, and it is important to learn the distinctions between income and transfer taxes, and when they would and wouldn't apply.

In addition to the personal level, transfer benefits and exclusions can also apply to business entities, which is an incredibly complicated topic out of this book's scope. But, to explain it briefly, if you already have a business and want to start a new company if you get an investor or otherwise change/divest ownership, but there's intellectual property and cash to transfer, you may be in store for entity-level transfer taxes that are completely separate from income taxes.

However, gift taxes deserve a mention, because they have been brought up in legal and taxation discussions on crowdfunding, fan donations, digital tip cups, and other aspects of the digital creator economy. When we get into the methods of funding a game, there's a chance you might be dealing with gift tax avoidance to some extent, which will be covered in the next chapter. Estate tax isn't discussed in this book, as it only affects a very minuscule amount of taxpayers, and inheritances generally do not trigger income tax.

*   *   *

While this isn't every single tax type under the sun, these are the types you should be aware of in going into business for yourself. You'll be picking up other pieces of tax lingo throughout the book too, but it's important to make the distinction between these different tax types since you'll have to deal with each type differently.

But just like the greatest strategy games of our time, you can devise a method that will get you the most points or the least damage taken. Because unfortunately, you can't ragequit your legal obligations, unless you'd like to make games from a jail cell.

Chaotic Neutral Married

Filing Statuses

Y OUR FILING STATUS IS a box that you check off on your tax return, which is indicative of your marital status and/or household composition.

Business taxation has its own nuances but also bleeds into personal taxation, especially as far as indie developers are concerned. How you set your business up and do or do not incorporate will affect your personal taxes, and, filing status can also have impacts, since certain business-related tax benefits are pegged to filing status.

While the depth of information about filing statuses and dependents could rival *The Last of Us*, you will have a basic overview in this chapter. Regardless of how you generate income as a game maker, many people frequently claim the wrong filing status, and it can have a massive impact on your tax bill and recordkeeping.

Putting on our programmer hats for a second, think of filing status as declaring a global variable in a script.

The filing status selected will define several local variables, some of which will be Booleans with a Yes or No answer, while others will be integers. The most prevalent local variable that filing status affects is how much the **standard deduction** will be worth (more on deductions in Level 5).

Originally, the next variable it would affect is the number of **exemptions** you can take, for yourself, spouse, and your dependents. They would phase out based on income level. Since personal exemptions were phased out in favor of a tax credit for children and other dependents after the 2018 tax reform, this no longer applies.

Regardless, if you are unsure who is eligible to be your dependent or whether you are using the correct filing status, you should check out the Internal Revenue Service (IRS) publications in the index and consult with a tax professional.

For brevity's sake and explaining the concepts, most of the scenarios will assume a single filing status. A majority of the concepts covered are irrelevant to filing status, but it may still arise, so it is important to be aware of the different filing statuses and choose the correct one.

SINGLE

Unattached, no kids, and don't have an elderly parent dependent on you? Single is your most likely filing status. This is what you'll check off, whether you live by yourself, with roommates, or with family.

But, even if you're not actually single, the IRS doesn't recognize serious romantic relationships whether or not you live together. Assuming no dependents, you and your significant other would likely file your own separate tax returns with single status, since you must be officially or common-law married to file jointly. You are still considered single for tax purposes.

MARRIED FILING JOINTLY (MFJ)

If you are officially or common-law married, you can choose to file your taxes jointly. This causes the IRS to treat you as one taxpayer instead of two separate individual taxpayers: Your income and deductions get merged. This can not only have serious benefits but also pitfalls.

Contrary to popular belief, it's not just higher income couples who have to worry about the "marriage penalty" when filing taxes. If you and/or your spouse are low-income, you may lose your eligibility for aid like the Earned Income Tax Credit, if you otherwise received it when you filed separate tax returns under single status.

As a self-employed person, you have both benefits and disadvantages in joint filing, depending on how your spouse makes money and how much both your incomes are. If your business that is reported on your personal tax return racked up a loss, your spouse can essentially use that loss to offset your joint income, assuming they work a regular job and/or have other income surpassing the amount of the loss.

Does your spouse also make games with you? You may be eligible to simplify your tax filing as a qualified joint venture, which means that you lose the non-tax benefits of incorporating, but it can save time and red tape when your studio is just starting out.

Newlywed? Congrats. You're treated as married for the entire year, even if your wedding was on New Year's Eve.

MARRIED FILING SEPARATELY (MFS)

Often the least beneficial filing status, you must use it if you are still legally married but separated, or if you and your spouse voluntarily keep your finances separate. Certain benefits become completely unavailable, such as the Earned Income Tax Credit. Other benefits that were easy to claim under single or MFJ status can become more difficult.

If you are unsure of your marital status and whether you should file as single or MFS, it's prudent to ask an attorney who practices in the state that you live and file taxes in.

HEAD OF HOUSEHOLD

Are you a single parent and/or caring for an elderly parent, and the primary breadwinner for your household?

Many single parents and caregivers accidentally file as single and end up missing out on the benefits of filing as a head of household. This is actually the correct status to use if you are unmarried and have at least one dependent child who lives with you most of the year. Dependent parents do not need to live with you to qualify, providing that you are maintaining a home for them and most of their financial support, such as paying for an assisted living arrangement.

In the event that the IRS calls your filing status into question, there is a concise list of eligibility guidelines and documents they may request on Form 866-H-HOH to prove your status.

QUALIFYING WIDOW/WIDOWER

If you were married and had at least one dependent child and then your spouse died, you can use this status for up to two years after their death, depending on the age of the child(ren).

* * *

This overview should cover the basics of how filing statuses work. This book relies on the assumption that most indie developers use single status on personal taxes; you should now have a clearer idea on what to research further if you're still confused over which status you should use. Or, in the case of couples, if you should delay or forego marriage for tax purposes. However, even if someone is eligible to be your dependent, it doesn't mean you'll necessarily be able to use a more beneficial status like head of household or qualifying widow(er).

Deductions, Credits, and Exclusions

THE CHIEF TAX BENEFITS at your disposal are deductions, credits, and exclusions. You've likely heard these terms before when discussing taxes but were unsure what the differences were.

Think of them as rolling the dice at the beginning of a game where stat modifiers are defined. Some will work to your advantage extremely well, while others are definitely shortcomings.

But, if you take a look at a blank Form 1040, it all makes sense. There's a reason why it's laid out the way that it is. Even though I'm discussing exclusions last in this chapter, they actually come first on the tax form. Deductions come before credits for a reason, and some will define more variables later in your tax return.

DEDUCTIONS

Simply put, a deduction reduces your taxable income. At the most basic level, if your income is $50,000 and you have $10,000 worth of deductions, you'd be taxed on $40,000. But there's two types of deductions: **above the line** and **below the line**.

Generally, an above-the-line deduction will be more beneficial to you for a couple of reasons. First, you don't need to **itemize** deductions to claim one that's above the line. The "line" being where you take the

standard or itemized deduction; you can take either and have above-the-line deductions.

You just need to meet the conditions to take that particular deduction. As a self-employed person, the one you automatically get is 50% of your self-employment tax, which is based on the grand total of all your sources of self-employment income. If you have self-employment income, and you are paying for health insurance for yourself or your family out of your pocket, you also get a valuable deduction for this. It usually outweighed the benefit of itemizing medical expenses, to begin with, but after the 2018 tax reform drastically reduced the number of taxpayers who could itemize, it is extremely crucial to take this deduction if you are eligible.

Other common above-the-line deductions include student loan interest and traditional IRA, and other retirement plan contributions. Moving expenses, if you move a substantial distance for a job, used to be deductible until the 2018 tax reform; now only certain armed forces members may claim this deduction.

These items were originally on the first page of Form 1040 and are now found in Part II of Schedule 1.

Above-the-line deductions are also referred to as **adjustments**. Adjustments are subtracted from your **gross income** to reach your **adjusted gross income** or **AGI**. (This book makes numerous references to AGI from here on out; so it's wise to bookmark this chapter in case you need to reference AGI calculations.)

Think of adjustments as close allies in a co-op game. There are many calculations in the tax code that hinge on your AGI, as you're about to see, which makes them an early and strategic tax benefit to take advantage of.

To illustrate this with a more detailed example, let's say that you netted $30,000 in self-employment income from your game-making activity, and that was your only income. You are uninsured, so there's no health insurance adjustment. Your self-employment tax comes out to $4,239, and you can adjust by half ($2,120). You also paid $700 in student loan interest. Your AGI is $27,180.

Below-the-line deductions are calculated after your AGI. There is the standard deduction and the itemized deduction. The standard deduction is a flat, precalculated amount based on your filing status, but it can be higher if you and/or your spouse are 65 or older. The legally blind also get a boost to the standard deduction.

If you are married and file taxes separately, your standard deduction is zero if your spouse itemizes. This means that you also must itemize, and it is likely going to be drastically less than the standard deduction for single status. However, fewer taxpayers are itemizing deductions after the 2018 tax reform, after both key and lesser-known deductions were reduced or eliminated, and the standard deduction amount substantially increased now that personal exemptions have been eradicated.

Itemized deductions are filed on Schedule A and attached to Form 1040. The form consists of various deductions that may or may not be based on your AGI. Medical and dental expenses (including health insurance premiums) are subject to 10% of your AGI, but state and local income taxes (SALT) have a flat $10,000 cap that also includes real estate taxes after the 2018 tax reform went into effect.

If you live in a state that doesn't have an income tax, you can claim the general sales tax deduction based on your state and county instead. Alternatively, if you have records of the actual dollars paid in sales tax that year, you can also use that. Returning to the example where you have $27,180 AGI, we will build on this example to illustrate how AGI works.

If your total eligible medical and dental expenses for the year were $2,000, that 10% of AGI threshold that acts similarly to an insurance deductible; coverage doesn't begin until after you exceed this amount. $2,000 of medical expenses is less than the $2,718 threshold, so there's no deduction.

However, if your medical bills were $3,000, instead, $282 is now deductible.

But just because you qualified for the medical expense deduction doesn't mean it's actually beneficial to itemize. Some taxpayers opt to itemize, despite it being less beneficial on the federal level if they have state-level benefits, such as the more generous medical expense allowance on New Jersey state taxes. Others are mandated to do so if they are married filing separately and their spouse itemizes, so they seek every possible deduction on Schedule A in which they are eligible.

If you donated money or goods like clothes, books, and household items to charity, you must itemize to be able to deduct it. There was a temporary deduction in 2020 and 2021 under the Coronavirus Aid, Relief, and Economic Security (CARES) Act to claim up to $300 in cash donations to charity as an adjustment, but all other donations must be itemized. You should still support causes you care about, even if you don't get a tax benefit, and long-distance moves or tossing items that no longer spark joy usually entail a trip to Goodwill. But, even if you donated profusely, the standard deduction is more likely to be beneficial with both the increase and SALT cap causing fewer taxpayers to itemize.

While donations and SALT are the most well-known deductions, there are countless oddball deductions hidden away in Schedule A. Some of them are rarely or never claimed, because virtually no one ever qualifies. One lesser-known deduction that was repealed in the 2018 tax reform was employee business expenses. This is bad news for employees who put a lot of time and money into their work at home spaces during the pandemic, and would like to stay remote, although, this generally must be for the employer's convenience rather than the employee's, in order to be deductible.

However, legal fees to fight for lost wages or back pay, appealing an unemployment board's decision, or other money you're owed is often deductible. It doesn't even have to be just wages or unemployment specifically; so long as the income is taxable then it's eligible. This is common knowledge to tax professionals, but a deduction the average person rarely takes advantage of.

A NEW BELOW-BELOW-THE-LINE DEDUCTION

The 2018 tax reform brought on sweeping changes to so many aspects of both personal and business taxes. As business taxpayers, you now have a new type of deduction that shows up on your personal tax return: the QBI deduction or qualified business income deduction.

Because there are numerous topics that must be covered first to better understand how the QBI deduction works, it has its own chapter. This deduction is uniquely calculated, and specifically comes after both adjustments and the itemized or standard deduction, and there are numerous conditions that must be met.

And yes, it's complex enough that it got its own chapter! Many game developers are likely to benefit from this deduction, if they haven't already.

CREDITS

A **credit** is more powerful than a deduction, because it is a dollar-for-dollar reduction of your tax bill. Just like how there are two kinds of deductions, with one being more beneficial than the other, the same is true of tax credits. There are **refundable** and **nonrefundable** credits.

The credits that most people, particularly most game developers, will qualify for are of the nonrefundable variety. This means that the credit can only be used to the extent that you are assessed income tax.

Originally, on the second page of Form 1040, refundable and nonrefundable credits are now differentiated in Parts I and II of Schedule 3.

Common nonrefundable credits include the lifetime learning credit for college and grad school tuition, and child and dependent care expenses. So let's say your AGI is $60,000, and you take the 2021 standard deduction of $12,550, which reduces your taxable income to $47,450. You are assessed $6,193 per the tax table and have no other taxes due, such as self-employment tax. You have a $200 lifetime learning credit from paying for grad school courses. Your tax liability is now $5,993, before determining eligibility for any refundable credits.

But let's change the scenario and include other expenses, such as having daycare expenses and paying foreign income taxes, both of which provide substantial nonrefundable credits. The child- and dependent-care credit provides $4,000 and the foreign tax credit provides $2,000, which wipes out your remaining tax liability. Unfortunately, the total of $6,200 in nonrefundable credits against a $6,193 tax liability doesn't make the mere $7 refundable or able to carry over to future years.

While the adoption credit does this, and the child tax credit has a refundable portion, most nonrefundable tax credits are true to their name. There are no carryovers, and it's "use it or lose it" in that, if your tax liability is less than your total credits, it will be reduced to $0, but the remainder doesn't get refunded to you.

So this means that you can't use nonrefundable credits against that dreaded self-employment tax, even if they beat your income tax to a pulp. This includes the oft-discussed R&D credit. It's nonrefundable; so, don't get starry-eyed at the prospect of funding a game with it, no matter how often the nice content on Gamasutra aimed at AAA studios talks about it being worth millions.

Refundable credits on the other hand are a huge boon. These will get you money back even if you aren't assessed any income tax and can be used to offset other taxes reported on your tax return like self-employment tax. The most common refundable tax credits are the Earned Income Tax Credit (EITC), net premium tax credit if you purchased a marketplace health insurance plan and the annual reconciliation went in your favor, and refund of excess Social Security taxes if you started a new job after already hitting the cap.

It's important to know the distinction between deductions and credits, because, as you can see, the way they're applied has a drastically different impact on your tax bill. Think of deductions as getting a promo code and seeing a reduced price at checkout, while credits are like getting a merchandise credit or gift card.

EXCLUSIONS

The best way to describe an **exclusion** is with a retro gaming analogy: it's like using a Game Genie *before* firing up *NES* game. It comes before you figure out credits and deductions, as in the Game Genie activates its magic before you press Start. For a more modern example, going to Nexus Mods and putting the mod in place before you open the game. While using anything other than a vanilla tax form will land you in some serious criminal penalties, the concept is the same in that exclusions come before you start filling out forms.

Exclusions determine your *gross income* after figuring out all your sources of reportable income, above-the-line deductions determine adjusted gross income, then below-the-line deductions, and then determine taxable income.

Despite its rank in the pecking order of determining one's tax liability, there's a reason exclusions came last in this guide. And it's because exclusions aren't as clear-cut as credits and deductions. Some require documentation and/or may involve receiving a tax form like a 1099, while others don't.

For instance, as covered in Level 1, you don't need to report a personal gift as taxable income on your tax return in a vast majority of cases. You don't receive a 1099 or any other form for that, either. This exclusion wouldn't need to be documented on your tax return or require additional forms.

On the contrary, if you owned your home and sold it, there are certain conditions to meet in order to exclude up to $250,000 of the profit ($500,000 if MFJ) resulting from appreciation in value. You'd have to report the sales proceeds, which get reported to you on a 1099 from the broker, even if you broke even or sold at a loss but you wouldn't be taxed on the proceeds. If you did profit more than $250,000 or $500,000 if MFJ, you'd only have to pay tax on the amount exceeding that limit, and this would require extra paperwork to properly claim the exclusion.

Just because something is *reported* doesn't mean it will be taxed.

But there are a wide variety of exclusions that can be murky to navigate, because they're not neatly listed in order for you to plainly see on a tax form the way deductions and credits are. Some exclusions could apply to anyone, while others only benefit certain groups of taxpayers.

*　*　*

In this book, we won't be dealing with exclusions much. The emphasis will mostly be on deductions, since they're the most common tax concept that freelancers and small business owners seek clarity on, and with the exception of the R&D Credit there aren't many credits that jump out specifically to game developers. But there are some exclusions that stand out for bizarre reasons, which you will read about.

To recap: the goal of this game is to get the lowest score possible. Deductions reduce your taxable income, which your score is based on. Kinda like *Oregon Trail*: the shorter the journey and the fewer resources you open the game with, the higher your final score will be. Above-the-line deductions are more powerful, because they reduce the next tier of your score base—AGI.

Then your base score is determined by below-the-line deductions and attacked by nonrefundable credits first. After that, your self-employment tax is added to your score, but, because it dodged the nonrefundable credits, it's now harder to get a low score.

Lastly, refundable credits take out whatever they can of your score. Does your score resemble that of the teacher or the banker? How many members of your party got dysentery along the way?

Solid Recordkeeping as an Important Framework

I F YOU COME FROM a AAA background, chances are that you've adhered to phonebook-size game design bibles. As an indie developer, you have more leeway in setting up your design pillars. You may have this equally colossal game design document, or you just doodled this neat idea down and it translated well to Unreal, so you built from there. Regardless of the method, you have some kind of framework.

Unlike game design, there are harder and faster rules about record-keeping when it comes to taxation and business. You're going to need a recordkeeping framework that works for you, and makes your and your tax professional's lives easier.

Keeping concise records is going to make your life easier and, more often than not, professional fees lower, since they won't need to allocate time to teach you about recordkeeping and building the recordkeeping infrastructure for a small business. Any dollar that comes in and out, you want to keep track of it! Anything concerning what you spend or earn, or getting traditional or alternative financing, record it.

The ultimate goal is the ability to easily locate transactions, contracts, and documents when you must reference it. For tax matters,

DOI: 10.1201/9781003335733-5

it's correctly sorting transactions and having the correct AMOUNT of information needed.

My old tax business was called Tax Solutions for Real People. I chose that name because something that always annoyed me about all these small business guides out there was that they virtually never discussed the utter necessity of good recordkeeping, record sorting, and why being able to find these things easily will make your life easier. And let's face it: real people generally aren't accountants and tax professionals who've had recordkeeping systems and requirements drilled into their skulls for years on end.

If you have poor recordkeeping habits, now is the time to improve them. Modern technology offers a plethora of recordkeeping tools that are free or very inexpensive. When you're just starting out, simply using a spreadsheet will suffice until you're ready to move on to a more robust recordkeeping system. The IRS will accept spreadsheets as "books and records," which you'll read more about in the business and hobby distinction.

Think of the numerous lists you have to make when you design a game: animations and sprite lists, rooms, audio assets, and then when you're further into development, QA tasks like bug fixes and ministerial tasks like sorting out your marketing plan and release notices. Let's apply that list-making skill here. These are the types of records you must keep track of and be able to easily locate:

- Expenses that led to the completion and release of the game

- Day-to-day expenses related to running your business

- Expenses related to finding work, making sales, and generating royalties

- Travel, convention, and expo expenses

- Large investments, such as computers and equipment

- Amounts you pay yourself from company funds

- Amounts you pay other people, and what their relationship is to the business

- Money earned from game sales, services rendered, etc.

- Sales and disposition of equipment used in your business, such as computers, consoles, audio equipment, etc.

- Sales of intellectual property rights and other intangibles
- Any changes in the ownership of your company
- Tax forms you've filled out or previously filed (must hold onto the last three years' worth for personal taxes, six years for business)

While this list isn't completely exhaustive, these are the types of records you must retain for tax purposes, no matter the size of your company, how many games you have for sale, and if you make most of your income from work for hire or royalties.

However, not all records are equal. Some transactions only require a receipt or perhaps your credit card or bank statement to back it up, while others have a higher burden of proof and require very strong documentation to pass muster with the IRS.

Travel and entertainment expenses immediately come to most tax pros' minds for transactions with a large burden of proof. This is because these items frequently have personal elements that cause the deduction to be reduced or totally disallowed. Unlike say, your Internet and hosting expenses, which are more straightforward because you pretty much have to be online to make a living in the digital sphere. Owning and maintaining websites, web content, social media, and game distributor pages is a necessity that is unlikely to ever be challenged in Tax Court. But going too far with claiming parts of your vacation for "game design research" is likely to raise red flags, which is why you'll read more about substantiation in general in Level 9 before honing in on travel and other categories of expenses specifically.

If you sell merchandise that necessitates keeping track of the purchase and sale of inventory items, diligent recordkeeping is extremely important. Selling inventory is also treated differently than if you sell something that you've used in the course of business like a computer or console, which you'd also need to keep tabs on.

At the time of publishing, more game developers and participants in the creator economy are utilizing outsourced print-on-demand and fulfillment outfits like Redbubble and TeeSpring. This is a drastic operational difference compared to the first waves of indie developers who had to source their own products, place an order with the manufacturer, and keep those T-shirts or books on hand. This is also creating interesting new accounting and legal challenges, not to mention potential sales tax nexus issues. Even though the 2018 Supreme Court case *South Dakota v. Wayfair* ultimately changed the game on this, which you'll read about in *Sales Tax: Torment,* this is a recordkeeping area you don't want to overlook.

Regardless of the complexity of your recordkeeping needs based on transaction volume, number of revenue streams, and types of revenues and expenses, it's crucial to keep the following principles in mind when deciding on a financial recordkeeping system and building a solid foundation that works for you.

KEEP BUSINESS AND PERSONAL EXPENSES SEPARATE

This is the first and foremost rule when it comes to making tax time easier, and overall simplifying your finances in general.

If game-making and other creative work is more of a side hustle and casual income to you, with little revenue or expenses to speak of and no formalized business entity, this aspect isn't as crucial, and you can file that Schedule C after going through your bank statements. But if you are doing a significant amount of business in games or other types of self-employment and want to make it your primary source of income or a major secondary source, separating business from personal finances is imperative.

This means separate bank accounts, PayPal accounts, and credit/debit cards. Think about the numerous items you'd have to scan through when analyzing your bank statements for business expenses. How do you know which of those two transactions at Staples were for your child's school supplies, and which one was the supplies you purchased for your PAX booth?

If you frequently dine out or order in, which one of those restaurant or GrubHub tabs was for a business purpose like meeting with a publisher or prospective client? Which one of those three-digit charges was indicative of buying dinner for your dev team or a night totally unrelated to doing business where you don't remember buying shots for an entire graduating class? Sounds like a migraine to sort out!

This is why it's integral to have separate accounts for business activity once you've reached the point that you have so many transactions, weeding out business transactions from personal ones becomes a major headache. The more transactions and higher value they have, the more you will also be prone to errors.

Establishing digital payment processor accounts, bank accounts, and credit/debit cards in your business name instead of your personal funds means that you can minimize headaches in separating page after page of commingled expenses. If you do not have a business entity yet, which you will learn more about in Level 7, or choose to remain unincorporated but want to track expenses on a separate credit card, you can open a new credit card that runs through your personal credit file but is used solely for business purposes. Since business credit is harder to establish for game developers as well, you may need to do this even after you've had your company for some time.

Regardless, keeping your personal and business finances separate is like smart level design. You don't want to constantly clear unneeded artifacts out of the way. In the event you are audited, you can also mount a much stronger defense if your business income and expenses are neatly kept separate by the entity, and away from your personal income and living expenses. Commingled bank and credit accounts tend to be frowned upon by the tax authorities and can even be treated as totally personal assets, depending on the auditor you wind up dealing with.

Additionally, if you get smacked with bank charges and credit card fees, you can fully deduct them if they're solely for business accounts. Fees may be deductible for mixed-use accounts, but would necessitate the onerous task of scanning your transactions to determine how much the account is utilized for business versus personal use. By having separate business accounts, you have a simple calculation of 100% for any maintenance fees, overdraft penalties, or other bank charges.

Having separate email accounts and cloud drives also helps you find documents and transactions more easily; wouldn't it be a pain to look up a very common search term, and you're digging through 5,000 results trying to find your deductible expenses, because your personal account has so many more receipts to muck through?

GO DIGITAL WHENEVER POSSIBLE AND KEEP RECORDS EASILY SEARCHABLE

This aspect has become colossally easier since the first edition of this book was published, although there are still concerns you'll have with digital records. There are also times when paper records will be unavoidable.

A vast majority of business records and transactions are kept in the cloud today, while older companies transitioning from legacy systems and actual paperwork are more likely to face challenges in digitizing. However, there are official documents and communications that are often only available on paper. There are some tax documents and information requests that require paper filing and mailing, or that you will only receive through the mail. IRS correspondence and some state tax matters, namely franchise taxes, are virtually always initiated through the mail. When you receive an IRS notice, you should note the postmark and date on the letter when you create a digital copy for future reference.

Keeping records digital facilitates your business processes and over-all preparedness for tax filings. Paperless bank statements are infinitely easier and faster to retrieve and compile. Now that online payments are the norm, and the way that game developers usually get paid as well, it is relatively simple to gather all of your necessary records in a central location. Having a well-organized cloud drive, or hard drive with cloud server backup, facilitates the retrieval process so that you won't need to visit every single distributor website to track down old and new 1099 forms, royalty statements, and other documents and communications.

Having specific websites or servers for certain types of documents will also simplify recordkeeping. For instance, many large and small businesses of all types transmit legal documents through services specially designed for them, such as SignNow and HelloSign. Having a professional and polished look for service contracts that makes fillable and signable fields easy to find and read is why this author uses one, and it also provides secure storage for legal contracts. Whether you're not being paid royalties you're owed, or the indies funding other indies movement has made your contract difficult to parse for tax purposes, you don't want to spend hours going through your email or a chaotic OneDrive looking for that contract and all of the relevant pages.

Know where your documents are. Build a system that works for both your business and thought processes.

Going paperless and centralized has other concerns, though. Information security has now become a major going concern in the tax and accounting field, since the rise of cloud computing went from a niche area of small software firms and game studios to a dire necessity most of the world now runs on. This is an important consideration when storing your data in the cloud. You will want to obscure personally-identifiable information (PII) like addresses, Social Security numbers, and payment details as best as you can before storage in the event of large-scale and targeted breaches alike.

Timeframes can also cause paper to be your only option. You should also note your financial institutions' limits on how far back they can go with your accounts, given the six-year guideline for business tax matters. If your 2015 bank statements are needed to back up claims you make for a deduction, but your bank's website only goes as far back as 2017, you may need to contact them and receive a paper statement.

Payments made with cash or money orders will require a paper trail that your card issuer or bank automatically provides with card payments and canceled checks. Receipts are another major source of paper-induced stress. You may not always receive a properly itemized receipt via email when you pay a vendor in person, and the receipt provides more context than your bank or credit card statement does.

If your activity generates a great deal of paper receipts, as is common if your career track happens to be travel-heavy with a major conference and convention presence, you may want to invest in a turbo-scanner system such as PaperPort to prevent spending days lining your phone up with photos of receipts. Having digital backups of receipts is prudent, because receipt paper and hand-written records will fade over time or get lost in moves, natural disasters, or spring cleaning.

Having too much paper laying around is a fire hazard, a stressor that affects your mental health, and a favorite dish of cockroaches. Digitize your records for simple retrieval!

WHEN NECESSARY, WRITE YOURSELF AN EXPENSE REPORT

Keeping personal and business finances separate is paramount. But real life happens. Let's take in the following scenario.

You have to leave for GDC in 18 hours, and your laptop just packed it in. You need a new laptop to show your game at the IGF pavilion, and the nearest electronics store closes in an hour. You find a suitable device there, but realize to your horror that you left your business credit card at home. It's in Apple Pay, but not all stores in your area have caught on with it yet. You must use a personal credit card or you're missing out on a potentially life-changing showcase.

Your GDC presence is a success. One of the attendees recommends some games to you to get inspiration for the mechanics you put together, along with some game design books. But that one-click ordering system means that your personal card automatically gets charged when you make your purchase.

Then a prominent Twitch influencer takes an interest in your game, and you offer to entertain them and their production team while they're in your city. Your personal credit card offers bonus cash back on restaurants, while your business credit card offers zero benefits, and you don't want to miss out on the rewards. Then you go out for drinks, and the bar's card processor is down, so you have to use cash.

This is easily hundreds of dollars in deductions that aren't seamlessly recorded on your business accounts like planned. What to do?

Breathe deep and remember this is why you built a recordkeeping system with processes and easy retrieval. You write yourself an expense report and then reimburse yourself.

It need not be as fancy or comprehensive as your average corporate executive expense report, since it doesn't have to be for solo business owners and small teams. It can be as simple as a Google Sheet, and there are plenty of free expense report templates for all major word processor and spreadsheet programs. All you need to do is label the expenses with dates, payment method you used in absence of your business credit/ debit card, and purpose. Also include the reason why you used a personal payment type, such as "it was cheaper with my personal store credit card" or "business Amex deactivated due to identity theft." Then reimburse yourself from the business funds, like the company bank or PayPal account.

If your report is on the long side, such as forgetting your business credit card for an entire trip, or a new card must be issued so you're using an alternate payment method out of necessity, make a memo on your receipt so that it can be matched to your expense report. Such as "PAX 2023 Event and Travel Meals" or "Dev Team Monthly Summit."

If you opt for a corporation as your business entity, the IRS will actually *require* you to do this. It is recommended you utilize the expense report method regardless of entity type however, if you must use a personal mode of payment for a business expense but still have separate business accounts to reimburse yourself from later.

Expenses that have unavoidable personal and business elements, such as your phone and Internet bill, need a simple allocation (usually 50%) without needing to fill out an expense report for yourself every billing cycle. It's pretty much accepted by the IRS to deduct half of your data and Internet bills, because it has become so vital to making a living in an increasingly digital world. However, if you establish separate Internet and data plans specifically for your business, then you can deduct all of it.

ISOLATE MULTIPLE VENTURES AND HUSTLES

Just like generally keeping business transactions separate from personal ones, if you're a hustler as most game devs are wont to be? You also have to keep your income and expenses for your multiple lines of work separate.

If you're making games but also must participate in the gig economy to pay the bills, such as driving for Uber, these are incredibly different activities where your income and expenses from each activity needs to go on separate tax forms. If you're taking on some freelancing or consulting in addition to selling your own games, it likely doesn't require a separate entity and mechanism for recordkeeping and tax filings.

But if you have a venture that departs significantly from game development and some form of sharing and being paid for your knowledge in the field, like breeding monitor lizards and selling sweaters for them on Etsy, you will likely need to isolate this venture into its own tax filing entity.

USE A RECORDKEEPING METHOD THAT FITS YOUR STUDIO'S COMPLEXITY...

Think about how you code scoring mechanisms in games. You have an integer or long value used to measure the player's score. A story-driven point and click adventure game is likely to have a simple mechanism with an integer value, and there aren't many events that affect the score. Picking up an item or solving a puzzle increases the points and that's about it. Then take a platformer that has randomly-generated levels with score multipliers that add or subtract points, depending on factors like how long the player took and if they picked up all the loot on the map, the score would be a long value that is frequently changing.

How you keep records actually has a similar dynamic. Is the mechanism going to be complex or relatively simple? Unlike score mechanisms, which can be flexible, tools appropriate for the recordkeeping realities of each studio are a necessity.

Let's examine a game developer who is employed as a narrative designer for a studio. They're not under a non-compete, so they take a few narrative consulting and freelance writing gigs per year, just some sporadic transactions. Someone fitting that description, where most of their income is from a full-time job, likely doesn't need to formally start a business and open a separate bank account. Noting expenses and income on an Excel sheet is fine if there's not much activity to account for. They'd have the point and click scoring mechanism: You use the right object on something and you get a point.

Then take an indie studio up for investors that has a corporate form and more than one owner. The studio not only successfully crowdfunded in the past but has multiple income streams and capital sources, with several repeat and one-time payees who've worked on games and receive royalties. This equates to a sizable amount of transactions every month. Their scoring mechanism would be something really complex, like *Heroes of Might and Magic IV*. Subsequently, professional accounting software is needed for recordkeeping, because an Excel sheet or two really wouldn't cut it.

A spreadsheet is what most new entrepreneurs use when they're starting out then gradually upgrade to a more robust system, as volume transaction and complexity calls for it.

...BUT MAKE SURE YOU'RE USING THAT METHOD CORRECTLY

If you're at the point of your games career where you need a more sophisticated accounting and recordkeeping system or plan to need one soon enough, be warned that you may not have the right skills along with the time and energy to handle it. When it gets beyond the point of recording, "I received this amount of royalties this month" or "I spent X on this conference," you'll probably consider a system that has a learning curve such as QuickBooks.

Speaking from professional experience, many a mangled QuickBooks once wound up on my desk. If I see one more, I could give Kratos from *God of War* a run for his money with the rage storm that will ensue. Free and subscription-based competitors like Wave, Xero, and Freshbooks entered the marketplace, but QuickBooks remains an institution of small business recordkeeping.

If you do not have a background in accounting, or at the very least a high level of financial literacy that will lend itself to ingraining accounting terminology in your mind, it's unwise to attempt using a system like QuickBooks or Sage on your own. It's dangerous out there. Take this knowledge of GAAP (generally accepted accounting principles).

Many of these systems lure you in with the promise that you won't need an accountant; this is untrue as many accountants' rent or mortgage payments come from fixing their clients' charts of accounts and transactions that were not correctly done the first time around in these systems.

Since most modern recordkeeping software has cloud features where your accountant can see real time updates, accountants are also pivoting to subscription models as well.

But if you lack an accounting background, be aware that you won't necessarily save money by using these systems. If your transaction volume and/or complexity increases over time as your studio grows, that's a cue to get the right professionals involved. If you or the dev team are unsure of whether you're using the system correctly and whether it follows accounting protocol, it's going to cause you more grief in the long run. You will also see higher bills from your tax professional, because improperly-entered records are incredibly time-consuming to fix. This problem also compounds faster than Sonic after an 8-ball soaked in espresso.

To provide some examples from professional experience: If you put your own savings into your new business, it's a capital contribution, not income. But I've seen it labeled that way on QuickBooks files I've received. If you get a royalty check, it increases the cash account, but it IS income, not a reduction of expenses. I've also seen that error, along with some truly bizarre entries like negative receivables and recording computer upgrades as inventory.

To reiterate the important point about keeping business transactions separate from personal: *don't pay personal expenses out of the business accounts*, even if QuickBooks makes it look like you can do so neatly. Always cut a check or digital payment to yourself first, referred to as owner drawings, then pay your personal expenses from your personal accounts instead of the company checking account. I saw this phenomenon too often on the job.

Some of you may be able to properly pick up how to use systems like QuickBooks or one of its numerous cloud-based competitors. Some of you may not, and there is no shame in it. There are many professional bookkeepers out there, a lot of who are QuickBooks Pro Advisors or are contracted with your provider of choice. For QuickBooks Pro Advisors specifically, they must pass a rigorous licensing exam by Intuit and are well-versed both in accounting principles and different grades of the program ranging from solopreneurs to enterprise level. These fine people will happily help you for a reasonable fee to ensure your books are done properly. Especially if you will need them on an ongoing basis.

They will review all of your records like receipts, information on people you paid and how much they received, how much money you've put in and taken out since inception, and all other relevant transactions. It will be correctly entered for you, which not only saves time so you can focus on making an awesome game, but then you also won't have to answer an additional fifty questions at tax time relating to breaking down an indecipherable file by some poor underpaid tax professional who's been working for seven days a week for almost a whole fiscal quarter, and just wants to lock herself in her apartment with *No Man's Sky* and not look at another mangled QuickBooks file for a very, very long time.

JUST BECAUSE YOU DIDN'T GET A TAX FORM DOESN'T MEAN YOU'RE OFF THE HOOK

If you're earning royalties from most of the major digital distribution platforms like Steam, Epic, Itch, and so on, you'll likely receive a 1099-MISC tax form. It is required once you've earned just $10 in royalties for the year.

Smaller publishers and bundle organizers may neglect to issue you a form even if they should have, or you received tiny amounts that went under the radar. Foreign publishers and distributors also aren't likely to send you American tax forms if they don't have any stateside operations or affiliates.

In any event, you must keep track of these earnings and report them, whether they were royalties or payment for services like consulting and speaking at conferences. It's also just a good idea to keep track of royalties that you're paid and owed, in the event you receive an incorrect 1099 form or didn't receive a royalty check that was due.

But just because you don't get a 1099 form doesn't mean you don't have to report the income. You still do.

CREATE A PAPER TRAIL FOR CASH INCOME AND PAYMENTS

Being in a primarily digital realm, game development is a relatively cashless line of work. If you're in the tabletop, card, and board game realm however, you are more likely to run into cash transactions at events where people may want to use cash to buy your games in person.

For a majority of game developers though, most of your transactions will be digital and thus easily traceable. But there's still potential for cash transactions like having to pay for meals at cash-only establishments on conference trips, or you pay or receive cash from the people you're traveling with to share the costs of gas and tolls. Cash is more common with expenses rather than income in this field.

If you've held a typical office job, many keep a petty cash drawer for cash-based transactions like this. But, since we're often one- or two-person companies, it can be a real annoyance to keep track of your own petty cash drawer. It would require making a separate account in your recordkeeping system and going back to the receipts you had on hand or hand-written records. Keeping track of your own cash with the company cash in the same wallet is a migraine waiting to happen. Don't design a shell game out of your cash management!

The best way to handle cash expenses harkens back to the section on creating your own expense reports. Use your personal cash in situations where you must, then make a report using any receipts as backup, and then reimburse yourself. In the event you don't get a receipt, such as if you're on the road and leaving cash tips for hotel staff, keep a log on your phone or through a spreadsheet of your cash expenses, and things like gas and lodging that people frequently split. Blank sales slip books are also good for keeping written records as they occur, you can always upload a scan with your phone.

As for cash income, it's less frequent outside the tabletop and card game space. But in the event you receive cash payments, you still have to report it just like any traceable income that you earn through digital means. Cash gets messy, both literally and figuratively. It's a pain to count and deposit. And there's a reason why cash-heavy businesses like coffee shops and laundromats are the most likely to get audited: that ever-present temptation to claim you're making less than you really are to skimp on both your income tax bill and sales tax tally, because everything is done in cash.

It's hard to make memorable games with high Metacritic scores from a jail cell. Don't try it.

Tax Impacts of How Your Game Gets Funded

INDEPENDENT GAME DEVELOPMENT REQUIRES money in a capitalist society. Even if you plan on a commercial release using nothing but free assets from the Unity Asset Store, Free Sound, and the Incompetech library of royalty-free music that has accompanied millions of YouTube videos, you still need money at the personal level to have food, shelter, and other basic living expenses covered.

The different tax types covered in Level 1 can come into play here, since money has to come from somewhere. Where is it coming from? Who is providing it, and what is their relationship to you? How will you be affected? These are the questions that should be answered before delving into what is and isn't deductible: all money is green, but tax law affects various ways to fund a project.

ME, MYSELF, AND MY MONEY: SELF-FUNDING PART 1

This is the most straightforward method tax-wise: If you pull money from your checking or savings account, it's tax-free as far as your business is concerned. This is referred to as a **capital contribution**. Because you own the business, putting your own money in as capital doesn't incur any taxes.

This remains true if your studio has multiple owners and each contributes their own money. It's capital and not income, and it's still capital whether the contribution is $1 or several million.

DOI: 10.1201/9781003335733-6

Friends, Family, and Fools: Is It a Loan or a Gift?

If you're lucky to have financial support from friends and family in your game dev endeavors, it's typically the next step in growing a business after you've put your own money in. After all, if you don't believe in your own project to put up your own funds, why would other people?

But it begs the question, are you getting a loan or a gift from a family member or friend? Are they writing the check to you or your company?

Let's say that you formed a corporation for your new studio, and your parents want to help out. If they write the corporation a check for $10,000, and it's meant to be both development funds and helping with your rent, the corporation would have to pay tax on that money. Despite the US having fairly lax corporate laws essentially saying that corporations are people, corporations still can't get gifts without paying up on them. But if your parents write that check to *you*, there's no tax, because it's a personal gift that falls below the taxable gift threshold.

By gift, it means that there is donative intent. Read: no expectation of repayment, whether it's through a revenue share or principal plus interest, or even a no-interest loan. Gifts also mean that they aren't expecting to get something of equal or greater value in exchange. This is more commonly expected from one's parents, although there have been wealthy gamers roleplaying the Medici family to their digital Leonardo.

On the other hand, if your parents want to loan your corporation $10,000 with a clear intent for you to pay them back, it's best to have a written loan agreement. Even if it's just your parents and not a bank, and they don't want to charge you interest, you would need to charge at bare minimum what's referred to as the **applicable federal interest rate** or **AFR**.

This rate changes every month and is not to be confused with the rate that changes every fiscal quarter for overdue tax payments. AFR is the minimum interest the IRS permits for private loans. It is actually the IRS that decides and publishes these rates under §1274(d) of the tax code, rather than the Federal Reserve or Congress, although it is based on market yields from US Treasury obligations.

There are three categories of AFR:

Category	Loan Duration
Short term	3 years or less
Mid term	Up to 9 years
Long term	More than 9 years

While your parents would want to let you off the hook for interest, they still need to charge you AFR for the month the loan is originated and determine a proper term. If that loan has a rate below the relevant AFR, the IRS may go after your parents for what's called imputed interest income. This would reflect the AFR rather than what you, the borrower, have been paying. Additionally, if the loan also exceeds the aforementioned gift tax exclusion for the year, it may create additional tax impacts and penalties for not having this acceptable minimum interest rate attached.

Repayment terms would also have to be clear, including the duration, so the correct AFR rate is used. You also need to issue your parents a 1099 for the interest paid. The loan proceeds are not taxable, and you'd be able to deduct the interest.

Because of the often informal nature of friends and family helping each other out, it's important to make the distinction between whether you or your business has to repay the money or not, and who the check was written to. Once again, if there's supposed to be any hope of paying the money back, even "interest-free", then it's a loan, not a gift. The gift tax limits wouldn't apply.

But if it's a very close party, usually a parent or sibling who doesn't expect to be paid back, then they are better off gifting you a sum below the annual per donee exclusion than creating a loan agreement. This way, you are free to use the funds for personal purposes or contributing some to your business as a capital contribution then one day you give them an awesome gift if you end up making *Stardew Valley* money.

Supportive Spouses

Hand in hand with friend and family funding, spousal support also comes into play, because there are two important considerations with the gift tax that you should be aware of: gift-splitting and unlimited spousal transfers.

Going back to the example with your parents, let's say one of your parents looks down upon game development and doesn't want to give or loan you one cent, but the other wants to help you however they can. You're the only one who has ownership of the company.

Recapping the per donee annual exclusion mentioned earlier, which is $16,000 for the 2022 tax year, your supportive parent can give up to $32,000 during the year without incurring the gift tax. This is despite the other parent not wanting to help at all, and it's because of the gift-splitting election. Since married taxpayers are treated as one taxpaying unit, it's basically as if both parents gave that money, despite one parent not giving any at all.

It also doesn't need to specifically be your parents. If you're friends with an independently wealthy married couple who want to help fund you, the same rules would apply.

When it comes to your own spouse, you can make unlimited gifts to each other and never incur gift tax, even if you file your taxes separately and otherwise keep your finances separate. If your spouse wants to give you well past the per donee annual exclusion, they can do so and not pay one penny in gift tax.

Loans and Credit Cards

If you take out a loan from a bank, credit union, or alternative lender to fund a game or pay other business expenses, you don't have to pay taxes on the proceeds and can deduct the interest paid. Since there is an interest rate attached usually far above the minimum AFR that must apply to loans from family and friends, the IRS is unlikely to intervene in these transactions.

To once again illustrate the importance of separating business from personal credit cards, credit card interest is deductible but only if it generated from business expenses. If you have $5,000 of business expenses racking up interest on the card and $2,000 in personal expenses, you could only deduct the interest applicable to the business portion. Because regularly charging personal expenses to the same card on a revolving balance can make it difficult to determine the applicable percentage every month, this is why you should have a separate card for business. All fees and interest will be fully deductible.

While you don't pay taxes on the money received from loans, or goods and services covered by credit cards, and deduct the interest paid, the proceeds can become taxable income in the event that you are unable to pay the debts and they get forgiven. You will receive a 1099-C tax form for the amount that was forgiven.

You may be able to legally exclude forgiven debts from your income, but this information is beyond the scope of this book. Regardless, you should be aware of this in the unfortunate event that your game gets trapped in Development Hell and you have no choice but to arrange debt settlement or file for bankruptcy.

Investors

Getting investors on board works similarly to putting your own money into your business, as far as taxes are concerned. They're now an owner of the company, so any funds they put in will not be taxable because they're capital contributions, not income.

EXISTING ROYALTIES AND OTHER INCOME: SELF-FUNDING PART 2

If your studio is already up and running, and you've already got games generating royalties or other income like ongoing Patreon support or websites that generate ad and affiliate revenue, all of it is generally considered taxable income in the year it's earned. If you have a game or digital income sources forming a nest egg in your business coffers for the next project, you pay the taxes on this income as you go and can deduct your business expenses.

Publisher Funding

If a publisher is paying you to make a game, it's considered payment for services and is therefore taxable as you receive the payments along with any royalties after the game has been released.

Even if the production gets canceled, you still have to pay tax on the money the publisher paid to you and deduct the related expenses you had.

Grants

With games gaining more legitimacy as a medium in the mainstream and video game programs cropping up in academia, there has been a significant rise in indie developers receiving government and private grants to make games. It has led to a slew of tax implications, depending on the conditions of the grant program and who the recipient is.

Generally speaking, if you're in the business of making games and you get grant funding, it is likely to be taxable income but not always.

Private grant funding, such as the Epic Mega Grant if you plan on making a game in Unreal, is the simplest tax-wise. These types of grants from private companies are always taxable, whether they're paid to you as a studio or an individual. They're intended to reward you for your skills or assist in taking your game to market.

If you are a game design student and receive grant funds from your department to make a game, the taxability becomes more of a gray area. It depends on the purpose of the project and who benefits (you the developer, the school, or the general public). In many cases, you will have to pay taxes on at least part of the grant, because you are likely providing services to your school. There are rules surrounding the treatment of taxable fellowship grants that are beyond the scope of this book, but more often than not these grants constitute taxable income unless you use them to pay for tuition, school fees, and the required equipment and supplies for your coursework. For example, if you received a $10,000 fellowship grant for the semester and it cost you $8,000 for tuition, you'd have to pay taxes on the $2,000 remainder, even if it went directly to development costs for a department-approved project rather than a personal one.

As for government grants, game development bleeds into technology and art as far as government programs are concerned, but the tax code sees the industry as just software. There may be a legislative exception for your studio to avoid taxation on the grant funds, depending on whether your studio received the funds directly or as a payment from a partner organization like a school or nonprofit. It also depends on whether the project is for profit or meant to benefit the public.

The complexity of government grants is outside the scope of this book. However, a simple way to know if you'll owe taxes on grant funds depends on whether your studio received the funds directly and what the purpose is, or if a partner organization paid you to provide development or support services (in which case it would be fully taxable).

Incubator Programs

Incubators became a popular method for startup funding when the first edition of this book was published. Now that this type of program has matured since, with some local programs designed particularly for game developers, the expectations of participating in one have become clearer. Depending on the terms of the program, and whether any ownership is exchanged, you may or may not have to pay taxes on incubator funds.

"Accelerator" programs frequently entail the program lead, usually an experienced angel investor, having some ownership stake in your company. In which case, the taxability is treated just like any other traditional investor that owns a larger stake; they have equity, so any cash they contribute won't create taxable income.

But some incubator programs will give you funding in exchange for your services, want ownership of the intellectual property rather than the business, or a cut of future royalties.

If an incubator program gives you or your business money in exchange for services like teaching or lending talent to the program, then these payments are taxable income. This context is not that different from free-lancing for a client or making a game for a publisher.

But, if receiving incubator funds comes with expectation of a royalty share or partial ownership of the actual copyright, it's a little more nebulous. Is any ownership of the company changing as a result of that revenue share? If the ownership of the business doesn't change, are there clauses in the agreement in the event of the game not making it to its release date? If there is no change in the ownership, you would likely have to pay tax on the funding, but then you can deduct any future royalties paid to the incubator per your agreement.

Crowdfunding

Crowdfunding was initially a "Wild West" concept of the 2010s that paved the way for many games to come to fruition that otherwise may not have been made. This is especially true in the tabletop and card game space.

With many prominent Kickstarter campaigns that failed to deliver or took significantly longer to deliver than expected, regulators took advantage of the crowdfunding fatigue that set in to start issuing guidance on the obligations campaign organizers are held to and relevant tax matters.

The IRS has since issued Tax Tips and fact sheets regarding crowdfunding, which can be found in the Index of Citations. When campaigns offer digital or physical goods to backers, it does create taxable income and you will receive a 1099 from your platform of choice.

You can deduct the fees paid, rewards, and other expenses incurred in running the campaign as well as the actual expenses of the project that you're funding; just be careful with the timing of your campaign and when you plan to spend the funds opposed to when you will receive them. The 2018 tax reform eliminated the ability to carry back net operating losses, if you end up creating one by not spending down the money until the next tax year.

* * *

This list should cover the most common ways an indie developer is likely to get their work funded. When in doubt, most funding methods outside of traditional lending and investors are likely to create taxable events. However, it's also important to make the distinction of whether your company is receiving the money opposed to you as an individual, and what the intent of that transaction is. Are you receiving funds because the giver wants to help you or to get something in return?

Most tax law applications and audit defense tactics ultimately boil down to intent, as you're going to see. But even the most plausible intents don't always mean the law is applied equally or in a straightforward manner.

Is Game Development Your Livelihood or Just a Hobby?

W E'VE DELVED INTO BASIC tax lingo and whether common methods of funding projects constitute taxable income. But taxes aren't strictly about filing forms and crunching numbers; there is a whole separate court dedicated to federal tax matters, where decisions made by the IRS that were upheld and appealed also have their own law libraries. This practice area is referred to as tax controversy, and there are numerous firms that solely specialize in it.

These libraries, now on the web such as Taxprof Blog and the Cornell University Tax Law Project, contain tomes full of case law. These cases not only concern whether a taxpayer improperly claimed credits and deductions, but also the intents, facts, and circumstances behind the taxpayers' decisions and how they framed their arguments. Typical courts of law have plaintiffs, defendants, and appellants. Tax Court has petitioners (you, the taxpayers) and the respondent, which is the Commissioner of the IRS then the United States, if the case gets escalated to the Supreme Court after appeal. There's going to be many references to these cases in the upcoming chapters and the citations.

It's important to know this, because before even diving into business entities and deductions, it's important to think about how the law perceives different degrees of game makers.

DOI: 10.1201/9781003335733-7

Semantically speaking, there's nothing wrong with dabbling in game making as a hobby. Independent creative work is hard, the media landscape keeps evolving, and living expenses continue to rise. Many game makers ultimately decide that they'll pursue their love of the medium through working with a team at a larger studio with AAA aspirations, or perhaps a different role in the industry like event promotion, streaming, or the games press.

Although, if you're reading this book and made it this far, there's a strong chance that game development isn't merely a hobby to you. But the eyes of the law hold a different view than your family, friends, and indie developer Discord groups. Particularly, the eyes of §183 of the tax code: Are you engaging in this activity for profit?

Because game development is often seen by outsiders as a very expensive hobby, the tax authorities feel no different. The fact that we don't have an industry code (more on this later in the chapter) actually works in our favor for once, because there are certain industry codes that the IRS flags for hobby versus business examinations.

Most game developers should be lucky enough to avoid needing a tax controversy expert, though it certainly couldn't help to have one in your network. Hopefully, no one reading this ever gets that level of examination. But it happens. And due to the extreme financial volatility the average indie developer experiences, along with many people being undecided on whether they should make games just for fun or if they should seriously pursue it for a living, you should familiarize yourself with the checkpoints for whether the IRS believes you have business and not a hobby.

Don't panic yet, though. Think of how the best games have some kind of clearly-defined goal, whether they're short indie narrative experiences or AAA blockbusters. Your strategy for reaching that goal could be talking to the correct NPCs or gathering a certain number of resources. Your checklist for proving you have a business is actually not as difficult or intimidating as it sounds.

DO YOU MAKE GAMES AS A HOBBY OR FOR A LIVING? (OR ATTEMPTING TO MAKE IT YOUR LIVELIHOOD)

Lots of people have fun, challenging, and engaging hobbies that can frequently be expensive. Game development is no exception, even though there's lots of free and low-cost tools laying around these days. People also band together on passion projects: That's actually how my old studio was formed, and many continue to do so today.

Unfortunately, passion projects may also lead people to get into some sticky situations with the tax authorities when trying to claim a huge amount of expenses for doing something out of love rather than the intent to make a profit. Any sort of gaming and gambling activity gets in the crosshairs along with extreme sports, reptile breeding, horse racing, and other expensive activities where it takes a long time to earn a comfortable living from it. Since it is very easy to rack up a substantial loss if you've got little to no income, many years of doing this and reporting it on your tax return winds up making you a stationary target for an audit, and this is something that should be of concern to every indie developer.

While making games independently for a living has gained more legitimacy in the mainstream, it's still not seen as real actual work by a significant chunk of society. You likely already know this, given that upon stating you're a game developer you will likely get the same looks people give five-year-olds when they say they want to be mermaids when they grow up. And unfortunately, the IRS is no exception!

Even though anyone who picked up this book knows how much eyesocket-grating labor goes into game development, to the tax man you're just pushing pixels for the hell of it until the money rains down. Especially if you're not generating royalties yet, and even more so if you have a big project in the works and it will be a long time before you start seeing any income from it.

So now, you have to ask yourself "Why do I make games?" Don't think too hard about the artistic and existential reasons. Do you just make games for fun and see whatever money you make from it, if any, as a nice bonus?

Is it something you do for fun but want to turn it into a side business or your main source of income? Or have you already quit your job and commenced development on what you hope will be the next *Hades* or *Paradise Killer*?

IT'S ALL IN THE INTENT

To make a profit, that is.

Even if you make games that put artistic expression first and profit second, you still need proof that you're in the business of game development. It goes a long way in case you consistently rack up losses then get pulled for an audit as a result.

Does this mean that you need to give up on making strange art games, or games with a strong social message, just because more mainstream-friendly genres seem more profitable? No. But you still need to show you have intent of doing this for money to some extent, whether you're a starving digital artist or the next Lucas Pope. If you don't really have the intent to make *a* profit, and you have other sources of income such as a job or another business, it's going to be harder to defend your stance that consistent losses should be treated as business losses instead of hobby losses.

Business expenses themselves, as you'll read about on a more granular level in later chapters, virtually always require having a profit motive to pass the smell test with the IRS, then with Tax Court if it reaches that point. This is why strong record-keeping is so dire. Expenses catastrophically outweighing your income are common with just about every new business. But especially so with game development, since it can be fraught with protracted periods of little to no income, and if these conditions continue for several years, it raises a red flag.

Interestingly though, what the law considers a trade or business has been fluid over time. The standard still used by the IRS was decided in the late 1980s after numerous appeals, *Commissioner v. Groetzinger*. Groetzinger was a gambler who spent about 60–80 hours a week betting on dog races.

Gambling income and losses are subject to slightly different tax rules than wages, business income, and self-employment income, but he earned about $70,000 from his wagers in 1978 after betting $72,032 throughout the year. Ironically, Groetzinger did account for this $2,032 gambling loss on his 1978 tax return but didn't even benefit from it.

He did not claim it as a deduction or utilize it to compute his adjusted gross income, since he was unemployed. The 1964 version of the tax code applied then, and he was selected for audit with the IRS claiming he was subject to a minimum tax due to gambling loss rules. Groetzinger could avoid this minimum tax by claiming business expenses for a trade or business, so he argued that he was in the business of professional gambling and shouldn't have to pay minimum tax. The Court of Appeals agreed with his stance, given the facts that his wagering was his sole source of income and he was betting for his own account, not a bookie or company.

The judge in the Groetzinger case interpreted the law as "to be engaged in a trade or business, the taxpayer must be involved in the activity with continuity and regularity, and that the taxpayer's primary purpose for engaging in the activity must be for income or profit. A sporadic activity, a hobby, or an amusement diversion does not qualify." While gambling at the track might be a fun or foolhardy diversion to many people, it happened to be how Groetzinger paid his rent and bills, pretty handsomely as well, given that $70,000 in 1978 was worth almost $320,000 at the time of this book's second edition in the 2020s. He was a professional gamer long before we had Twitch and esports programs in schools.

Groetzinger's intent was fairly easy to figure out; he intended to earn a living from wagers and had no other income. When your overall intent is examined, there is a nine-factor test. These nine concepts are not of equal weight, and each have been applied to every Tax Court case differently depending on the facts and circumstances.

1. Are You Operating in a Business-Like Manner?

This doesn't mean getting up at 5 AM every day and putting on a suit to design levels, though you do you if that's what works.

But this part does mean that you don't treat making games as something you sporadically work on then forget about. You're keeping actual books and records, getting a separate bank account when it gets to the point that you need one, and doing a lot of the same things other game developers are doing to build up their reputations and get noticed. You're also looking at successful indies and examining how they achieved that success, or what you can learn from games that didn't sell much.

If you're just treating game development like something you do on the side for fun, there's nothing wrong with that morally speaking, but this factor will hurt you when it comes to tax filings. If you want to be considered an actual business, you need to formalize that intent with a business entity and an employer ID number, have business cards and other promotional materials made, separate email and social media accounts, plus a website.

If you have a build you're ready to show the public, seeking signs of fan and press interest with Steam wishlists also helps your case. Even if you don't generate many email sign-ups or wishlist tallies, showing your intent to gauge marketability helps prove that you're business-like. It need not be a fancy, expensive marketing plan from an agency with a five-figure price tag.

All of these actions demonstrate that you're not just doing this because you like making games. Putting actual branding together, and separating your business from your personal life and finances, shows you're serious about going indie and want to make money off your creations. You don't have to prove that you want to make *Call of Duty* money. Just that you want to generate some palpable earnings.

2. **Industry Expertise vs. Business Principles**

Are you invested in learning about the business environment of game development, particularly for indie games? *Zidar v. Commissioner* is an oft-cited case that established passionate involvement for many years isn't enough to prove that your venture is a business and not a hobby.

Even if you've been playing games for multiple decades, worked for large and small studios, and frequently speak at games conferences, you need to demonstrate attempts to familiarize yourself with the business end of indie games. The Zidar case isn't just legal precedent for why business expertise matters, it's a tragic cautionary tale:

Tony Zidar was passionate about racing stock cars and had been doing so since he was very young. He was an expert on racecars, so he pursued racing on his own and attempted to get some sponsorships, but didn't miss a day of work at the concrete business he co-owned with his brother. Despite taking drastic measures like remortgaging his house to build a custom stock car, he couldn't find any racecar drivers interested in taking it to the track. There's more money in sponsorships than prizes, especially when drivers reasonably receive most of the prize winnings, but Zidar only garnered a paltry sum of sponsorships. Dejected, he listed the stock car for sale, having never even raced it.

He figured that showing it during peak racing season would generate interest in potential buyers. On the day of the race, a driver took it around the speedway for a test run. It summarily crashed into another stock car and got demolished. The car was also uninsured, so he didn't recoup the loss in any way.

Although Zidar had a variegated business background, with the concrete business plus multiple rental properties and other ventures he co-managed with his brother, he didn't invest any time or money into learning about the business specifics of professional racing. While there was no YouTube or Skillshare in 1992, there were speed racing consultants and you can still find them. There's books on the topic. Failing to learn about the business end of racing ultimately struck down Zidar's ability for his other business income to absorb the consistent net losses from his stock car endeavor.

There are many lessons to be gleaned from this Tax Court case, aside from the importance of insurance whenever large and expensive assets prone to catching fire, like vehicles, are involved. One of them is that the business of games is another discipline of the games industry, just like how programming isn't the only skill needed to make a game.

While it's important to know how to make good games and improve your skills in various disciplines of game making, it's crucial for indies to understand the economic aspects of how to make a living as a game developer and the financial realities of indie life. Are you taking business courses, whether they're industry-specific or not? Working with business consultants who specifically know the games industry (http://sonictoad.com/consulting)? Buying books and constantly combing Gamasutra for reading material about running a game studio? This book counts! No one reads about industry-specific taxes for fun.

Even if you don't understand the business aspects very well and just want to concentrate on making a game, you still have to demonstrate that you made some effort to become familiar with the business side of your industry. This includes taking classes, retaining a consultant, buying books, going to conferences, and other actions that show you want to do this for a living and not a side hustle. Proof of at least making that effort works in your favor, if you ever wind up fighting this issue out in Tax Court.

3. Time and Effort Investment

How much time have you put into forming a studio and making a game?

Going back to Groetzinger, the OG professional gamer in the eyes of Tax Court, he didn't have a job or do any freelancing or consulting. His gambling income was his bread and butter. But we have a far different economy in the 2020s compared to the 1970s.

Regardless, Tax Court frequently looks at whether you've quit your job to substantially work on your new business, or if you still depend on the income. It's hard to make a living in this business, due to how long it takes to make a game. A vast majority of indie developers frequently need a job (or series of jobs and/or other freelance gigs) to subsidize their efforts. If you're ever audited, point out how common this is. Tell your tax professional so that they know what strategy to take with the auditor; this factor virtually always ties in with the financial situation factor of whether or not you were also in a position to quit your job or perhaps had been fired and had no choice but to take on self-employment.

Another aspect the court examines is whether your personal relationships suffered as a result of pursuing entrepreneurship. Your friendships and marriage don't have to tank while you're holding onto a day job as you work on your game and building your following. But it happens frequently, and this is also a good defense against this factor. It's an unfortunate reality some of us have had to contend with; the ways that starting a business often impacts your interpersonal relationships is a topic for a whole other book. But showing that your friendships or romantic relationships suffered as a result has been used as a valid defense.

No less, whether you quit your job or not, or your relationships suffered or didn't have an idea of how many hours per year you put into the games and building up your fan base, and those hours being indicative of building your business plus working on the game.

4. **Expectation That Assets Will Appreciate in Value**

So you've made your games, and in some cases turned them into franchises, and built up your brand and community. Do you expect them to make you money in the future upon protecting your intellectual property with copyrights and trademarks?

In the old days, game sales would tend to taper off after the first few months post-release. But, the digital media landscape by the late 2010s drastically changed where a game doesn't find its audience until long after it's been released. *Among Us* is probably the most prominent example of this that could be cited in Tax Court. Suddenly, the copyright is worth a great deal of money. Or if you utilize your intellectual property in other ways that consistently make you money, such as merchandising, it's a given that your intangible assets have increased in value.

But if you're not formalizing your development pursuits as a business, and don't bother to protect your work with a business entity and copyright filings, it's hard to say if the value would appreciate and this factor would rule against you if you wound up in Tax Court. Filing copyrights and, if applicable, trademarks also goes back to the first factor and proving that you have business savvy by legally protecting your creations.

5. **Your Success in Other Activities**

Is this your first foray into indie dev life, or have you done this before with another dev team as a principal or as an employee? Have you ever gone into business for yourself at all, like having a side hustle in addition to a job? And were you profitable, even if you didn't earn much?

If you've made games before, did you work for studios or with publisher funding on your own or other indie projects where the games sold many units?

Prior business success didn't help in Zidar, probably because he somehow managed rental properties yet didn't think to get insurance for his stock car or research how you actually make money with them. But if you have proof of success within the same industry, it will help more than hurt.

Fortunately, this factor is often neutral in many Tax Court proceedings, because a lot of people frequently have only started one business in their lifetimes. But it's still on the books, so if you've had previous success, it will help your case.

6. **History of Profits and Losses (3 Out of 5 Year Rule)**

The IRS looks at how your activity is doing in five-year intervals. If you made a profit, even just a few dollars, in three out of those five years, then your loss is less likely to get the book thrown at it.

Industrial norms are also factored in. While game development isn't understood that well by the professional sector, there is more than enough authoritative literature from IGDA, local game developer collectives, Gamasutra, and the like to prove that it can definitely take more than three years for game developers to turn a profit. Even the IRS has frequently cited the start-up phase being between five to ten years or exceeding that. If development timeframes and costs wind up spiraling out of control, defend your loss by proving that it resulted from an exceedingly long start-up phase, not because you're doing this as a hobby.

Going back to the first factor, operating in a business-like manner also means that you chose to abandon unprofitable methods; this really gets factored in if you have a long history. Many indie developers attempt to live the *Stardew Valley* dream of making a game that size, then eventually decide to avoid large, epic projects in favor of smaller projects that can be pushed faster, so that it's generating royalties along with discussion on social media and the games press.

No matter how you decide to make games, consistent losses over a five-year period can represent just finishing up one large project or slowly working on it while you're at your day job or seeking outside funding like publishers and investors. So, if you didn't profit in three out of five years you've been around? You'll have to prove that the potential is there, and that this is an industrial norm.

Once again, you don't have to prove you'll make *CS:GO* kind of profit: just **a** profit.

7. **Amount and Frequency of Incidental Profits Earned (If Any)**

This factor sounds rather Kafkaesque or like one of those sliding puzzles where the piece you need is all the way on the other side of the board, and there's no reset button.

The best way to prove you have the intent to make profit is to actually...make a profit. Even if it's just $5. But the big picture is examined here, plus the five-year intervals, in determining if you have a real business or just a very expensive hobby.

But to sidestep the obvious, it's worth going back to Zidar. Zidar got walloped by Tax Court because his stock car activity was determined to be "highly speculative" in terms of having any ability to make a profit whatsoever. In other words, if Tax Court deems that there is no opportunity to ever make a profit, either just for you or for your activity in general, that's where you'll get a smackdown.

Fortunately, you have plenty of proof all around you that games are a viable industry and indie developers can indeed be profitable to various degrees. Games are a crapshoot: you can have this massive epic narrative adventure that's a darling of the games press, wins all these awards, and deployed a strategic marketing plan...then the project lead laments at a GDC talk how the game barely earned back its development costs.

Then you have a guy who just wanted to make something fun for his girlfriend who liked word games, suddenly it takes the Internet by storm and gets bought by the New York Times for over $1 million. (And millions of people are still playing Wordle!) One of my consulting clients had about 1,100 Twitter followers and 70 people who wishlisted his game on Steam, then he made over $200,000 in his first month of sales and never even saw it coming. You truly don't know what will happen until you put your game out there.

It's safe to say that games have an extremely high potential for profit and are not speculative at all. Risky, but not speculative: look at how many six-figure and seven-figure crowdfunding campaigns for games are out there. AAA and indie development mashed up together have a larger economic output than film and music COMBINED. Despite the stigma we deal with? If you ever find yourself mired in Tax Court, you shouldn't have to worry about this part if you're demonstrating effort to make a profit.

8. **Your Financial Status**

This somewhat goes back to the time and money investment, and whether you're going to have what Tax Court often refers to as a "detrimental reliance" on this income–or the wealth you hope to build from starting a business.

If you're not relying on your royalties and payment for services, how many sources of income do you have? Moreover, is the loss from your game development activities providing you a massive tax benefit to net against these other sources of income? The appeals department and Tax Court have seen it happen time and again, where people try to deduct expensive hobbies and use those hobby losses against income like a high-paying job or significant investment income. Take Zidar, he was making over $600,000 a year from the concrete business plus another $50,000 from the rental properties.

Stock car racing was a major passion of his that was just a fun hobby, even if he took it incredibly far by remortgaging his home to get a custom stock car built. It wasn't so much that he quite literally crashed and burned in this venture, but Zidar both lacked opportunity to make a profit, and he had absolutely no detrimental reliance on the income. Unlike Groetzinger—our OG pro gamer, where he did prove he was engaged in a real trade because he had no other income and could demonstrate detrimental reliance.

For an interesting detrimental reliance case, *Shane v. Commissioner*, the case escalated to Tax Court on the questioning of whether horse racing and breeding was engaged in for fun or profit. Shane was of fairly modest means and didn't have much to lose by investing in his horse racing venture. His primary income was a full-time programmer job with Maryland's government, supplemented by a part-time job at an insurance company. Shane was passionate about breeding and racing horses, even taking two years off university to get a horse trainer license and travel around the east coast to work with renowned equestrians.

He had to learn not just how to handle various types of racehorses and stable equipment, but also receive training from veterinarians on how to diagnose and treat various equestrian maladies. Even though Shane's bills were ultimately paid by his skills as a programmer, he pursued this passion and credentialing for almost 20 years and eventually earned horse trainer licenses in five different states. He dreamt of professionally training and competing with his own racehorse and made this dream come true, with this horse winning tens of thousands of dollars in prizes after he trained her. A few years later, Shane owned eight pedigreed horses and got into breeding foals after he didn't have as much success with his new horses. He also didn't have much success selling foals, even though he put countless hours per week into maintaining their stables, feeding, training, and grooming, while he had to hold down a full-time job.

Shane also never rode his horses or allowed other people to, unless they were jockeys racing them. They weren't for entertainment. In using the nine-factor test, they found he did intend to make a profit and the Court of Appeals in *Nickerson v. Commissioner* was cited in this case with, "Common sense indicates to us that rational people do not perform hard manual labor for no reason, and if the possibility that petitioners performed these labors for pleasure is eliminated, the only remaining motivation is profit." Remember this next time someone tells you that game making isn't real work. Maybe it's not the same as mucking stables, but would you want to turn on Unity after being mentally drained at a tech company all day if you didn't have this unsatisfied desire for game development?

Citing *Engdahl v. Commissioner*—another horse breeding case, except it concerned a couple who planned to supplement their retirement income but also racked up huge losses, this was ultimately how Tax Court decided that it was highly unlikely Shane would engage in such an expensive, back-breaking hobby if he didn't want to make a profit. He had detrimental reliance on his two jobs and was hoping his horses would take him to greener pastures after the first one was successful.

Bet Shane would love that horse game made by an actual horse girl.

Indie developers span an economically diverse group from welfare recipients to the independently wealthy who live off inheritances or well-to-do spouses, with a majority in between who subsidize their endeavors with jobs or other businesses. So this factor varies by case depending on income, wealth, and other aspects of your financial situation.

9. **Personal Pleasure Element**

Okay, that heading sounded like one of those full-motion video 3DO titles from the 90s that were only in the very back of select Electronics Boutiques, complete with the adult-only (AO) rating from the Entertainment Software Rating Board (ESRB) that was retail suicide in the 1990s. But this part is ultimately what causes a lot of people to lose their appeals either by itself or in conjunction with one of the other factors in the test: Is your activity seen as a fun thing rather than endless toil? And game development definitely is by mere perception.

It'd be easy enough to prove to Tax Court that while you're passionate about making games and love working on them, you're not sitting there playing *Animal Crossing* for 12 hours a day. The articles, tweet threads, and whitepapers against crunch time and the countless indie dev logs out there about mainlining espresso and ramen to just finally hit that release date will help prove this.

It's only human nature to gravitate to things you like; it's safe to assume that one would like making games wherever they please rather than sealed in a fluorescent-lit box all day with tax forms and fax machines that predated the Louisiana Purchase. It's reasonable to expect that someone is going to enjoy crafting, horse racing, or making games far more than working as an insurance adjuster or ditch digger. These jobs deserve respect like any other, but it's safe to assume that most people don't pursue them for fun.

Going back to Shane, the judge remarked that Shane enjoyed working with computers just as much as he did with horses. That it's human nature to gravitate to jobs we enjoy and avoid the ones we find less appealing, but that just because you derive pleasure from what you do it doesn't mean it isn't labor-intensive or intended for recreation. Since Shane didn't ride the horses in his spare time or allow other people to, they were clearly for business and not living out that *My Friend Flicka* dream.

This idea is inverted with game development, since the whole idea is that we want other people to play our games whether they were purchased off Steam or made available for free because of grant funding. If our activity is construed as making games for no one but ourselves, then this factor is less apt to rule in our favor.

Ultimately, it boils down to intent to make a profit as soon as possible no matter how much fun you're having. Or how much you start sympathizing with all the parents of toddlers in the Discord server, because you too have been hearing the same song in your game twenty times a night as you're testing and catching bugs.

HOW TO SAFEGUARD YOURSELF IN THE EVENT OF A HOBBY VS. BUSINESS AUDIT

For most readers, this should hopefully not be an issue as you're going to get your game businesses in order correctly and be able to demonstrate that you've made an effort to generate a profit. There's also the whole act of formalizing your business, which is something a lot of creatives need to be extremely careful with, since creative professionals can become easy targets without even realizing it. But if you're coming up short year after year, you need to be mindful about your intents as well as straightening out your business finances.

Here's what you can do to minimize your risk of having your game dev endeavors viewed as a hobby:

- **Formalize your business.** Form an actual entity and get a tax ID for it, open a separate bank account followed by choosing a recordkeeping system, and have something of a business plan even if it's just some scribblings in a sketchbook or a Google Doc and not a high-level, multi-page document from a consultant. Entities and business formalities will be covered in depth in the next chapter.

- **Get a website.** A nice-looking one with slick design that fits your studio's style. It's not only a good idea to do so anyway for the sake of building up your brand, showcasing your work, and giving your fans a place to go aside from store pages for the game, but it also proves that you've made the investment in yourself. While hobbyists have websites, having a professional-looking website with your own domain demonstrates that you are serious about making games for a living.

- **Keep good records.** There are so many reasons for this, and proving you have an actual trade/business is one of them. Hobbyists keep minimal or no records. Are you a hobbyist or trying to transition to working in games for a living? For records beyond receipts, mileage logs, and so forth, this is why it's a good idea to have a separate email address for your studio if you don't already get one through your website. Being able to pull up proof of industry communications and all the time you're putting in can be done from a simple email search. Spreadsheets also help to keep track of your activities, such as meetings you had with other people in the industry, and what you did or tried to accomplish. One of my colleagues even has a whole spreadsheet where he inputs the information from business cards he collects at every event he attends along with what he remembers discussing with that person. Not only is that an effective method for nurturing business relationships and collecting emails for your mailing list, but it's also a great way to prove you do this for business and not as a hobby!

- **Make efforts to learn more about the business environment of indie games.** If you don't live in an area with a significant indie game scene, or a local IGDA chapter or Meetup group to attend, there's plenty of Discord servers, Twitter and Facebook groups, TikToks, and other resources for game developers of all skill levels and entrepreneurial aspirations to learn about the business aspects of games. There's plenty of free content, as well as books, classes, and private consultation.

SO WHAT IF GAME DEVELOPMENT IS JUST A HOBBY TO YOU?

You still have to report the income, whether you receive a 1099 or not. However, there's two sides to this.

One upside is that you won't have to pay self-employment tax on the income like you do when you have business income as an owner, principal, or partner. Because it's a hobby, not a business, you therefore don't have to pay business taxes or file overly complex forms.

But as of the 2018 tax reform, it also means you can no longer deduct hobby expenses. Prior to the reform, you could claim hobby expenses if you took the itemized deduction. Hobby expenses were only deductible to the extent that they pass 2% of your adjusted gross income and limited by the amount of your hobby income.

Let's say that you have a full-time job in an unrelated field that pays $60,000 per year and that is your only income. You make games for fun and don't intend on making a business out of it. Working by yourself with the help of the Unity Asset Store, you incurred zero dev costs. Then a games event a few states away is giving out cash prizes for the most innovative game. Your game wins! You get a $1,000 prize after you spent $400 on travel and lodging to attend and submit your game.

Had you officially been in the trade, your $600 profit would be subject to self-employment tax of $85. Then 50% of it ($43) would reduce your adjusted gross income (AGI): $60,000+$600 - $43=$60,557.

But as a hobbyist, you have to add the full $1,000 into your AGI: $60,000+$1,000=$61,000. Had this taken place prior to the 2018 tax reform when you could still deduct hobby expenses, 2% of your AGI is $122. If you took the standard deduction, it makes no difference whether you had hobby expenses or not, because you won't deduct these expenses. Whereas if you itemized, you could only write off $278 ($400 profit - $122 2% AGI threshold=$278). The higher your AGI, the less you'd be able to write off for most items with the itemized deduction.

After the 2018 tax reform, no one can deduct hobby expenses. But it's worth noting that like most of the reform's provisions, this will sunset in 2025 so you will be able to deduct them again after 2024.

Regardless, imagine if you had just pushed your game onto any of the major platforms after the success at the event, and it winds up becoming a major sensation that sets the groundwork for a franchise, like *Monster Prom*. Your royalties suddenly eclipse what you make at your job or at least come close to it. It then opens a lot more debate between Tax Court arbitrators and tax controversy experts for whether an amount of money that large is really just an expensive and shockingly lucrative hobby, or the dawn of a new indie games powerhouse. But despite the pain of self-employment tax you'd have with that amount? So many beneficial deductions and credits hinge on the adjusted gross income: which business expenses then help knock down.

* * *

Most people who picked up this book are serious about making their game development dreams into a business and have plans to rely on it financially to some extent. But just in case you change your mind or wind up consistently racking up losses, it's important to know the distinction the IRS makes regarding whether you have an intense hobby or an actual business.

With much talk of properly formalizing your business to prove that you have one, that is what the next chapter will focus on.

Business Entities

Formalities and Setting Up

W HEN YOU'RE STARTING A new business or have been engaged in an activity for a long time but never formalized it as is common with some game makers, one of the most pressing issues is deciding which **business entity** is right for you.

A business entity is the structure that your endeavor will take. It's set by a binding document that is sort of like your company's birth certificate. This determines how it will appear on official documents, along with how it will be taxed and regulated.

Most American business owners choose entities that are called **flow-through** or **pass-through** entities. This means that your share of income, deductions, and other items that the entity generates or incurs will flow right to you, the taxpayer, where you must pay federal income taxes at the *individual level* rather than the business level. The same goes for racking up losses and depending on what type of entity you have, items like gifts to charity and nondeductible business expenses, and capital gains and losses, which have different treatment than normal business income.

INDIE DEVELOPERS ARE PRIMARILY NON-EMPLOYERS

This is actually a distinction that the Small Business Administration (SBA) makes, not the IRS. Most indie developers fall into the **non-employer** category of small businesses; it means that your business generates at least

DOI: 10.1201/9781003335733-8

$1,000 in revenue per year and has no employees regardless of how many principals or owners there are and how many independent contractors you pay.

While not a formal entity type, you should definitely become familiar with this term because it comes up again in this book, and the SBA estimates that about 75% of all small businesses in America are non-employers regardless of what entity type they've chosen. This would also include anyone who has some self-employment income or loss that they're reporting so long as they had at least $1,000 in revenue and never bothered to set up a formal entity, because it's a side hustle to them. So the statistic about 75% of all small businesses is honestly a little misleading on their part, it doesn't mean that every non-employer sets out for their small business to be their chief source of income. Still, this is an important term for you to know; all business entities can choose to be non-employers, and you can opt not to form a business entity if the administrative burden doesn't seem worth it in the beginning and you don't plan on hiring employees.

But if you want to join the 25% and hire at least one employee in the future or right away, forming an entity beforehand is going to save you a lot of headaches.

Whether you're going to hire employees may also factor into which entity you choose not so much for tax concerns but for liability reasons. You, the employer, are held liable for the actions of your employees, so an entity that provides more shield from liability like an LLC or C corporation would be preferable.

However, your tax situation will still drastically change when and if you hire employees. You will also have increased tax obligations resulting from payroll taxes. This is primarily your share of FICA as well as 6% in federal unemployment insurance, and you also need to factor in state and local taxes. Having employees entails additional administrative burden on both the federal and state (and possibly local, like city or county) levels, such as the filing of quarterly payroll tax statements. Your life will look like *Papers, Please* if you don't have the right professionals in your corner helping you out with this.

Also, you can always kill off your current entity and start a new one down the road if need be. Depending on how many years you've been in operation along with income, expenses, activities, and headcount, it can become a very cumbersome and expensive process. But many companies do this to reflect changes in ownership or location, one or both of which has made a different entity type more favorable. Switching from being a non-employer to an employer, and the other way around, are also valid reasons for winding down and starting up again.

My professional experience has shown that most indie developers are non-employers and plan on staying that way. It's very common for indie developers to have strong relationships with the people they make games with, but on paper you might have a payer-contractor relationship if they opt not to own part of the company with you. Non-employer or not though, having employees is merely one factor that goes into choosing the best entity for your operation.

SOLE PROPRIETORSHIP (NO FORMAL ENTITY)

If you are self-employed and never set up a formal entity, you would be what's called a **sole proprietor**. It's just you who owns the ship and runs it, even if you have employees. (You can still request an employer ID as a sole proprietor; you just won't get the liability shield of an entity.) You report your income and expenses on a form called Schedule C that goes with your personal federal tax return, and your profits are subject to self-employment tax.

If your operations are still pretty small with not many transactions yet and don't foresee that changing in the near future, and/or you don't want a whole lot of administrative burden to deal with, sole proprietorships are frequently the way to go. When you're starting to make more money, other entities become more preferable because of liability protection, and self-employment tax can also take a massive bite out of your earnings.

Self-employment tax won't be your only concern, though. Most indie developers tend to reinvest significant profits. A game that sells well easily self-funds the next game. But because sole proprietorships are taxed entirely on the profit you netted, this means that you'll be in for some disappointment if you were purposely conservative with your take-home drawings.

If you operate as a sole proprietorship and your studio nets a $200,000 profit but you only drew a $40,000 salary, you still have to pay taxes—both income and self-employment taxes—on the full $200,000. You can't deduct the amount you pay yourself as a sole proprietor, and it won't matter how much you withdrew in most cases. That could put a serious damper on your plans to self-fund your next title.

You'll have the same concern as a single-member LLC as well, since sole members of LLCs are usually taxed as sole proprietors.

LIMITED LIABILITY COMPANY (LLC) AND DEFAULT RULES

LLCs need their own section because they are the most common type of small business entity but present interesting challenges and flexibility when it comes to taxes.

Subsequently, LLCs have equal amounts of blessings and curses. For business formality purposes, they're perfect for getting your company up and running with fairly minimal formality in most states. Most American small business owners opt for LLCs over corporations and partnerships, because they have less administrative burden while offering greater legal protection and authority than having no entity at all.

But in terms of taxation, LLCs are fairly amorphous. They are what the IRS calls a **disregarded entity**, in that the IRS does not recognize LLC status. When you form the LLC, you must choose how it's going to be treated for *tax purposes.*

You still have an LLC as far as business law goes, along with proving your intent with both the government and the business world. But tax-wise, you must decide how your LLC will be taxed or follow the **default rule** based on the number of owners.

Sound confusing? It is at first, but this is the perfect opportunity to analogize it to operating systems: readers born after 1995 probably don't remember when cross-platform computer game development was a rather difficult and expensive endeavor. DOS held the majority of the market share, and ports for Macs often took more than a year to come out, if they did it all. It was rarer for Mac-native games to get ported to PCs since it required significant investments in middleware at the time. Modern operating systems are more agnostic compared to yesteryear, where cross-platform capabilities are achieved by selecting a tab or radio button in the engine.

Think about making a game in most modern engines like Unity, Unreal, or even more niche engines like Ren'Py. It no longer matters which operating system you used to make the game. You can make a Linux build from your PC upon clicking that compile button. Porting to consoles and devices like the Switch is a whole other discussion; but for simplicity's sake, this analogy just uses computer builds. The days of needing expensive middleware and at least one or two years to port to other operating systems are gone.

This concept works similarly with LLCs.

You can use the default rule, which is akin to staying native: PC to PC, Mac to Mac, and Linux to Linux. Or, you can opt to create a build for a different operating system, but it doesn't change the *original* operating system.

What this means is that, under the default rule, a single-member LLC is taxed as a sole proprietorship. LLCs with two or more members are taxed as partnerships.

Single- and multiple-member LLCs can elect to be taxed as S or C corporations instead of sole proprietorships and partnerships, respectively. It isn't as seamless as clicking the correct tab in Unity, but you will need to file Form 8832: Entity Classification Election which will cause your LLC to be taxed as a C corporation. To elect S status, Form 2553: Election By a Small Business Corporation must be filed after this form has been processed.

If you want to be taxed as a sole proprietor, or a partnership if you have two or more owners, then you don't need to do anything after forming the LLC. No additional IRS forms are needed. But if you want to be taxed as an S or C corporation without actually forming one, you will need to file the first entity selection form with a second one for S status.

Why would an indie developer, or any other business owner, put themselves through the trouble of going through this classification process for an LLC instead of just forming an actual S or C corporation?

It's because there will be situations where it's too much administrative burden, or the actual structure of the corporation doesn't make sense. There's no federal agency dedicated to forming entities. That must be done by a state government. Because LLC status is recognized by the state, but not the federal government, that means you can reap many of the same corporate benefits but without additional corporate burdens and franchise taxes. Some states make this more beneficial than others.

As your studio grows, you may also decide to change how you are taxed without having to interrupt operations because you had to start a new company from scratch. Sole proprietorships and partnerships aren't designed to exist in perpetuity like corporations. But by choosing an LLC, they can take on similar characteristics by giving you the option to change how you're taxed without actually forming a whole new company!

Bucking the default rule can either save massive amounts of money or create unnecessary headaches. It ultimately depends on the state of incorporation along with the locations and financial realities of the studio and the owners.

PARTNERSHIPS: STRUCTURE, BASIS, AND LIMITS

Partnerships are formed between two or more individuals or business entities. "Pure" partnerships are relatively rare in the gaming industry, since LLCs and corporations provide more flexibility in case the ownership changes.

Partnerships also present a plethora of complex taxation issues that make most business owners gravitate to S and C corporations. While these entities have complexities of their own, they frequently offer greater financial and administrative benefits than partnerships. One of the most palpable administrative benefits of choosing a multiple-member LLC over a partnership is that partnerships must dissolve in the event a partner dies or wants out, or new partners enter the picture.

A whole new partnership must be formed in all of those scenarios. This makes partnerships incredibly unpalatable to game developers planning to onboard investors ASAP, and a roadblock if you plan on growing the studio and decide to give more responsibilities and equity to a key team member.

However, many studios are formed as multiple-member LLCs then taxed as partnerships without having to follow through on partnership laws and subsequent tedious dissolution rules if the ownership changes. Hence, the following partnership taxation principles apply whether you choose a partnership or multiple-member LLC.

Each partner (or member, if an LLC) reports income or loss according to their ownership percentage, referred to as partnership (or LLC) interest. (*For simplicity's sake, I'm using "partner" from this point onwards.*)

Unlike a sole proprietor who will report all of their revenue and expenses directly on their personal tax return using Schedule C, the partnership will report all income and expenses at the entity level first. This is an information return called Form 1065, used by partnerships or LLCs taxed as such.

Federal income tax isn't paid at the partnership level, but the information about the partnership's or LLC's income must be provided on this partnership return regardless. After the 1065 partnership return is filed, all partners receive a form called Schedule K-1 that itemizes your share of the company's profit, deductions, and other items that are passed through to your personal level.

Partners also have to deal with the concept of **basis**, which comes up in several areas of taxation, but in this case refers to how much cash and/or other property the partners have invested into the business. Partner basis must be recalculated at the end of every tax year, as well as before sale or disposition of the interest. **Basis should be noted on your K-1 every year**.

Let's start with this year. You made a friend at a game jam, and you both decide to take your jam project and turn it into a commercial one, and formalize it into a two-member LLC taxed as a partnership. After you get your LLC papers and open a bank account in its name, you deposit $10,000 from your personal savings to pay for game assets and marketing. This increases your basis by $10,000. Your friend contributes $7,500, their basis is now $7,500.

Basis increases whenever there's a profit and is calculated by your ownership percentage. If you and your friend each own 50% of the LLC, then get the commercial version of the game released at the end of the year resulting in a $5,000 profit; both of you see a basis increase of $2,500. Your total basis is $12,500 at year-end and theirs is $10,000.

Conversely, losses decrease your basis. So if that $5,000 was a loss instead, your basis would be $7,500 after your share of the loss and your friend's would be $5,000.

Now let's recap the section on sole proprietorships, the difference between drawing money and being taxed on the actual profit that year regardless of how much money you actually took. It's pretty similar to partner taxation, except the latter can affect basis calculations.

Going back to the first example with your studio posting a $5,000 profit, you would report that $2,500 share of the profit on your personal tax return. Since expenses are reported at the entity level, you can't deduct anything else and must pay self-employment tax on this amount. Even if you didn't withdraw any money! But if you had a loss that could be netted against your other personal income just like a sole proprietorship loss would.

However, if you have a sole proprietorship, then you have the advantage of being allowed to withdraw however much cash you'd like from your company accounts so long as it's properly labeled as a drawing. This is because you're always taxed on whatever profit you earn that year regardless of how much you pay yourself and how much you initially invested. If you withdraw more cash than the profit you earned this year, it doesn't trigger a loss. It just needs to be properly labeled on the books.

Whereas partners have consequences for taking too much money out of company coffers, depending on what their basis is. These withdrawals are called **distributions**, rather than owner drawings, and they reduce the partner's basis.

If you have a positive basis both at the beginning and the end of the tax year, this isn't that big of a deal. Assuming our $5,000 profit and 50% ownership once again that leads to a $12,500 basis, let's say that you take a $6,000 distribution for living expenses. Your basis becomes $6,500.

While the $6,000 distribution is reported on your Schedule K-1 and happily sitting in your personal bank account, only your $2,500 share of the profits was taxed on your personal tax return. Unfortunately, the same would also rule true if you took zero distributions; partnership income is taxed *as it's generated* just like a sole proprietorship does, except that you now also have the annoyance of basis calculations to contend with.

Because in this next example, we're going to up your distribution to $15,000 since you found the home of your dreams and need a down payment. This distribution completely wipes out your $12,500 basis and actually leaves you with a negative basis to the tune of -$2,500.

That $2,500 in the red created a taxable gain. You'd have to report not only your $2,500 share of the studio's profit, but an *additional* $2,500 for exceeding your basis. (This law was essentially designed to create a disincentive for business partners taking from the pot if the business is floundering.)

And these are just the simplest and most common basis issues you're likely to deal with. This is barely the tip of the iceberg! Partnership taxation requires *Return of the Obra Dinn* levels of deducing, minus the sea monsters! Even the crab riders would run away screaming from basis calculations.

There are other transactions and events that affect basis, so if you want to form an LLC taxed as a partnership? Grill your prospective tax professional on how well they understand partnership taxation and request that they do a basis calculation for each partner at tax filing time every year. Whether you stay with the same firm or eventually switch professionals, you're going to be very glad you did this.

There are also **general** and **limited** partners when it comes to partnerships. Most readers would be considered general partners in that you spend a considerable amount of time on the studio and have an active role in its operations. Limited partners would be investors who don't materially participate, which is IRS lingo for that last sentence. They can be friends or family members who put up funds to help you, or professional investors.

This brings up the **at-risk limitations** for partners like these, because a business you don't have an active role in is considered passive activity. Deducting losses from passive activity is extremely limited if not completely disallowed. Limited partners generally can only take a loss to the extent of their investment (basis) in the partnership, while general partners can claim their share of losses in full.

Partnerships are killer. They'd make Guiles weep.

S CORPORATIONS: BENEFITS, LIMITATIONS, REASONABLE COMPENSATION RULES

S corps, named for subchapter S of the tax code, have become a very popular business entity in recent years, because while they're flow-through entities just like partnerships and sole proprietorships, they have the unique aspect of profits being totally exempt from self-employment tax.

Don't get too excited yet. S corps can carry a fairly high administrative burden. Those irksome distribution classifications and basis calculations in partnerships? Guess what, you have them too even if you're the only person involved in the company!

S corp payments and distributions frequently come under scrutiny because of the **reasonable compensation** rules, and having to open a payroll account to pay yourself and the other officers, because corporate officers are always treated as employees. This means dealing with payroll taxes and the administrative burden of having employees, including having to buy workers' compensation insurance.

Yes, even if it's just you. Even if you want to remain a non-employer! But once you start earning significant royalties, S status can convey many benefits that make this additional burden worth it.

The reasonable compensation rule states that you have to pay yourself a salary similar to what someone doing comparable work and holding comparable credentials would be earning, further shaped by facts and circumstances of your business environment.

To exemplify that in English, a full-time game designer in the author's metropolitan statistical area would easily receive $90,000 a year at a typical AAA studio. If they got a more generous employer that's not super layoff-happy, another $20,000 worth of benefits. So if you have a comp sci or game design degree, and do most or a significant amount of the coding, your reasonable compensation would be close to $110,000. Even if you paid yourself a far lower amount than that, especially when comparing indie to AAA profits, this would still be considered a reasonable compensation baseline.

The reason why reasonable compensation is such a sticking point with the IRS and S corp shareholders is because corporations can issue dividends to shareholders, and these dividend payments are often used to disguise sole owners' actual compensation and skirt onerous payroll taxes. By instituting "reasonable compensation" requirements, it ensures that you're still paying some form of self-employment tax.

The IRS has gone after thousands of small businesses where the owners didn't give themselves a salary at all, or they did but it was deemed inadequate. One such case was *David E. Watson, P.C. v. United States of America*, which is an interesting lesson on both partnerships and S corps.

Ironically, Watson was an accountant who should've known better than to bring his case all the way to the Supreme Court, given how much accountants tend to get paid: he left a Big 4 accounting firm background and made partner at a new small accounting firm in Iowa, LWBJ. As one of four partners, he initially didn't receive a salary, because the new firm had no money to pay him. It would be considered reasonable not to have a salary in that event.

But Watson then started his own solo firm—a professional corporation taxed as an S corp, where he also transferred his 25% partnership interest in LWBJ. The entity then replaced him as an individual partner in LWBJ, and LWBJ's cash flow eventually picked up. Watson determined that his S corp should receive $2,000 a month from LWBJ regardless of business volume, although it was never put in writing. As the firm grew and Watson received larger payments from LWBJ through his S corp, which effectively paid him his salary rather than LWBJ itself, the S corp paid the remaining cash to him as dividends. Watson reported his salary as $24,000 per year based on this $2,000 per month informal agreement, even though he received anywhere from $175,000-200,000 or more in profit shares from LWBJ. They were classified as dividend income, not distributions or wages.

The IRS determined Watson was delinquent on payroll taxes, since the governmental authority on reasonable compensation examined data from the American Institute of Certified Public Accountants and researched how much an owner or director in Watson's metropolitan region would earn for his services. They determined that the actual market value of his services was around $90,000, which not even the most exploitative regional accounting firms would pay $24,000 for an entry-level job let alone someone from a Big 4 background who made partner. This case also reaffirmed the IRS' right to recharacterize S corp dividends as wages, if they believe the shareholder is trying to skimp out on reasonable compensation rules.

Obviously, gaming industry norms are radically different from those of the professional sector. Pay grades and how much indie developers make from game sales are all over the map. A game studio can also be miles apart from another that makes the exact same genre as far as royalty payments go, just like how countless games quietly rake in six figures a year (or even month), while some games press and awards show darlings didn't sell nearly as much as the developer or publisher thought they would.

The number of people on the dev team, even if they're independent contractors, can also affect what the IRS and courts see as reasonable compensation for sole shareholders. An interesting case where this was presented was *McAlary LTD v. Commissioner*, McAlary was a real estate broker with an S corp where he managed all of its core duties. He was the only licensed real estate broker present, but he supervised eight sales agents who worked as independent contractors, half of which landed him some sales. McAlary made the same underpayment mistake as Watson in that he paid himself only $24,000 that got reported on a W-2 form and took another $240,000 in distributions. Ironically, Tax Court actually gave him a more lenient reasonable compensation figure than the IRS: the IRS said that $100,000 should've been his reasonable compensation based on the median hourly pay for California real estate brokers. Tax Court said that it was $83,200 based on $40 per hour in a 2,080-hour year, given their panel's findings. However, since McAlary had other people working for him, only part of his distribution was recharacterized as a salary.

Because many indie developers handle every single production aspect themselves or use prefabs, this is an important factor if you are considering an S corp. How many people are helping you generate income, even if you have an independent contractor relationship? What was the significance of their roles in making the game, or helping you in sales or administrative capacities?

In the partnership tax example in the last section, a $5,000 profit is exciting news for that dev. It would be reasonable to expect that you wouldn't draw a salary period, let alone a AAA salary, if we look at the profit alone.

Going by indie game norms, the general consensus is that you pay yourself whatever you can afford.

But many of us frequently opt to hold onto our profits in good times to self-fund future games. That means paying ourselves a modest salary relative to our credentials, and what a larger and more profitable studio would pay, like $30,000-$50,000 in comparison to that $90,000 estimate. Holding funds for reinvestment would constitute a reasonable circumstance for giving yourself a low or non-existent salary. After all, you can't generate and be taxed on more profit if you don't have more games to sell.

Because even an operating loss didn't save Glass Blocks Unlimited. In *Glass Blocks Unlimited v. Commissioner*, the company president and sole shareholder was a non-employer, just like most of us. He didn't give himself a salary, but he did take out about $30,000 in distributions from current year profits and accumulated earnings. Glass Blocks actually had a small loss in the year these distributions were examined and reclassified as a salary, because the owner was doing all the work. He didn't have employees or even freelancers who were making his sales or helping with support tasks. As a result of reclassifying his distributions as wages, it actually created an operating loss when he previously posted a modest profit.

One thing that game developers don't have to fear when looking at *Glass Blocks* is that this guy had a finished product he was already selling. Your reasonable compensation worries won't ratchet up until you start building up a back catalog or work-for-hire roster. The facts and circumstances of any indie developer's financial performance in a given year vary so wildly as well: Was that sudden jump in profits from a marketing plan you executed, because your game was randomly picked up by a well-known Twitch streamer and found a rabid new audience, or your Steam numbers just completely blew up out of nowhere like what happened with one of my clients?

Taking note of these events is critical when you choose S status. You want to be able to prove how much of the profit was a factor of your own hard work, other peoples' hard work, and forces you cannot control.

With all of that said, how do S corporation profits get taxed after a reasonable compensation is determined?

Let's evolve that example of the two people who met at the game jam and built a business together. So successful was your project that evolved from a game jam that it's now a franchise with a very dedicated following. With mounting self-employment taxes, the two of you agree to change the

LLC's tax scheme from partnership to S corp to avoid disrupting operations and creating more paperwork than you have to.

Still having 50-50 ownership, the studio posts a $400,000 profit before officer compensation is considered. You pay yourself $100,000 and your friend opts for $80,000, all correctly classified as wages, leaving a $220,000 profit. You would not only like to take some cash distributions out for living expenses, but also leave plenty to fund the next installment in the franchise.

The S corp paid the employer's share of payroll taxes on the salaries, while you and your friend pay the employee's share. Your 50% share of the profit comes to $110,000, and it is NOT subject to self-employment tax. But when combined with your $100,000 salary, it can push you into a fairly high tax bracket. Avoiding self-employment tax is frequently why people choose S status, which also makes paying yourself a very low salary appealing, but you'll be taxed on your share of the profit regardless of how much is earned.

If you have a net operating loss, the loss will also go in your favor just like it would if you had a sole proprietorship. But depending on how it comes out on paper, you might still be subject to reasonable compensation requirements as Glass Blocks proved. Especially since being able to rack up a loss may ironically give you more incentive to give yourself a salary, to create that loss and avoid more taxes, depending on what the corporation's income and the rest of its expenses were like. This is a sharp contrast with C corporations when it comes to choosing how to pay yourself.

Lastly, another consideration when choosing an S corp is that S corps have restrictions as to who is allowed to start one. Only US citizens are permitted to be S corp shareholders, and you can't have more than 100 shareholders. You also can't form a dummy corporation or LLC to buy the shares.

The 100 shareholder limit might not be of concern to most indie developers, unless you plan on getting an investor and/or going the equity crowdfunding route, but if you have offshore team members, this is definitely of concern to you. You'd have to go with a partnership, or LLC taxed as one, or a C corporation.

You should also pay close attention to whether your state or locality recognizes S status. In New York City, New York State recognizes S status but the City does not, meaning that the City will tax it as if it were a C corporation. It can be a few hundred dollars to the City when you're just beginning, but quickly mount to tens of thousands of dollars after your studio takes off.

New York City's refusal to recognize S status doesn't stop people from living and making games there, or running millions of other different businesses for that matter. But it is an aspect you should be aware of to make an informed decision whether S status is right for your studio, and a reminder to research how S status is considered at different state and local levels depending on where you live or plan to relocate.

C CORPORATIONS: THE TRUTH ABOUT DOUBLE TAXATION, BENEFITS, AND PITFALLS

C corporations, named after subchapter C just like S corporations have their subchapter, tend to get a lot of hate in the business world but sometimes this hate is just plain undue. You may have considered a C corporation but were scared out of starting one if you've already had this discussion with a lawyer or accountant.

C corps do have some disadvantages, such as having a higher administrative burden and formalities compared to the other business entities. But the biggest and most profitable companies in America are C corporations, including almost every stateside AAA studio. If you have the right people and planning on your side, C corporations can actually be an enormous boon to you, although this entity type also comes with more pitfalls than *Dark Castle* if you're not careful.

After the 2018 tax reform, hate toward the C corp from the tax pro community also vastly lessened because of the changes to corporate income tax rates. While a majority of the provisions in the tax reform are expected to sunset in 2025 unless extended or made permanent by Congress, the reduction in corporate income tax rates is permanent. These rates may still change in future Congressional sessions, but at the time of publishing this book's second edition, the top federal corporate income tax rate used to be 35% then fell to 21%, among numerous other corporate tax benefits.

Pre-2018, the lowest corporate income tax rate was just 15% if your profit was $50,000 or less but increased to 25% if your profit was between $50,000-75,000. Then an extremely wide range in the 34% bracket if profits were $74,000-10,000,000. *The corporate tax rate is now a flat 21% regardless of how much profit is earned.*

With the slew of changes that also affected personal income taxes after the tax reform was enacted, many entrepreneurs found themselves questioning if it was worth it to continue using a pass-through entity if the entity rates were so much lower and didn't involve self-employment tax or reasonable compensation rules.

They might also be your only option if you aspire to be more than a company of one and S status won't work, such as if you have a team member who is not a US citizen. If you plan on getting investors or considering equity crowdfunding, C status is definitely more attractive than S, since there's no limit on the number of shareholders and almost anyone and anything can own shares in a C corporation.

Directors must be appointed when you have a C corporation to decentralize the management, but if you have a **closely-held corporation**, which is usually the case for a vast majority of indies, you don't need to have a board involved. A closely-held corporation is one where at least 50% of the voting stock is held by five or fewer individuals. While other entities can own your stock, a majority must be held by no more than five individuals to get this distinction, which cuts down on the formality requirements and overall administrative burden.

C corps are their own entity, unlike all the flow-through entities you just read about. This means that whatever happens with a C corp at the entity level stays there, on their own tax return, which is Form 1120. (S corps use Form 1120S which, like a partnership's Form 1065, is a required information return that must be filed first before the Schedule K-1s get filled out for the shareholders' personal taxes.)

Unlike S corps where you will be taxed on both your share of the profits and your reasonable compensation at the personal level, C corps utilize a similar concept except there are entity-level taxes.

Officers are treated as employees in both C and S corps so you do need to pay yourself a salary if you are an officer like CEO, CFO, COO, or CTO. But if you elect not to take one or it's low pay relative to what the C corp earns, the reasonable compensation laws you read about don't come into play. This is because there's no self-employment tax to skirt, but there are entity-level taxes to chase.

If you pay yourself a salary, you are only taxed on what you paid yourself. The same goes for payments characterized as a dividend (corporate share of profit), which is more likely to get examined if a C corp studio isn't very profitable yet, and you've got little or no salary to speak of.

Interestingly, C corps have an inverse of the S corp reasonable compensation issue—the UNREASONABLE salary conundrum. The IRS may deem your salary too high relative to the services rendered, size of the company, and financial performance, because there's more incentive to reduce corporate profits and get the officers to pay a lower rate at the personal level. In which case, the IRS or Tax Court could recharacterize what they deem "excessive" as a less-preferential distribution rather than wages or a dividend. But now that the 2018 tax reform drastically reduced corporate income tax rates permanently, to the point that it may even be favorable for small business owners to use a C corp when it otherwise wouldn't have been, excessive salary has become less of a concern.

Nevertheless, what the C corp earns will only affect your personal tax bill *if you take money out of it.* If you take nothing out, because you want to keep your business and personal finances completely separate, and dedicate corporate funds to business expenses and development costs, your personal tax bill is completely unaffected. **It doesn't even show up on your personal tax return.**

Going back to our successful developer example where you have 50-50 ownership with a friend and post a $220,000 profit after expenses and your salaries, all you report on your personal tax return is your $100,000 salary assuming that you received no other payments from the C corp. However, the corporation does have to pay corporate income tax on the $220,000 profit. This is the infamous double taxation aspect of C corps that makes people want to send it to the same void the Stadia went to. But with 21% of $220,000 coming to $46,200, this is actually far lower than the personal tax rate for the same amount of taxable income (35% for 2022, assuming single filing status).

On the flipside though, if the C corp creates a net operating loss, then you can't use it to offset your personal income because that loss doesn't directly flow through to you. You'd still owe taxes on that $100,000 salary you received, whether the corp was running in the red or making money hand over fist.

While there's obvious financial benefits and disadvantages to C status that are immediately visible, there are some hidden personal benefits as well which make indie developers opt for it instead of S status or an LLC. For one, it's easier to pay yourself a low salary for reinvestment purposes or skip out on a salary altogether. S corps incentivize you to pay low, C corps to pay high, so it's the latter that'll keep those pesky reasonable compensation deficiency notices away.

You may also have personal reasons for wanting to keep the income reported on your personal tax return on the low side, such as retain eligibility for housing or artist grants. If you have a foreign business partner, they not only cannot use S status, but they may also not be ready to handle US tax obligations yet and would like to keep their offshore ownership out of their foreign tax matters until the royalties roll in and it must be reported. C corps offer more leeway when it comes to financial planning both for studio and personal finances, although it comes at the expense of losing the pass-through status.

Dividend payments also come into play with both S and C corps. Dividends are earnings that you receive when you own stocks, and being the owner of your business you might own 100% of the shares in your C corp or a certain amount of them. If you have a brokerage account or retirement investments, you've probably seen dividend payments on the statements.

Dividends are based on profits, so you need to define your dividend policy when you set up your articles of incorporation. Dividend policies could include rules such as dividends will only be paid if the company posts X in profits. Dividend income also isn't subject to self-employment tax.

Dividends are taxed at a lower rate than what you'd earn from wages or 1099 payments, with a 0% tax rate on qualified dividends if you're low or middle income. But unfortunately, you can't deduct dividend payments from the corporation's tax return like you can with salaries.

It's important to keep track of your dividend policy, because refusal to pay them out over a protracted timeframe can wind up getting you smacked with the **accumulated earnings tax**—a 15% flat rate tax on accumulated cash that only applies to C corps. Don't worry about it too much: indie developers constantly reinvest significant sums into new games, so you're not that likely to get an accumulated earnings audit if that's your reason for not making payments beyond your salary.

One last advantage that C corps have over the other entity types is that hobby loss rules completely vanish. No one starts a C corp as a hobby, unless they're a total masochist. If you consistently rack up losses at the corporate level, it also doesn't flow to your personal taxes so the IRS isn't that pressed about potentially lost revenue.

BOTCHED LOCALIZATIONS: LOOK OUT FOR PITFALLS IN YOUR CHOSEN BUSINESS ENTITY

A question that I have frequently been asked since founding my consulting business is, "What is the best business entity for an indie game developer?" And it unfortunately has the same answer as almost every unclear tax law quandary: it depends.

Because the US doesn't have a federal business register like many European countries do, this means that your location (and your co-owners' locations, if applicable) plays a major role in this decision.

- **Incorporating in a state where you do not live isn't a failsafe method for tax avoidance.** If you're in a state with high business taxes at the state level, such as California or New Jersey, you may be looking at incorporating in Delaware or Nevada which are known for being corporate tax havens. It may even be a good decision if you want to keep business formalities low and have foreign business partners. But in most cases of solo ownership, you still need to file with your state of residence as a "foreign corporation doing business," which entails extra fees, and still needing to pay those state taxes anyway. Tread carefully, because you may end up with twice the state-level paperwork. This approach tends to work best if there are multiple owners spread across different states or countries, because Delaware and Nevada corporate law is the gold standard among business attorneys, so you can get help with legal issues almost anywhere.

- **Your state or locality might require you to publish the formation of your new business in a newspaper, and it's expensive.** New York State does this; they require a publication affidavit for LLCs but, interestingly, not for corporations. Under $206 of the New York State Limited Liability Company Law, you have to get two newspapers to publish the joyous news of your game studio formalizing— one with daily circulation and another weekly. Your announcement has to run for six consecutive weeks within 120 days of the date on your LLC's birth certificate. The newspapers also must circulate in the county where the business is located, so if you're in New York City limits, this announcement fee can skyrocket: anywhere from $1,000-2,000 is the norm! It's far more than the actual incorporation fees you'll pay to the state. Look into your state's laws so you'll know if you're required to do something similar, and how much this would cost upfront versus the foreseeable future.

- **If you don't want to incorporate, because you're not ready to make the official leap into the business world or have other reasons, consider a DBA.** DBA is "doing business as", also referred to as "fictitious business name filing". It is a method that individuals and both incorporated and unincorporated businesses use to lend an air of legitimacy or capitalize on a brand they built up. This process is handled through your County Clerk for a nominal fee, sometimes with multiple fees if there's more than one owner.

- **Regardless of entity type, if you move, you need to manually notify the IRS.** Usually, when you relocate, the IRS will automatically update your personal address when you file your next tax return or you filed a change of address with the postal service. But this process is NOT automatic for your business, whether you use your home address, a registered agent service, or rent a co-working space or dedicated office. One of the worst things that happens to game developers is when distributors with super sensitive ID verification like itch.io and Amazon suddenly can't issue your 1099 or verify your W-9 because the information doesn't match. Without that verification, you don't get paid. What usually messes it up is that you're entering your new address, and it doesn't match the old one in the IRS database. IRS infrastructure is painfully outdated, so you need to file Form 8822-B (https://www.irs.gov/pub/irs-pdf/f8822b.pdf) with both your old and new addresses, match it to your EIN, mail it to the IRS, and wait four to eight weeks for processing; then your verification should go through.

BUSINESS FORMALITIES

You've seen this term crop up often by this point of the book. What are formalities beyond starting a business entity?

Basic formalities include the foundation discussed earlier like record-keeping, separate bank accounts, and digital or physical presence. But, depending on the state where you set up your business and what entity it is, may be subject to potentially higher degrees of formality. We went over a lot of the basic formalities such as keeping good records and forming an entity, as well as establishing a presence with separate bank accounts, emails, and a website.

As far as the tax code is concerned, "formality" means that you are observing those mundane little rituals such as having meetings and keeping minutes. Corporations have the largest formality burden, because you can have your corporate status (and thus all the relevant benefits) revoked if you fail to observe certain formalities.

If you've set up a corporation, you've likely seen all these different positions to appoint: treasurer, secretary, chairman, and the like in addition to actual corporate officers. Since most indie studios are very small noncorporate businesses or closely-held corporations, and thus don't need to worry about this, you'd just need to appoint the person who is most responsible for handling the business side of the studio. Or yourself, if you're a one-person operation.

But depending on the state where you incorporated, you might have to hold an annual meeting where you discuss the state of affairs and have the secretary keep minutes. This could easily be done over beer and nachos at the local pub, and using a napkin then snapping a picture with your phone if you've got nothing important to discuss and think it's pointless and taking away from development time. COVID also normalized holding such meetings over Zoom, Discord, and the like.

But if you plan on making some serious changes to the studio, like issuing shares to a new team member, appointing a new secretary, changing your dividend policy, and so forth, then you'll need to keep strong records of it. Preferably, in a place where it can be easily found and referenced. So if your studio's revenue increases dramatically, and you want to raise the threshold in your dividend policy, note in the minutes how much money you estimate will be allocated to a new game, expansion, or other major business expenses to keep the accumulated earnings tax monkey off your back.

Obviously, keep good records, no matter what! But you'll want to bear in mind that this is one of the downsides, if you opt for a corporation to be considered alongside the benefits. Still, is a meeting over good food and beer or maybe Discord really that high of a price to pay for being able to decide when and how much to pay yourself?

EMPLOYER IDENTIFICATION NUMBERS (EIN)

After you've arranged your incorporation papers and operating agreements, you need to get an employer identification number (EIN) once the entity's "birth certificate" is in your hand. Conversely, if you don't plan on incorporating but would like to shield your Social Security number when filling out paperwork, you can also request an EIN.

Most incorporation websites will offer to get you an EIN as part of your startup package for anywhere from $35-200. Don't do this! Once those papers are in your hands, go to irs.gov and simply choose what kind of entity you have, and there's a few other questions to answer. You should have an EIN in less than five minutes for free. There's plenty of other times you'll need to hire professionals for tax matters and document prep, but getting an EIN is easier than a hidden object game with halos on all the items.

You need an EIN to hire employees, and issue 1099s for freelance work and if you issue royalty payments. Even if you're a non-employer, an EIN is just going to make your life a lot easier when establishing things like your new bank account and publisher agreements, and having payments routed to the EIN instead of your Social Security number to help keep your finances organized.

INDUSTRY CODES

Despite how much video games now eclipse film and music *combined*, we don't even have our own industry code! When you go to file your business returns, you have to use a code set by the North American Industry Classification System (NAICS code) that best describes your business activity.

This doesn't sound like a big deal at first, but actually, it would be nice if game developers could have their own industry code for statistical tracking. Such as how much the average game developer spends on things like meals and entertainment and general supplies, the entity type most associated with this code, and how sharp income and loss swings tend to be year-over-year.

If you're planning on applying for government grants and contracts at some point, you will also need to regularly use an industry code.

But we don't get one. Nope. We're lumped in with every other software publisher, regardless of whether you're an indie developer making less than $10,000 a year or a AAA studio. We have to use the same industry code that Microsoft does.

So when you're sorting through that massive list trying to figure out what code we fall under, **511210** for software publishing is what typically gets used. This is the same code Activision and EA use, even though we don't just make software; we make cinematic software that could fall under film and art! Why DON'T we have our own code?

It's ludicrous that NAICS makes a distinction between whether laundromats are coin-op or not, and still has active codes for blank video tape manufacturers; but game developers don't get their own code.

* * *

This should give you a thorough understanding of how the most common business entities work, at least at the federal level. Whether you decide on your own or with the guidance of an accountant, lawyer, or business consultant, pick the entity that seems like it'd be the best for your current needs and foreseeable future. If the facts of business and life change, you can always wind down the business and start a new entity. Or if you chose an LLC, change the way it gets taxed without having to start a whole new company.

There's a learning curve to starting a business but after you do it at least once, starting a new one isn't nearly as difficult. So long as you keep detailed records that are easy to search and retrieve, your studio will be off to a fine start.

The Load Screen

Startup and Organizational Costs

B EFORE WE GET INTO more granular level design in the form of common business deductions, there's the whole notion of start-up costs. Accounting for **start-up costs** can be like a fantastic level-up bonus or a piece of utterly masochistic design with slippery controls.

This is the load screen. This is what goes down before the game actually begins, and it gets treated a little differently than the business expenses you'll be writing off. You opened the game but didn't actually play it yet. Though we know you want to play.

Let's press Start.

WHAT IS A START-UP COST?

There's technically two classes of start-up costs: **organizational costs** and actual **start-up costs**.

As the name implies, organizational costs refer to the expenses incurred when you set up your business entity. This would include the actual incorporation fees paid to the state, professional fees if you hired a lawyer or accountant to handle it for you, and using incorporation services to help bring your game studio into existence. As you're about to read, there's a reason these costs are accounted for separately.

DOI: 10.1201/9781003335733-9

Start-up costs are most other business expenses that you incur before you're officially in business. Here are some common start-up costs:

- Market research, including hiring marketing consultants, social media experts, and branding artists

- Building websites and purchasing domains

- Traveling to games events to get people to play the game, find investors or publishers, etc.

- Professional fees to lawyers, accountants, consultants, etc., for getting the studio up and running

- Wages, salaries, and freelancer payments, if you've hired people right away

- Rent on office or co-working space, if you aren't working out of your home

This list isn't fully exhaustive, as there are other business expenses you might incur before making yourself available for hire or working on the game under a formalized entity. However, start-up and organizational costs *do not* include interest (such as if you're bootstrapping with your credit card or qualified for a loan), taxes, and research and experimental costs.

Because many areas of game development tread what's called R&D, research and development, along with research and experimentation, there will be a section dedicated to that at the end of the chapter.

DEDUCTING AND RECOVERING START-UP COSTS

What separates start-up costs from your other common business expenses is that while some may be recurring like professional fees and conference attendance, these are the just the costs you've incurred prior to either that first dollar in revenue or officially being open for business.

Think of a game that has fighting mechanics where you or an enemy can regenerate health or hit points, preferably something turn-based. I'm a *Heroes of Might and Magic* fan, at least until the fifth installment and the removal of town screens.

We're going to get more into **cost recovery** methods in the oncoming chapters, since there's different rules of varying complexity that will apply to you depending on what you purchase or acquire for your studio; but there's a cost recovery move with some stipulations that you need to be aware of first.

Cost recovery is a fancy term for deducting major purchases, like equipment and vehicles, over a longer timeframe. For instance, a high-performance computer tower meant for pro gamers and industry professionals who would constantly strain weaker processors can easily cost over $2,000. You might be able to deduct all of it in the year you purchased it or deduct portions of this cost over a couple tax years. This process is called **amortization**, which will come up again.

It works similarly with your start-up and organizational costs, except that you MUST do so, and we've got a bit of a building puzzle, or stat modifier puzzle if you will.

You can elect to deduct up to $5,000 of start-up costs, <u>and</u> $5,000 of organizational costs, with a phaseout range, if your total start-up costs exceed $50,000.

Since this is elective, it means that you can choose to deduct up to $5,000 for each type (unfortunately, not $10,000 combined–$5,000 for organizational costs and $5,000 for start-up costs uniquely); but this deduction gets reduced if your start-up costs exceed $50,000. It can phase out completely if you have incredibly high start-up costs, which is relatively rare for indie game developers, especially those starting out with more humble amounts of money. But think of more speculative industries that require a physical presence, like chemical plants or opening a restaurant. There's far more compliance requirements, potential land surveying, and other costs that could quickly fly past $50,000. Studios starting out with significantly larger coffers could also easily exceed $50,000, particularly in the MMO space where team size and testing require significantly more resources than the typical art game made by one or two people.

Regardless of size and starting capital though, game developers have some advantages with being able to start lean but also potentially reclass some of our development expenses as "research and experimentation," if you are starting with a large and expensive project.

Now to illustrate these concepts with examples:

After a game jam last fall, you decided to turn it into a commercial project and wait until January to officially incorporate. Working with placeholders and free assets, you continue development; so technically your operations began right after incorporation.

You hire a lawyer to handle your incorporation process for $1,000, where you had to pay the state an additional $250, and they required one of those annoying and expensive publication affidavits where the newspaper charges you $800 to run the ad. After incorporation, you spend $2,000 on travel and conference fees to attend GDC and grow your network while learning new techniques, $100 on office supplies, and $500 on a gaming industry consultant. Meantime, you're working on the game and garnering interest on Steam and Itch. Your website costs $15/month, and you earned your first dollar in March after a fan tips you on Ko-Fi in encouragement.

Your organizational costs are $2,050 since that publication affidavit is a condition for incorporating, along with the legal and state fees. You have another $2,600 in fixed expenses, and another $30 (two months of website costs) that could be considered start-up costs, since they were incurred before your first dollar in revenue for a total of $2,630.

Conversely, you could claim $0 in start-up costs, and just deduct these items as normal business expenses since you were technically open for business on Day 1. This tends to work differently for studios that operate out of physical spaces or aren't open to the public yet; the interpretation is a little harder with digital creators and businesses.

Regardless of the interpretation though, you can deduct both your start-up and organizational costs in full with no issues, because they're both under $5,000 for each category. They'd just need to be labeled appropriately on your tax return. Alternatively, you can elect to amortize these items instead, because you anticipate having more revenue the following year after the game gets released.

Start-up and organizational costs are amortized over 180 months, which is 15 years, but the IRS insists on draconian monthly calculations for many business deductions. For the start-up costs, the deduction is $11.38/month ($2,050 / 180, rounded down to $11 since IRS rounding conventions round down for less than $0.50, round up for $0.50 or greater) for $132 per full year since the studio incorporated in January. For the organizational costs, the deduction after amortization is $14.61/month ($2,630 / 180, rounded up to $15) for $180 per year. Deducting a total of $312 over 15 years might not make much sense, since it's a relatively small amount.

But let's say that you're from a AAA or tech background with indie aspirations and are subsequently opening a new studio with more resources to create a much larger game. You hire some of the best lawyers that

January to take on all those pesky legal processes and affidavits, for a total of $6,000. Your start-up costs are also $40,000, because you're building a proprietary engine, renting an office, hiring employees and freelancers to build websites and branding, and other qualified start-up costs before the studio is officially considered open.

Unlike the average indie example, where both the start-up and organizational costs were less than $5,000 each, $46,000 combined definitely passes $10,000 combined. You're definitely going to amortize some of this but won't hit the phaseout range. You can deduct $5,000 upfront for the organizational costs and amortize the remaining $1,000 for $72 per year for 15 years ($1,000 / 180, rounded up to $6); then for your start-up costs, deduct $5,000 upfront and amortize the remaining $41,000 for $2,736 per year for 15 years ($41,000 / 180, rounded up to $228).

You can also make the election to just amortize 100% of these amounts, if you feel it would be beneficial to stretch them out over 15 years compared to deducting them upfront. The decision ultimately depends on the business entity, reasonable expectations of future revenue, and your personal finances as well.

But if your start-up and organizational costs were even higher than this, those $5,000 deductions get reduced by the amount exceeding $50,000, until you're forced to amortize everything. Let's repeat the same scenario as our AAA developer going indie, where you still have $6,000 in organizational costs, but your start-up costs are now $51,000, because MMO server testing took longer than expected and that was more months of rent, wages, and so on. You're still amortizing that $1,000 in excess organizational costs over 15 years and deducting the first $5,000. But your start-up costs in particular are over $50,000, so you can't deduct $5,000. $1,000 is the portion that exceeds $50,000, making your upfront deduction $4,000, and the remaining $47,000 gets amortized over 180 months.

To go even further, let's say your start-up costs are now $60,000 because that MMO server really decided to make your life hell while the engine just went through another update that rendered a whole bunch of code useless. You now have no choice but to amortize the entire sum of start-up costs over 15 years: No upfront deduction, but you can take off $3,996 per year for 15 years ($60,000 / 180, rounded up to $333).

Sound a little confusing? Let's bring it all back to gaming lingo: think about combat in turn-based games and how you have spells or maneuvers where you can deal damage in one go, or you "set it and forget it," and that spell keeps sapping at the enemy's hit points every turn until they run out.

The aforementioned *Heroes of Might and Magic* franchise comes to mind, particularly *Heroes of Might and Magic IV*, where so many spells utilized the turn-based mechanic rather than dealing damage upfront. Think of the tax year as one turn in combat, and your Hero and their army are doing a town siege, which is when turn-based spells tend to work the best. With beefed up Death Magic skills [the *Heroes Wiki* (https://mightandmagic.fandom.com/wiki/Death_Magic_spells) comes in handy for this if you aren't familiar with the design or play], the Poison spell lasts several turns, while the Hand of Death spell deals a vast amount of damage in one turn.

There's situations where one spell will be more efficient than another. With so many enemy stacks to take out, that Poison spell only needs six or seven turns to completely eliminate that stack while you're working on the others. Then, when that slow but threatening enemy stack lumbers closer to you, like Behemoths, the Hand of Death spell is a better call.

That's more or less how it works with amortization versus expensing. Will it pay to take it all out in one go or slowly deal the damage over several turns? We'll revisit this concept again when depreciation comes up, but this is for your start-up costs only. Then once you're past $50,000 in start-up costs, you have a limit on that upfront damage; but, after $55,000, turn-based amortization is your only option.

ACTUAL GAME DEVELOPMENT COSTS: ARE THEY EXPERIMENTAL OR PROVEN?

There's an entire chapter dedicated to research and development, or R&D, matters. Special attention has to be paid to development costs compared to your organizational costs, and other business expenses that are both ongoing and crucial to starting up. This is because it might pay to treat them differently.

Unlike how start-up costs that have an option for you to expense up to $5,000 then amortize the rest over 15 years, providing that it's under $50,000, dev costs work a little differently. You can choose to expense them in their entirety or recover them over five years, if they are not experimental. If they are considered experimental, then you can amortize over 10 years' separate of your start-up costs with no expensing.

This option is there for you for projects further down the road, but has a unique aspect in that it must be treated this way whether your business is brand new or long-established. Dev costs have a shorter amortization term than the start-up costs and is all-or-nothing in that sense. You also cannot lump your development costs in with your start-up costs, even if you have a brand new company. You have to expense them in full when they occur, or amortize them over 5 years, 10 years if experimental.

The R&D chapter goes over this concept in more detail; but in short, you have to separate your dev costs out even if you plan to amortize over 15 years. For most indies working with fairly small budgets, this isn't going to be a major concern upfront, but can become one once your studio grows.

*   *   *

Basically, once you're open for business or made that first dollar in income, now is when the real fun begins with what you're allowed to deduct. The load screen's done: We're moving onto the actual game now!

The Main Event

Business Expenses

Now we're at the part most readers were waiting for: What am I allowed to write off, aside from my development costs and actually forming my company?

But before you start bouncing like Qbert over what kind of tax hacks are in store, we need to have *The Talk* about business expenses as a generality first.

If you recall from all those hobby loss court cases, the thing that killed most of the petitioners' defenses was that there was no way to prove there was a profit motive in what they were doing. That same core concept is going to apply here again: Is there a profit motive behind what you're spending money on? This is especially critical for the audit "appendage hits" that deserved their own chapters, like extensive travel, coffee addictions, and tasty food you don't have to cook and having a home office.

If you're in doubt about whether something is deductible, consider the following questions:

- Was it necessary to keep your studio operational?

- Was this expense helpful to your career or business in any way?

- Did it make it easier to run your studio, like automating or hiring help?

DOI: 10.1201/9781003335733-10

- Was it something legally obligated, such as local taxes and annual LLC filings?

- Do you think that by incurring that expense, you'll be able to make money more easily right now or in the future?

If you're unsure of the answers to these questions, or they're a flat-out "no", you could have a harder time defending it if you wind up getting audited. But, just because you answered "Yes," it's not necessarily a cheat code to bypass stringent auditors. Even though there are actually troves of tax deductions you likely weren't even aware actually existed!

But whether it's a little-known provision in the tax code or a more well-known one, especially travel expenses, people unfortunately get a little zealous with their deductions and try to claim things that flagrantly don't qualify.

Just like how those hobby loss cases are about your right to simply exist as a game developer and prove you have a real business, now it's time to delve into its distaff counterpart: substantiation.

WELCH PRECEDENT, COHAN RULE, AND HAVING ALL THE RECEIPTS: ORDINARY AND NECESSARY BUSINESS EXPENSES AND SUBSTANTIATION

While the chapter on travel expenses includes a deep dive of how you substantiate travel and event expenses *in particular*, your "save early and save often" moment is here: it's time to become familiar with the concept of substantiation ahead of time.

§162 of the tax code is what allows you to deduct all expenses considered "ordinary and necessary". Both "ordinary" and "necessary" are subject to interpretation, and this is why there's entire libraries of Tax Court cases and internal IRS documents dating back to when the federal income tax was first enacted in the early 20th century.

§262 the tax code is the boss battle that lops off personal and household/family expenses, while §274 comprises the boss' minions who ultimately nerf your tax-slaying weapons. This is the code section that vaguely informs taxpayers that they have the burden of proof to prove they're eligible for deductions. You'll learn more about §274 in Lost Levels, which is a tax code section where the Cohan Rule you're going to read about doesn't apply.

Basically, what was the time and place where you incurred that expense? What was the actual business purpose for it?

The 1933 case *Welch v. Helvering* is what ultimately shaped the way that Tax Court interprets "ordinary and necessary." To give you a TV Tropes "Laconic" page for what transpired in this case, Welch was a small business owner whose first company went under. The debts he incurred in his company's name no longer were obligated to be repaid. But Welch did something that would stoke endless discussion on social media almost a century later by repaying his creditors anyway once he started a new company, to demonstrate he was an incredibly solid guy to do business with. Subsequently, Welch's new company deducted these payments, and the authorities challenged him on this repeatedly until it escalated to the highest court.

Ultimately, the case ended with Welch being unable to deduct the payments because they weren't considered *ordinary*, let alone *necessary* since his obligations ceased with his first company's closure. The judge ruled such payments as "extraordinary," although it was open to interpretation whether the repaid debts could be considered a foundation for the new business (referred to as a capital expenditure that builds on the new company's basis).

On the other hand, there were no Glassdoor or Google business reviews in the 1930s, so business owners needed some way to prove that they were worth dealing with to both customers and the business world. Word of mouth and advertising were how both large companies and small business owners gained reputations. But whether you think Welch was a foolish glutton for punishment or an intrepid entrepreneur creatively used what few reputation management tools that were available at the time, *Welch v. Helvering* is the precedent still cited in courts to this day that states the law trusts tax examiners more than the taxpayer. Especially if the latter cannot produce proof that such payments are ordinary and necessary in nature.

The ultimate clinch in Welch was that it set precedent that you are always on the hook for proving you're entitled to any deduction no matter the nature or amount. The house rules by default, even though there is a Taxpayer Bill of Rights.

If Welch was the Nintendo of business expense substantiation in that this case still gets cited almost 100 years later, Cohan was the Atari in that it's equally cited as often. *Cohan v. Commissioner* was decided in 1930, long before we had endless digital paper trails with our credit and debit cards, Apple Pay, Zelle, CashApp, and the endless list of digital payment methods where we don't even have to put our phones down to pay for anything from a latte to mattresses.

Where Welch was about the substance of your business expenses, Cohan was about having proof of payment and being reasonable about it. His expenses made more sense than Welch repaying his forgiven debt, because he worked in theater and claimed on his tax returns that he spent a great deal of money entertaining actors, critics, and his employees in addition to traveling for shows he produced, directed, or attended for networking or research purposes.

But because Cohan couldn't Venmo the *New York Times* critic for his share of the carriage ride or pull up a GrubHub history of Russian Tea Room orders, he provided estimates for a majority of his business expenses since he didn't have receipts for every transaction. When he was challenged by the IRS, they agreed that his expenses would be deductible otherwise; but he lacked evidence that he actually paid that amount.

He appealed again, and the Second Circuit Court upheld the Cohan Rule ever since: that provided your deductions have merit, you can rely on a reasonable estimate if there's factual basis for it, and Tax Court will decide this. For example, many games composers charge around $600 per finished minute of original music, with the price point varying on experience level plus awards and notable franchises they worked on. If you lost your payment records and claimed $2,000 per minute, that would be more plausible for AAA development. The IRS or Tax Court would then get estimates from composers or use one as an expert witness, relative to how much finished bespoke music was done for your game, instead of completely throwing out the deduction just because you don't have the receipt.

The Cohan Rule is there to protect you in case of cash transactions we previously went over, and in the event you lose your records. But with modern paper trails, expense tracking apps, and cloud storage for business records, it's less of a concern than Welch matters like proving that those hats you bought on Etsy for your pet frog have actual business substance. (Perhaps less so for a game developer, more for PetTube influencers.)

The Cohan Rule not only lets you be reasonable with estimates but also for the recordkeeping realities of the era in which you're being examined. Cloud computing wasn't in the same place in 2010, but online payments, spreadsheets, and smartphones with cameras were definitely in use.

But in spite of the vast technological improvements since that have made recordkeeping much faster and simpler than it used to be, like the normalization of digital payments and receipt apps, enough people still keep poor records that *Cohan v. Commissioner* keeps being cited almost a century later.

Now that you know what your responsibilities are in terms of claiming your deductions, let's get ready for some football!

BUILDING YOUR DIGITAL PRESENCE: INTERNET AND WEBSITE

You need a place for your fans to go, and show off what you've done. Your web-related expenses are definitely deductible: How else can you make money if no one can see your games and what you're up to?

Website-building expenses for your main site and any additional micro sites, webpages, and domain purchases are deductible, along with your ongoing hosting bills and things like domain transfers and back-end maintenance. Whether you hire a professional or do it yourself with free or paid templates, the expenses incurred are all deductible.

Subsequently, your data plan and Internet are also deductible. Because phone and Internet packages often have unavoidable personal elements, it's the gold standard to deduct 50% of your phone plan whether you reimburse your personal account from the business one or split the bill across personal and business credit cards. However, if you establish separate Internet, data, and phone plans in your studio's name, then you can deduct 100% of the expense whether you're placing that router at home or an external office.

ADMINISTRATIVE EXPENSES

Has your studio or other creative work gotten to the point that you need a virtual assistant to help you field emails, manage all your social accounts and game distribution pages, and keep your mailing list updated? It's definitely deductible along with those other costs of doing business like registered agent services, mail forwarding, document preparation, and other aspects of participating in the business world.

Also called "office expenses," administrative expenses include postage, faxes, notary fees, bank charges and digital payment processor fees, check printing, and others in this vein. If it's just one of those day-to-day things, you don't really think about until you need it, like a HelloSign account to send and retrieve legal contracts, it's likely a deductible administrative expense.

BUSINESS TAXES

When you read about the different tax types at the beginning of this book, you discovered that there are all kinds of different taxes out there. You can deduct some of them on your business tax return.

If you paid state or local corporate income taxes, you can deduct them and the same goes for any local business taxes such as New York's unincorporated business tax and Delaware's corporate franchise tax. However, you can't deduct personal state or local income taxes. Only state or local level corporate taxes, franchise taxes, and other business-related taxes.

When it comes to sales tax, it doesn't get a special deduction when it comes to the purchases you make as a studio. Whatever sales tax gets tacked onto the purchase, you treat it as part of the total price and don't account for it further.

SUPPLIES

Beyond our desktop machines or laptops, most indie developers don't tend to have "hard" supplies that we use in our day-to-day work like a nurse or handyman might. But we buy office supplies to some extent: binder clips and paper clips for those sprawling game design documents. Envelopes for the mailing of official documents. Speaking of which, mailing supplies also count: stamps, labels, and packing materials.

If you're doing your own art for your games that involves physical supplies like sketchbooks, pencils, markers, and mixed media, you can deduct them because they went into your final product Or in the case of doing your own branding art, something that your business used.

Paper for your printer counts too. Just like with the Internet and phone expenses, you may have to allocate both your printer and paper for business and personal use, since it's pretty inevitable in home office settings. The paper would get expensed, but the printer gets depreciated (deducted over a longer timeframe, but not as complex as those start-up costs). This is true even if you buy a massive carton of paper that takes over a year to go through.

Big ticket items like computer towers, motion capture equipment, and other major investments will be discussed more in depth in Level 12, since you'll have to differentiate what gets depreciated opposed to what counts as supplies. But typically, if it's something you'll use up relatively quickly opposed to gear you'll expect to use for a couple years, it'll be considered a supplies deduction.

RENT

Do you pay for co-working space or a dedicated office? It's a deductible rent expense!

Rental of a PO (Post Office) Box to keep your business mail separate and your address private is also deductible, typically as an administrative expense. If you rent any equipment such as furniture or TV screens for conventions, you can also deduct it. Indies as a whole don't tend to deal with long-term equipment leasing, so tax treatment of that is beyond the scope of this book, but providing that you pay your rent as it's due on both space and equipment, you can deduct this expense normally. Then if you have an actual office, rent on this is also deductible whether it's ongoing or you're just renting a room for the day for your team to meet in person.

How you can deduct your residential rent if you work from home is discussed later, because home-based businesses have enough regulations and case law to merit their own chapter.

MARKETING AND ADVERTISING

While there's plenty of differences between the two, for tax purposes we treat them as one and the same: deductible. How can you make a profit if no one's heard of you?

Marketing materials like business cards, stickers, convention banners, and other promotional goods (shout-out to the infamous transparent green Sonic Toad chip clips given out at every convention) are deductible, because they're just one method of many that helps establish your branding and get your name out there.

Speaking of chip clips, swag that you plan on using for marketing rather than offering for sale is deductible as a marketing expense. Aside from chip clips, this could include promotional t-shirts, keychains, USB cables, and other interesting goodies that will raise awareness of your studio and provide a creative outlet as well. But if you do plan on selling these items rather than giving them away for marketing purposes, check out the chapter on inventories.

The same goes for digital marketing: so many indie developers create dedicated social accounts for both their studio and each game, especially if they anticipate them having different audiences. It's often inevitable that you'll work with a freelance social media manager or marketing firm to help you manage all those accounts when release day is coming closer and you're wearing yourself thin. Adsense, Facebook ads, sponsored placement on Amazon, and promoted tweets are just a handful of examples for digital advertising and paid content. Making videos to promote your studio, work-for-hire services, or just to use as game trailers? ALL of these methods count as deductible marketing and advertising expenses.

What makes marketing expenses fantastic is that a marketing expense doesn't have to be successful to be deductible. You just needed the intent to get your name out there. Be it through attending or even hosting your own events, sponsorship, digital and physical ads, you name it.

Most entrepreneurs, indie developers certainly included, frequently have to try different methods of growing both digital and physical presence. For us in particular, there's no magic bullet solution for this. Whether you hire an agency, a freelance marketing operative, or take a DIY approach, all of these options are deductible because you have a profit motive to get your name out there.

Do you have an off the wall idea for how you want to sell your game? Such as going up to people in a public space in costume, or hiring someone to do this, or using props? Making really weird TikToks? So long as you can prove it was part of a guerrilla marketing effort, you should have no problem deducting it!

Deductible marketing expenses also include getting headshots and other professional photos taken of you and your dev team as part of your image. Retouching and printing fees are also deductible.

But unfortunately, stylist and makeup artist fees aren't deductible, unless you're having some really extreme makeup or hair styling done that was clearly related to marketing your games. Like a character with blue skin and hedgehogs for hair that would require professional assistance. Simply wanting to look your best using normal makeup and styling tools for the shoot doesn't count. Tax Court frowns upon stylist expenses for pretty much any industry that isn't modeling or film.

NETWORKING AND LOOKING FOR SALES OR WORK

Some indie developers place all of their focus on the craft and don't prioritize making industry connections. Which is valid if you don't have much industry presence where you reside or are on the introverted side, but many devs want to get out there and network.

Meet people and follow up with them in order to get gigs as well as engage with people in person to generate interest in your games and your other endeavors. You'll also expose each other to your cool projects, maybe even collaborate in the future.

With many game developer events permanently pivoting to Discord and Meta formats to keep costs down and ensure access to high-risk individuals, chances are that you can find some great free events without ever having to leave your bedroom. And if that works, that is great! But for live attendance, be it local or needing to book a flight, networking has a cost that is at least tax-deductible.

Are you an IGDA member or plan on becoming one? Membership is deductible, along with any other professional societies, trade organizations, and developer collectives that charge for membership or nominal fees to attend events like mixers, demo showcases, and meet and greets.

Getting into conventions is a biggie for both finding fans as well as other devs and publishers who can provide opportunities and improve your skills. If you're paying for a booth or admission, you can deduct it. The same goes for shorter events where you don't have to do extensive travel; we're going to talk about conventions and travel in the next chapter more in depth, but the basic gist is that you can write these events off.

If you're trying to land work-for-hire gigs or freelance work, any expenses you incur when looking for work also counts. Such as signing up for platforms that charge monthly fees, hiring a professional resume writer, and all of those aforementioned expenses in marketing yourself and your studio.

Just like the marketing methods, you still get a deduction even if you were not successful. You have no way of knowing if that publisher who was incredibly interested and responsive at PAX ends up ghosting you, or if you're going to land a more lucrative deal because someone you met at Indiecade three years ago suddenly remembers you.

BUSINESS GIFTS

Many of us foster business relationships through gift-giving: you'll get your business partner a gift card for their favorite restaurant to show your appreciation, give your accountant a bag of artisan coffee to tell them you're thinking of them during tax season, and the like.

But there's a limit on this deduction: $25 per recipient per year, although you can give to as many recipients as you like.

For instance, if you buy a case of 10 Funko Pops and each one cost $35 apiece but you gift them to 10 different colleagues, you don't have a $350 deduction. You only have a $250 deduction, $25 per person for 10 recipients. Then, if you decided to be really generous to these hardcore collectors and make it two Funko Pops for five people, your deduction is limited even more: it's now worth $125, as your limit is still $25 per person.

While you can still ostensibly buy that colleague or client a gift costing more than $25 to foster a relationship or curry favor, just be aware that the portion above $25 per person won't be deductible. Whereas if you bought two $10 gifts and gave them to the same person throughout the year, you'd still fall under that $25 per person annual limit.

The exception to the $25 per person annual rule are small items like pens, keychains, and other small tchotchkes primarily meant to market your business that are worth $4 or less. (Like those chip clips! Comes in handy when you're in San Francisco all week for GDC, doesn't it?) If you give another dev you met at a show a T-shirt with your game's logo on it, it wouldn't be considered a gift and you'd just write off, however much the T-shirt costs you to print. But if you went out and bought them a T-shirt that doesn't promote your work, you couldn't deduct more than $25.

PROFESSIONAL SERVICES

Lawyers, accountants, consultants, business service firms: you can deduct the amounts you pay to these professionals throughout the year. Most of the time, particularly for indie devs who are just starting out, you will get billed for each service and simply pay as you go, which means you deduct as you go. This is usually the case for tax prep, consulting services, and having a lawyer review that first publishing contract.

While many solo attorneys and small law firms have adopted the pay as you go format in the 2020s, working with larger firms typically means you work with them on retainer. You need to keep track of how much is in the retainer and how much you're being billed for each transaction, since deducting it isn't as simple as when you pay as you go.

Let's say that your counsel requests a $2,000 retainer in January. You are billed $500 in February, $750 in June, and $250 in November. Summing up these bills, you can deduct $1,500 for the year, not $2,000. This is because you can request release of the retainer at any time, so that $2,000 initially becomes an *asset*, not an expense. The amounts you get billed then wear that asset down. We're going to explore this topic further near the end of the book, where you'll read about the timing of income and expenses.

INSURANCE

General business insurance, liability insurance, and similar policies paid on an annual or monthly basis are deductible. One-time product-based insurance purchases, like the plans you can purchase for your electronics and business travel, are also deductible.

If you receive any payments from your insurer that exceed what you paid for that item or trip, then the excess amount is taxable. This doesn't happen frequently, but it's happened enough that the IRS codified it. You can also deduct any expenses associated with filing insurance claims, like postage, notary fees, and the like, although smartphones have expedited this process.

Health insurance is discussed separately at the end of this chapter.

RESEARCH AND REFERENCE MATERIALS

The Internet has opened up the floodgates of all the free material you could possibly muster, and even then some. There's so much Internet now it's impossible to keep up with.

But when you want to really dive into a game's setting, the Internet and the library might not cut it. Movies, books, magazines, other games, going to museums, and events–they can count as tax-deductible research if you can prove they're indeed part of what made your game come to life.

Supporting other indie developers not only feels great, but you'll also want to know why a game sold so well or why it did or didn't get praise from critics. Or you just got a recommendation from a friend, because they told you it has similar mechanics to what you're working on.

Hold onto those Steam, Itch, and Epic Store receipts. While other industries likely don't have carte blanche to deduct video game purchases, WE DO!

Any other topical, cultural, and academic research that entails hiring a researcher or perhaps a language or diversity consultant also counts. If it helps with making the game, non-game content, or community management and discussion on the game? It's all deductible research!

EDUCATION AND SKILL-BUILDING

These expenses need to be differentiated a little, because figuring out which educational tax benefit is best depends on whether the expense is for classes or a degree program at an accredited college or university, or more informal private education like self-study on Udemy and Skillshare, or attending live classes and workshops.

If it's any of the latter, you can simply deduct it. But if you went to an accredited institution, it could be a different story, depending on who paid for it.

For the simpler business deductions first: if you attend workshops, seminars, classes, or hire private tutors to help you with various aspects of game development and overall industry education, you can deduct these expenses normally. The same goes for continuing education courses related to game development and running a studio like project management, marketing, and general business.

If you're buying subscriptions to game-related magazines to keep up with the latest development techniques and market data, these are also deductible as skills-building expense. The same goes for buying books (including this one!)

As for collegiate game design and business education, the details of the Lifetime Learning and American Opportunity Credits are beyond the scope of this book. However, you need to weigh if it's more beneficial to deduct your accredited educational expenses as a business expense or just take them on your personal taxes. While the Lifetime Learning Credit applies to most indie developers since you don't need to be a degree candidate and can claim it at any age and timeline in your educational pursuits, it doesn't net much back in most cases although there could be state-level benefits that would make it worth not claiming as a business expense.

Regardless of which method you choose, university-level education expenses generally can only be deducted if they improve your skills in your current profession or business. They can't be deducted if they're meant to train you for a new career.

HEALTH INSURANCE

Health insurance is treated differently than your routine insurance expenses, as well as your medical expenses that you may or may not be able to take as an itemized deduction on your personal taxes. If self-employed people ever received a cheat code, this is it.

Unlike your liability and device insurance expenses that get treated like any other business deduction, your own health insurance is an above-the-line deduction on your personal tax return for this.

Now, if you are being treated as an employee by your own corporation, then the corporation can pay for your health insurance premiums and deduct them as business expenses. These premiums would be included in your income on your W-2 form. It's straightforward for C corps, but S corp shareholders need to be particularly mindful about this. Depending on how the S corp performed that year, it can look like double-dipping to the IRS and could nullify this personal deduction. After all, your share of S corp profits transfer to your personal tax return, which isn't the case for C corps.

But if you pay for your health insurance yourself at the personal level, and file Schedule C because you're taxed as a sole proprietor, then you can take an above-the-line deduction based on half of your self-employment tax and the amount you paid for health insurance for both yourself and your spouse and/or dependent children.

Let's say that you bought a self-only marketplace health plan for $450/month ($5,400 for the year.) Your only income was from a single-member LLC, and it posted a profit of $40,000. Your self-employment tax would be $5,652, half of that is $2,826.

Your self-employed health insurance deduction will be the lesser of what you paid for insurance OR your Schedule C profit after you take away half your self-employment tax and contributions to self-employed pensions like SEP and SIMPLE plans. After deducting the $2,826 from $40,000 in profit, you get $37,174, so your self-employment health insurance deduction is the full $5,400. It was designed this way to also cover people who have self-employment income in any capacity, not just the full-time hustlers, so you can take this deduction even if you just do some freelancing or gig work on top of a regular job.

Assuming a situation like that, if you have a smaller profit, then you have a smaller deduction. Let's say you're making games on the side from your job, which doesn't give you insurance, so you need to buy your own health plan anyway. If your profit was $2,000 instead of $40,000, then your self-employment tax is $283 and half that is $142. Taking $142 away from $2,000 comes out to $1,858, which is a lot less than the $5,400 you're still paying.

Your self-employment health insurance deduction is $1,858, while the remaining $3,542 could then be taken as an itemized deduction with your other medical expenses. If you're still working for someone else and have no health coverage, this deduction can provide you some relief because you don't have to itemize to benefit from it. At least you get something of a cheat code while having to pay for your own insurance.

But if you work for someone else, have no self-employment income at all, *and* have to buy your own insurance, then you'd have to itemize for all of the premiums. With the 2018 tax reform causing most people not to itemize, most people then see no benefit.

That example I gave also assumed that you didn't receive Advance Premium Tax Credit (APTC). In the event that you bought an exchange plan, and your family status and income level qualified you to receive this subsidy, you need to subtract any APTC payments from the total amount paid. Assuming you had the full $3,000 credit paid to you in advance, then you'd use $2,400 for the premiums paid instead of $5,400 to calculate your deduction.

One last pitfall to keep in mind: if in all this time, you had access to an employer-sponsored plan, or were eligible for a spouse's or parent's employer-sponsored insurance, you have to snip off the months you were eligible from your deduction.

PAYING IN KIND: TRADING SERVICES AND STUFF

Every business and individual collects payment for their work and goods. No one wants to be paid in "exposure," something that people die from. Most of the time, you'll be paying your business expenses out of your (separate and strictly for business) bank and digital payment accounts or credit/debit card.

But indies are a community-oriented bunch, and not everyone is starting off with a safety net from an old job, a spouse, or parent. Time could be traded rather than money, instead of the "exposure" lie. Indie developers tend to be sympathetic to one another regarding dev costs and will help each other out by sharing knowledge bases since a majority of us left other fields or are trying to leave them to pursue our common dream of making digital toys in pants-free bliss. When this occurs, the IRS refers to it as payment in kind.

If you're making a payment in kind to someone whose help you want with the game or a non-game aspect of getting your studio up and running like building a website, be advised that you can only deduct your expenses related to the service. You can't deduct the value of the time you normally would've charged someone.

For instance, an artist agrees to make some of your art assets if you help them with web coding that you charge $100/hour for. The task takes five hours. You don't get a $500 deduction for your time. However, you spend $50 buying a template and $100 subcontracting bug fixes to finish the job faster. You could write off the $150.

The same concept rules true of game keys that you give to colleagues, beta testers, the press, streamers, and so on. While game keys might not represent payment to someone, you can't deduct what you would've earned had those copies been sold on Steam or any other distributors.

There's no deduction for what would've been, only what is.

* * *

While this list isn't completely exhaustive, these are some of the more common business expense deductions the average indie developer is likely to encounter. You have many more of course, but they deserved their own chapters because there are different rules and substantiation requirements when it comes to travel, meals, and entertainment plus taking deductions for a home office.

The Lost Levels

Nondeductible Items and Net Operating Losses

A S IS EVIDENT THUS far, most business expenses are deductible when they are ordinary and necessary in some capacity, helpful in keeping your studio running, and can be substantiated to some degree. You can't make a game for free, right?

Finding out about more esoteric deductions is like a bonus round. But the game also isn't without some baddies: Where's the challenge and balance without them?

In going over business entities, I gave an overview of how you would go about deducting your own pay. In some cases you can't, such as with a sole proprietorship or receiving dividends instead of a salary. Your own pay is often the first nondeductible item you'll have to deal with. But there are plenty of others that also fall under §274, which is the tax code section that nerfs all those lovely deductions you were stockpiling for the big battle.

Then for deductions that are eligible and legal, you might rack up a loss with them and there's limits on what you can do with that loss, which is at the end of this chapter.

DOI: 10.1201/9781003335733-11

FEDERAL INCOME TAXES

Whether it's corporate or personal federal income taxes, these tax payments are never deductible. It would defeat the entire purpose of having them.

FINES AND PENALTIES

No matter what the penalty is, no matter the jurisdiction: whether it's a $20,000 federal fine for copyright infringement or a $200 parking ticket from your city, you can't deduct these fines.

The only penalties and fines you could deduct are those set by a private company as part of doing business, such as late fees on an overdue bill, or if you're renting office space and break the lease so you have to pay penalties to the landlord.

But if any level of government hits you with a fine or penalty, there's no deduction.

EXPENSES THAT LACK COMMERCIAL SUBSTANCE

This pretty much goes hand in hand with the ordinary and necessary clauses you read about in the last chapter. If you can't demonstrate there was an actual business reason for that deduction, it won't stand.

In the 2014 case *Peppers v. Commissioner*, Peppers was an accountant with the Securities and Exchange Commission who did some freelancing work for a travel agency. She had expenses that seemed totally ordinary for a travel agent: extensive travel plus phone and bank charges. But she couldn't prove they had commercial substance. Part of this was poor recordkeeping, and the other part was that she didn't really *need* to incur some of these expenses that she had in order to get her work done: the phone and bank charges were upheld, but she lost her travel and meal deductions. She claimed that the trips were for helping the travel agency get reviews and foster customer trust. But her family members accompanied her on every trip, which didn't help her claim that it was all business travel.

Even if you have a day job like Peppers, good recordkeeping should save you and you'll learn more about travel deduction precautions in the next chapter. Still, "lack of commercial substance" is an area you could easily fall into if you get a tough examiner or judge.

EXPENSES THAT ARE OBVIOUSLY PERSONAL

You're bound to hit some gray areas in travel and meal expenses, not to mention the device you use to make games with, and any games purchased for review and reference. But there is still commercial substance to these costs: You need an Internet connection to make a living. You need to see why a game did or didn't sell, which aspects of its narrative or mechanics appeals to you as a developer. You can't make games without a computer or tablet. Going to events is how you network and get a fanbase, even though you're having fun going to them.

Even if you end up just playing *Overwatch* instead of it inspiring you for your next game, you're at least in the industry and making some good faith effort to only deduct business expenses.

But that doesn't stop some of the utterly absurd deductions people will try to claim. Citing my professional experience, I saw plenty of things in peoples' expense folios and QuickBooks files that were like something out of a movie or a comedy game, like the partner in a law firm who used her business Amex to spend an ungodly sum on her daughter's prom dress and didn't reimburse out of her personal account. Her justification when I inquired? Buttering up a dressmaker client. It's the tax professional's job to help you defend your deductions, and we have to issue warnings when one's going to crash and burn like the sprites in many unforgiving NES cartridges.

If you invite your entire development team and all your colleagues to your or your child's wedding, it's not going to magically turn it into a deductible business mixer. Seen this so many times despite the fact that literally every single case has been thrown out every time this happens. The only way it would possibly pass muster with Tax Court is if every person in attendance is actually part of the Wedding Industrial Complex.

There's expenses with personal portions, like Internet and data if you don't have a separate plan in your company's name. But if it's a living or recreational expense which is THAT obviously personal like mass catering pack lasagna at an overpriced banquet hall, you don't get a cheat code.

POLITICAL, ELECTIONEERING, AND LOBBYING EXPENSES

Despite all the legislation that gets bought today, you can't deduct any efforts to advertise or endorse a political candidate. Nor can you get a write-off for promoted tweets and other paid agitprop encouraging people to vote for or against ballot measures.

ILLEGAL PURCHASES

There's people who try to claim things that are far more outrageous than a prom dress or wedding caterers: If you "entertain" an associate with an escort service, it's not going to be deductible. Same goes for that wonderful strain of indica you just picked up, even if it inspires the greatest game or jam album that ever existed.

No matter how you feel about drug use and sex work, it actually raises some interesting questions with both unclear legality and what would constitute a personal expense. *R.L. Vitale Jr. v. Commissioner* is a fascinating case, definitely as far as Tax Court cases go, even having the distinction of making Wolters Kluwer CCH's Wackiest Tax Cases of 1999 list: Vitale was a former federal employee who quit his job at the Treasury to become a novelist. Going back to those pesky hobby vs. business rules, the Court did determine him to be in the fiction writing business, even though he didn't seek advice on how to start a writing career. The judge said that it worked against him, but he overall conducted his new writing career in a business-like manner.

So much so that it didn't affect Vitale when he racked up losses from not having the book published yet, and the joy he got from writing was irrelevant. In researching his book, he took some trips to Searchlight, Nevada, which was the book's title and setting. Some of his travel expenses passed muster, but various business expenses like advertising and supplies were thrown out, because he didn't substantiate them. What he DID substantiate?

Visits to brothels. He posed as a client and took detailed notes on how he agreed to pricing and the terms of sessions with sex workers, the house rules, popular menu items, and other information. Given that patronizing and working at a brothel is legal in Nevada, it doesn't seem like it would be an issue.

But although Vitale could deduct some of his travel expenses for book research, the judge struck down his deductions for the brothel visits on two counts: illegal goods and services are not deductible, and he felt that visiting a brothel was so personal in nature that there was just no way it could be deductible, even if sex work was at least decriminalized on the federal level. After all, this was a good 20 years before we got all those Abroad in Japan videos rating love hotels and the influencer economy as a whole.

So when you're in doubt, stick with this simple guideline: if you saw it in *Hotline Miami* or *Grand Theft Auto*, you probably can't write it off.

NET OPERATING LOSSES: ARMOR OR NERF?

A **net operating loss** (NOL from now on) isn't a deduction, it's a *result*. A game over, in a sense.

It's not necessarily a fail state, because a lot of new businesses and game studios struggle to make a profit. But as far as your annual tax returns go, it's a negative number that results when your allowable business deductions exceed your revenue. (Some deductions are not allowed to create a NOL, such as expensing that new laptop instead of depreciating it.)

It's time to bring up those hobby loss cases again: Why do you think the IRS was so adamant about going after gamblers, horse racing enthusiasts, and other activities that tend to be expensive hobbies to determine if the taxpayer was actually in a trade or business? Because NOLs have some intense superpowers, like being able to absorb your and your spouse's [if using married filing status (MFJ) filing status] other personal income.

Yes, you read that right!

This is a good time to mention that this book solely focuses on business-induced NOLs, but you can actually end up with a NOL on the personal level. Namely, through losses on rental properties or casualty and theft losses that were the result of a federally declared disaster. Prior to the 2018 tax reform, having excessive business expenses as an employee and moving expenses could also create a personal NOL, but these items aren't bouncing back until 2025.

From this point forward, NOLs refer to the ones generated by your business. There are several intricacies to personal NOLs that fall outside of this book's scope.

The prime reason that hobby loss rules don't apply to C corporations is because if they have NOLs, they cannot be used to offset personal income. This isn't the case for the pass-through entities that you read about: That NOL is all yours when you're taxed as a sole proprietor, and your share of the loss when you're taxed as a partner or S corporation shareholder.

So if you're just starting out in game-making and rack up a $20,000 NOL while your spouse has $80,000 in wages, your joint adjusted gross income would be reduced to $60,000. This same concept would apply if you were unmarried but had other personal income, like in the Shane case where he worked two jobs plus his expensive and risky horse-racing venture. The NOLs he had offset the income from both jobs.

But NOLs can also be nerfed, or *be* a major nerfing force, with legislation as well as enforcement. First, there's the timing aspect of NOLs, which is covered in the upcoming section. Then there are enforced limits as well as the impact that NOLs can have outside the taxation realm.

Generally, NOLs cannot exceed your total personal income (single or joint) for the year. If your excessive business loss wipes out all of your and your spouse's income, the remainder has to be carried forward to the next year on your personal tax return. Let's say that you're starting a new game studio with more resources than the average "garage indie". You quit your AAA studio job in June before the second quarter axe falls, your W-2 reports $50,000 in partial-year wages. Your spouse has a full-time job that pays $100,000, and the two of you get another $10,000 per year by putting up a spare bedroom on Airbnb. Your new studio needs full-time employees, equipment, and frequent server testing, so your total deductible business expenses are $200,000, while you haven't gotten any revenue yet.

As a single-member LLC taxed as a sole proprietor, your $200,000 business loss can't completely offset your combined $160,000 in personal income. The remaining $40,000 would need to be carried into the next year.

The 2018 tax reform also instituted limits on how much NOL you can deduct in a year and eliminated the two-year carryback, meaning that losses can only be carried forward if they were incurred prior to January 1, 2026 (when this provision sunsets). Small businesses were suddenly on the hook to cover that permanent reduction in the corporate tax rate: noncorporate business NOLs that were generated after 2020 and before 2026 not only can't be carried back, but there is a set dollar limit and how much you carry forward is limited as well.

$500,000 of nonbusiness income can be offset for married taxpayers, $250,000 for every other status. If a loss is being carried forward, only 80% of it can come with you!

It's also worth noting that the Inflation Reduction Act of 2022 (IRA) has **extended** this limitation until 2028, promising to index those $250,000 and $500,000 thresholds for inflation. However, the IRA does not extend that 80% limit on importing your old NOLs into a new tax return.

IMPORTING OLD SAVE FILES TO NEW GAMES: CARRY-FORWARDS VS. CARRY-BACKS

Have you ever worked on a game, or just played one, where you had campaign or map content that allowed you to transfer a character's save file to new maps or perhaps to a new game entirely?

Game developers who grew up with the *Quest for Glory* series have the best frame of reference for this: You were able to create a save file when you finished the game, then import it into future installments so the Hero character could retain some of their statistics, but it was also the only way to become a Paladin. You couldn't start a new game with this class.

That's similar to how NOLs work. They're a save file that you can hold onto for the future, and when you're calculating the next tax year's deductions, you import that save file and start with it! But the 2018 tax reform said that you can only take certain inventory items with you, you don't get a carbon copy of your old hero.

Until 2018, NOLs could be carried up to two years back (backwards compatibility, importing your character from the fifth game to the second game to annihilate those behemoths! Or self-employment taxes, in this case) and 20 years forward. 20 campaigns of tax-busting fun!

But then the 2018 tax reform happened, and now you can only bring them forward if the losses took place in the aforementioned years, because the CARES Act in the wake of COVID granted some temporary relief for NOLs generated in 2018, 2019, and 2020. NOLs generated in this period can be carried back up to five years, and an unlimited carry-forward, so if you're of many people who used job loss or other COVID-induced life changes to go indie, think carefully about whether it makes sense to go backwards compatible or save that NOL as a lifeline for a year your game attains *Among Us* levels of finding a huge audience long after release.

Going back to our former AAA employee with a $200,000 NOL, this is a great example of the limitation in action: While the amount falls under the $500,000 limit for married taxpayers filing jointly, the $40,000 that would carry forward normally now cannot be carried back at all to when both taxpayers had a higher joint income and would probably want to use it. Moreover, the full $40,000 does not come with them in the pursuant tax year: $8,000 is lost to the tax gods, 80% of the NOL comes to $32,000, which can be used to offset business and personal income in the next year.

* * *

As you can surmise by now, some attempts at business deductions are pretty audacious, but many are rarely as black and white as this. We're going to be moving into pretty nebulous territory with the different travel deductions as well as the home office deduction where it's a business deduction that is rather personal.

The Bonus Round of Travel, Meals, and Entertainment Expenses

REMEMBER THOSE BONUS ROOMS from *Donkey Kong Country* that opened whenever you collected three identical animal statues, then you had a time limit before trying to grab all the golden rhinos, ostriches, and sundry to get extra lives? How the screen would blink in semblance of shock before you went postal, trying to snap up all those tiny rhinos before the time ran out?

That is how people react when finding out about the ensuing deductions. And just like those enormous frog and ostrich statues that would double your points, these tax breaks can be just as deviously hidden.

But instead of a time limit, you have some sneaky baddies that could throw you off the swordfish cavalry and into a chasm quite easily, for these expenses are frequently audit risks. Many people fail to properly document them, then defend them if petitioning IRS appeals or Tax Court.

Travel easily gets reclassified as a personal expense if you bring family members, and/or you lack a real business reason to make the trip in the first place. New entrepreneurs also tend to flat-out misuse travel deductions, simply by not keeping good records or lacking business substance for what's often a very large expense.

DOI: 10.1201/9781003335733-12

The Cohan Rule also does not protect you for travel, meals, and entertainment. It did in the 1930s when it was established, because there was no Excel, Expensify, or Venmo back then. But now you must substantiate beyond having your receipts, and can't estimate how much a conference costs even if you go by an industry peer's numbers.

So, you need to keep extremely militant records for travel, meals, and entertainment expenses to meet substantiation requirements. In order to qualify for that deduction, it has to meet certain rules or else there's no gold ostrich statues to accumulate.

You must carefully note the purpose of your jaunts and what you're doing with the people involved. *The Last of Us* sized accounts of the trip, dinner, or coffee run aren't necessary: one to three sentences on a spreadsheet or the notes section of a digital payment processor payment or reimbursement should be sufficient. You can also write it on the receipt itself, if taking pictures with your phone or using a digitizing system like Paperport.

Such as, "Chatted with Ms. Jones over coffee. I critiqued her game and she gave me insight on my marketing strategy. It was just the two of us." If you're with a large group, something like this would work: "Post game jam beer and nachos, event was packed! Gave out lots of business cards, and I told everyone about my game then directed them to my website. About 50 people were at the jam and 20 came to the after party, most got my card."

We're going to start with relatively local travel that doesn't involve overnight stays. One of the greatest things about the indie life is that it's ultimately up to you how much local and faraway travel you want to do. More travel means higher burden of proof and better record-keeping than you engaged in before: but they can be like an endless bonus round in terms of writing them off your taxes. It's like hurling a barrel on the ground and finding a golden rhino statue!

TRAVELING BY CAR: WHAT IS YOUR CAR'S BUSINESS PERCENTAGE?

Busy self-employed people like us frequently have to travel: constantly running around to gaming conventions, local developer groups, meeting up with your dev team to work on the game, and meeting with professionals who want to help you grow your business such as consultants and publishers. It all adds up if you're not digitally getting together on Zoom.

If you don't live in a major urban area where you have your choice of rideshare and public transportation if you can't just walk there, you're more than likely driving to and from these places. You probably don't have a company car like a AAA studio would offer to their executives, although buying one to use solely for business IS an option.

But for most indie developers, you need to figure out a business percentage for your personal car. While it's pretty simple to just do 50-50 for direly necessary expenses like phone and Internet where that's a reasonable assumption, it's definitely not the case for your car. Almost no one in the gaming industry buys or leases a car solely for business reasons like one would in a more physical job like landscaping or plumbing, unless you're doing lots of filming or have regular presence at events where you're constantly loaded down with boothing supplies.

When determining your business percentage for your personal car, it isn't done through an approximation like "I mostly use my Nintendo Switch for leisure, about 30% for testing my own games so I can sell with Nintendo." There's a specific procedure that has to be followed: it's also one that CHANGES year to year, which makes keeping a mileage log incredibly important.

Today, there are several different mileage apps to choose from so you should pick the one that you like best. Keeping a manual mileage log, like recording mileage in a spreadsheet you can access with your phone, is also helpful in case you're driving in areas with spotty connections and you can easily ascertain trip length with map apps of your choice.

First, you need to know how many miles you drove during the year with your personal car, period. If you just got started with the indie developer life later in the year, then a partial year from the moment you went into business.

Relative to those total miles driven in that full or partial year, how often are you driving to events, workshops, and business-related meetings? Are you frequently on the road for conventions, games events, and so on, or do you keep things primarily remote and therefore don't drive for business that much? Out of all the long-distance trips you take, how many are for your game development career, and how many are for personal purposes? Asking yourself these questions will help determine what your business percent should be.

Also, just because you deck out your car with stickers and a paint job that blatantly advertises your studio or next game, it doesn't mean it makes your car-related expenses 100% deductible because you now deem it a "company car." No, you still have to use a percentage based on how much you drive for business reasons, although you can deduct the car-size stickers as advertising expenses.

According to Metro Mile, which interprets data from the US Department of Transportation, the average American driver puts 13,500 miles on their car in a given year. Let's use that figure in our example along with a January launch, so we're working with a full year to make this easy to understand.

You're a solo indie developer in the New York City metro region. You're going through your mileage app after the year ends, seeing that you drove 13,500 miles throughout the year. Of that 13,500 miles, you took the following business trips:

- 20 miles round-trip to your nearest biannual IGDA meeting: 40 miles total
- Monthly local games event with playtesting, showcases, and other meet and greets: 10 miles round-trip, 120 miles total
- Making that trek from NYC to Boston for PAX East: 830 miles round-trip
- Various PAX-related car trips, which encompass everything from picking up your co-designer at the train station to frequent trips to and from your hotel, their hotel, PAX itself, restaurants, Boston-based studios, and convention booth rental facilities: 80 miles
- Driving to the airport before leaving your car in the lot there: 40 miles round-trip for three conferences, 120 miles total
- Miscellaneous car trips for various business activities, like picking up merchandise samples and visiting your accountant: 100 miles total

The grand total comes to 1,290 miles traveled for business purposes. 1,290 business miles over 13,500 total miles comes to 9.5%, which following IRS rounding conventions, is rounded up to a nice and even 10%.

It sounds like you won't get to deduct much from your personal car expenses at just 10%. This is why there's two methods of calculating personal car expenses, and then some expenses that you can also deduct no matter which method you use.

STANDARD MILEAGE VS. ACTUAL COST

Whether you are traveling locally or farther away and travel by car, you must use *ONE* of these methods: the **standard mileage** method, or the **actual cost** method. At the time of writing the second edition in 2022, there was an interesting deviation with the standard mileage rate.

Normally, there's one uniform rate for the entire year. When the first edition of this book was published in 2015, it was $0.56/mile. But with record inflation and gas prices causing crises in 2022, the IRS instituted two different rates for the first half of 2022 and the second half (https://www.irs.gov/newsroom/irs-increases-mileage-rate-for-remainder-of-2022).

Driving for business purposes has a rate of $0.585/mile for car trips that took place between January 1, 2022 through June 30, 2022, then it bumps up to $0.625/mile for car trips between July 1, 2022 to the end of the year.

Normally, you'd apply one annual rate to the total business miles you drove in the year. Using our NYC-based indie developer in the last example who drove 1,290 business miles, if we pulled a *Steins;Gate* and put a banana in the tailpipe of the car, to go back to 2015, you'd have a nice and simple deduction of $722 using that $0.56/mile standard mileage rate.

But you got a slightly higher, albeit tougher to calculate, mileage deduction for 2022 that proves the importance of mileage apps that also include dates, not just number of miles driven. Let's revisit your business trips:

- **IGDA meetings**: 20 miles before July, another 20 after

- **Monthly local games event**: 60 miles before July, another 60 after

- **PAX East schlep**: 830 miles before July

- **The PAX-related car trips**: 80 miles before July

- **Airport driving**: 40 miles round-trip for three conferences, two were before July and one was after for 80 miles and 40 miles respectively

- **Miscellaneous car trips**: Let's say 50 miles pre-July, 50 miles post-July

1,120 miles used the January-June rate, and the remaining 170 miles used the higher July-December rate, coming to $655 for the first half of the year and $106 for the second half, making your total mileage deduction $761.

So, why did you need to figure out how many TOTAL miles you drove, if you were just going to use the mileage calculation?

Because the actual cost method doesn't rely on mileage calculations, where your deduction depends on the IRS' arcane processes of determining that standard mileage rate. Rather, the actual cost method uses your business percentage against your numerous car-related expenses.

The following items can be used with your business percentage:

- Gas and oil

- Tires

- Interest on car note

- Insurance

- Repairs

- Maintenance (inspections, washing, tire rotation, etc.)

- License and registration

- Wear and tear (depreciation, which is discussed at length in the next chapter)

If you use the standard mileage method, then you can't write off any of these things.

The only exceptions to this are parking, tolls, and personal property taxes. If you have to pay a property tax on your car, such as the vehicle tax in Connecticut, you can also deduct the business percentage of this tax, regardless of which method you use.

While it's a good idea to keep records using both methods to figure out which one nets you a bigger deduction, you can't claim both mileage and actual car expenses in the same year.

You must pick one and stay with that method, making a note on your tax return if you switch methods the following year.

It's a lesson in always keeping good records regardless, especially if you want to change strategies in the ensuing year. Because the IRS already sets the standard mileage rate for you, you don't need to worry about whether you kept all your gas receipts and how you have a cash-only mechanic who makes it harder to produce a paper trail.

But you still have a high burden of proof to correctly record your mileage, how much you used your car for business reasons, and what the purpose of each trip was. You might as well also keep track of the actual expenses, so you can compare whether you'll get a better outcome with standard mileage or the actual cost method.

Like many tax problems, the answer tends to be "it depends" when it comes down to which one is better for you. Most tax professionals who have clients who drive a lot for their work, like real estate brokers, find that actual cost tends to be more beneficial if they're not shelling out for a business-specific car at that point of their career.

But burden of proof aside, it really boils down to how much things like gas, repairs, and insurance cost where you live. Compare this to the total number of business miles that you drive during the year and how often you use the car for your studio and games industry things in general, so you can figure out which method is the best for the foreseeable future. If you move to an area with higher car maintenance costs like one of the coasts and/or foresee a lot more use of your car for business reasons, it would make sense to consistently stay with actual costs.

Revisiting our scenario with a NYC area developer who drove 1,290 business miles with a business percentage of 10%, let's see how the actual cost method scores in comparison to the standard mileage method which amounted to $761 with two different rates that the IRS assigned for 2022.

While your business percentage is just 10%, you live in a notoriously car-hostile area with incredibly high car expenses plus record inflation with gas exceeding $6/gallon. Your car insurance is $2,000 for the year and you spend $400/month on gas because inflation hit incredibly hard. Repairs, inspections, and vehicle registration came to another $1,800 then just your luck, your tires packed it in so you got new ones which came to $750 after sales tax and service fees. With $4,800 spent on gas alone for the year, your total eligible car expenses come to $9,350. 10% of that is $935, so even at a fairly low business percentage it beats the standard mileage method.

Had you taken more business road trips, be they local game developer meet-ups or faraway games cons, then stayed home for more personal purposes, raising that percentage could equate to a major deduction. If that percentage was 25% based on this change in behavior, coming to 3,375 miles out of 13,500, then you'd have a $2,338 actual cost deduction and a $1,974 standard mileage deduction (using just the January-June rate for example's sake).

You might as well keep extremely detailed records with your mileage app of choice, noting the date, mileage per trip, total miles driven in the year, and purpose of each trip in your log, so you can have an accurately-computed and watertight deduction, and see which strategy is best every year.

LEASING A CAR

There are situations where you can't use the standard mileage method, and leasing a car is one of them. You *can* use the standard mileage method if you want to, but if you already deducted actual costs in a prior year while leasing a car, then you can't make the switch to standard mileage in future tax years. But you can allocate that business percentage to the leasing cost along with your other car expenses.

Whichever method you choose, if you lease your car then you must use it for the duration of the lease. You can only switch methods the following year if you're not leasing.

PARKING AND TOLLS

When it comes to deductible car expenses, you can always deduct parking for business trips regardless of whether you use the standard mileage or actual cost method. (But remember, you can't deduct parking tickets under any circumstance.) It doesn't matter if it's $2 to use the parking lot while you're visiting your lawyer for an hour and they won't validate parking, or you have to pay by the day or week when leaving your car at the airport. Parking is always deductible for bona fide business trips!

The same is true of public and private toll roads. You're stuck using them regardless, so you can get a deduction for all of your tolls paid during local or faraway business travel. If you use a system like EZ Pass for cashless toll payments, the statements can help keep track of your personal and business tolls by date and time. However, you'd have to use your business percent on the purchase of the device and any set-up or maintenance fees.

CAR RENTAL, TAXIS, RIDESHARE, AND PUBLIC TRANSPORTATION

These expenses are more straightforward than using your own car: you simply deduct the actual costs.

Whether you're taking a local bus or a Greyhound to a farther destination, the subway, an airplane, regional rail or Amtrak, you just deduct what you actually paid. That's it.

It's incredibly simple, unless you're buying a weekly or monthly transit pass which you'd have to allocate between personal and business use. There's otherwise no mileage records required. You approximate like you would with your phone and Internet, if the pass is for where you actually live. But because public transit cards are so much cheaper than driving, deducting 100% of a weekly Metrocard while you're in New York for five days for Indiecade East wouldn't raise eyebrows.

If you take a taxi or rideshare like Uber, the deduction is just as simple. No draconian calculations necessary, you just deduct the actual cost of the ride. If you're splitting it with other people, most rideshare apps have a cost-sharing function with other users. If it malfunctions, or you forget to use it, you can always reimburse one another with something that has a paper trail. Or you cover the ride, they cover dinner.

As you can see, expensing your own car is like a bullet hell shooter. Expensing taxis and public transit is like a point-and-click adventure. In terms of mechanics, at least!

If you're renting a car to booth at a games show and need to transport things like expo supplies and equipment, deducting the rent is pretty simple as you're clearly doing a rental just for that event. But if you're renting a car for extended travel like a convention or multiple business trips on the other side of the country, you'd need to allocate the rental cost between business and personal use.

Before I moved to California, I'd often come for the entirety of a conference and catch that redeye back to New York with several hours to kill, in case any colleagues wanted to get together or I could explore on my own. When I had to trek across the country, I'd deduct my airfare, Lyfts to and from the airports, and the subway fare to and from the Staples Center and my hotel. I'd usually get Lyfts back from the developer parties at night.

But I couldn't deduct the fares for personal trips like searching for old punk scene landmarks, and locations from favorite movies. (That's why I live there now.) There's nothing wrong with doing some personal travel while you're·away on business trips. But if you have that rental car for an extra day and use it to see a friend before you move onto the next conference, you won't be able to deduct your travel and meal expenses for that personal day. But you're good for the day you bring it back to the rental facility at the airport, and any other days you're driving that rental for events and meeting with clients, publishers, and other developers.

It's the personal car use that's the real boss battle here. I wouldn't worry about examining rental car expenses too much if you're just coming for the event and likely don't have too much time for sight-seeing, and aren't staying many extra days if you are at all. When you're mostly getting between the train station or airport, hotel, the event site, and offshoot events like those infamous GDC parties where much of the real networking happens, then most if not all of your car rental should be deductible.

ENTERTAINMENT EXPENSES

In the original version of this book, meals and entertainment were grouped into one category under one header, because that's actually how they were for decades until the 2018 tax reform. Meals now got their own separate heading because COVID created some special rules there as well.

Whereas it felt a lot like the "All sports canceled!" moment on *Futurama* when the bill rolled out, because a crucial networking method for small business owners was toppled overnight (which often includes sports tickets and season passes). Between 2018 and 2025, business entertainment has been made completely nondeductible, unless it's a party held at your office with just your employees, or a type of event marketing meant to elevate your business: like the Sonic Toad 2018 GDC party. It was full of branding, including company colors, and the entire purpose was to get its listing seen by thousands of people scanning those party spreadsheets, even if they didn't attend! The pizza and arcade games were just a bonus.

But until 2025 comes, you can't deduct 50% of those Broadway tickets, escape room experiences, or other fun bonding activities with your potential teammates or publishers.

But if we're going to put that banana back in the car's tailpipe to travel back in time in a *Steins;Gate* manner, if not surging forward to the end of 2025, here's a great example of seemingly normal business entertainment deductions gone wrong. One of the most infamous cases that still gets frequently cited is *Danville Plywood Corp. v. United States* in 1989.

The company claimed to hold a "Superbowl Sales Seminar" for a select group of customers in New Orleans in the early 1980s. But neither Tax Court nor the Supreme Court saw it that way.

A closely-held corporation owned by a few siblings, Danville Plywood didn't advertise in trade magazines or journals, or create long-term sales agreements with their customers. Their plywood prices varied heavily as a result because products were sold to wholesale distributors based on their specs. Like most small businesses, their marketing was primarily being very personal with their customers and communicating mostly by phone with some salesmen making in-person visits as necessary. Because of this, the company kept marketing costs fairly low. This is important, because it was likely what struck a huge blow to the ill-fated Superbowl Sales Seminar.

Danville Plywood paid for a three-day event in New Orleans covering airfare, ground transportation, food, and lodging for 120 attendees, with the main attraction being the Superbowl. Per court documents, just under half of the attendees were actual customers or their representatives (e.g. buyers for the wholesalers). There were some customers *of* those customers and Danville shareholders, but most of the attendees were Danville employees and executives, spouses and children of Danville customers, and friends of Danville's president along with the employees' spouses and children.

The president of Danville Plywood testified that he wanted the seminar to be a way for customers and employees to connect with one another, and see how the company could do a better job serving them, such as improving business processes that could cut down on the salesmen's travel time and expenses. So he hired a travel agency in New Orleans to orchestrate a package deal and all of the logistics in putting such an event together for 120 people.

While the company president wrote to the travel agency that he planned to invite about 120 customers to the Superbowl and dictated what he wanted the agency to provide, like banquet facilities and a riverboat cruise, the letter of intent didn't reference any business purpose or even refer to the event as the Superbowl Sales Seminar. There wasn't any request for meeting rooms to conduct actual business at the hotel the president requested or perhaps conference area space to showcase Danville's products.

Danville's success as a plywood seller that didn't report significant advertising and entertainment expenses in the past also worked against them, along with owning numerous sister companies in the plywood industry. If the company was successful with their current marketing methods, there's nothing wrong with trying a new one. But they weren't really building a case to prove that the Superbowl Sales Seminar was for marketing purposes, when they were inviting existing customers. The claim that the event's purpose was to find ways to improve business and sales processes *could* have saved them in court, but it wasn't made clear from the outset, and saying it was "promotional" didn't work when we didn't have fancy terminology for inbound marketing yet in 1981. The salesmen just did their jobs with almost no advertising budget.

The court therefore found that Danville's prime purpose for the trip was to attend the Superbowl and get a corporate tax deduction for it without having a real business purpose. While the company's president did invite customers and employees, they didn't comprise a majority of the attendees. The intent just didn't look like it had any business substance. (This is why I put in all of my event space inquiry emails that Sonic Toad was hosting a *promotional* GDC party.)

When we get business entertainment deductions back after 2025, or you're using this book as a guide for tax years preceding 2018, bear all of this in mind when claiming business entertainment deductions! The following section applies to both meal and entertainment deductions, but it is especially crucial for entertainment in the eligible years, because meals are still allowed given the whole "we have to eat to live" thing.

WHO WERE YOU WITH AND WHAT WAS THE FUN TIME FOR?

Until the Reagan era, you could deduct 100% of your meal and entertainment expenses. But then the taxpayers got sick of subsidizing corporate executives' three martini lunches, so the meals and entertainment deduction was subject to a phaseout over the years, starting at 80% of these expenses until it fell to 50% and remained there ever since. So, you're typically limited to 50% of the actual costs, whether it's $200 worth of beer and burgers with your entire dev team or $3 for that cup of coffee you bought to discuss potential collaboration with a publisher or streamer.

In order to be deductible, there has to be some kind of business relationship with this person or group of people. Are they one of the following?

- Publisher

- Investor

- Customer, client, patron, or fan

- Colleague/fellow developer

- Employee
- Contractor
- Press, reviewer, content creator
- Influencer
- Members of your dev team, business partners
- Professionals who serve you in a non-dev capacity (lawyer, accountant, etc.)
- Someone who is going to give you work or a speaker slot

And, was this get-together primarily for business?

Did you actively try to conduct business in some manner, with the expectation that you would benefit in some way afterward? Or if you were the one providing the benefit to the other person/people, did this breaking of Doritos and Mountain Dew result in solidifying your business relationship in some fashion?

"Benefit" doesn't necessarily mean that this person will pay you sometime soon. But it can mean that they teach you a new skill, offer input on your game so you reach a larger audience and thus become more profitable, work on the game or help you with finding someone who can, or provide something like a review or social media boost.

Whether you're going out for beers with hundreds of other developers after a conference or having a more intimate coffee talk with an animator you're hoping to work with, those three key business elements need to be present to defend your deduction to avoid the same fate as Danville Plywood:

- **WHO** you're dining with (or entertaining, if in a year outside of the 2018-2025 tax reform range) and what your relationship is to them
- **WHY** you are dining with them
- **WHAT** was the business purpose or benefit

Even if that person is in a non-dev capacity such as your lawyer or the printer who creates your promotional materials, the benefit might not be games-related but still be a benefit to you on the business level. Maybe you're getting useful information about legal concerns you have about a publisher contract while you get coffee, or trying that new pizza joint with your printing professional leads to a substantial discount on your next order. Information and discounts are certainly benefits!

On the flipside, if you buy an investor a round of drinks or tickets to a show because they expressed interest in you, but they end up not funding you? You can still deduct it: there was a business reason for that treat.

Just because you weren't successful in getting money out of them doesn't mean you didn't have the reasonable expectation to benefit in some way, even if that benefit was merely telling you how to improve your studio's business profile and getting a lesson in what gaming industry investors want to see in potential investees.

COOK, SERVE, DELICIOUS TAX DEDUCTIONS: MEAL EXPENSES

In the wake of both the 2018 tax reform and COVID relief bills that impacted the tax code, meals needed their own section. While typically lumped in with entertainment, this is not the case anymore.

Unlike going out to a baseball game or doing something really out there, like scuba diving, we have to eat to live. It's expected that you'll need to eat on your business trips whether you're alone or have company, and you definitely can't count on hotels, events, and your mode of transportation providing meals for you. It's also reasonably expected that hotel and convention center commissaries will price-gouge attendees, along with area restaurants.

So if you were looking for a tax-deductible excuse to go to a fancier restaurant at GDC or PAX compared to how you'd normally dine where you live, it's definitely the right time and place! You're just not allowed to deduct what the IRS deems "luxurious" or "excessive" food costs, no $600 beluga caviar for your That Party TikToks.

But if your taste is more humble, like that $9 burrito bowl because it's the only place that's open and doesn't have a line snaking around the block when you have to be onstage for your talk in 20 minutes, that too is deductible and subject to the same 50% limit.

Because food can be bought in multiple places that aren't restaurants, like convenience and big-box stores, this is why keeping receipts is so important. Going to grocery stores for long conferences so that you can stay alert, energized, and hydrated and not be gouged $3 for a lukewarm bottle of Aquafina and $8 for a slice of supermarket pizza that's been laying under a heat lamp longer than it took the *Duke Nukem* follow-up to lose vaporware status? It can save you time and money over going to restaurants, and is still 50% tax-deductible.

UNDERSTANDING THE DIFFERENCE BETWEEN A TRAVEL MEAL AND A BUSINESS MEAL

While "business meal" is used as an umbrella term for both, it's important to make the distinction between the two.

Travel meal costs can only be deducted when you are away from home for business purposes *at least one night.* All of your basic life-sustaining costs become deductible once you're gone at least one night, which is what can turn them into a major bonus round.

So let's say you take a day trip two hours from home to show your game at an event there. You pack up the car when the event is over, get dinner by yourself, then go home. Because you came home the same day (or if it was after midnight, you at least left with no plans for an overnight stay), you can deduct just about all of your event-related expenses, EXCEPT that dinner. It seems a little weird, but that "life-sustaining" element in the law doesn't think it should sustain your life if you'll be home again the same day. It doesn't show concern for you until you're away from home for one night at minimum.

Even if the event was just two hours away, opposed to four hours, staying with a friend in town or getting a room for the night would then qualify all of your meal expenses until you get home.

If you're otherwise headed back to your own place after the event, you'd only get a deduction as a *business* meal if you went with one of the other attendees, exhibitors, or other industry people to talk shop.

Business meals can take place as an incidental expense when you're at home, local business travel where you're headed home afterwards, and during personal travel if you happen to meet up with a colleague at your destination. That's when you're still in your home city, but your publisher rep wants to meet for coffee, or you order pizza for the voice actors after a productive recording session to say thanks.

Travel meals you can have by yourself and deduct them, business meals require at least two people and identifying that "who, why, and what" in order to pass the smell test.

THE DUTCH RULE

The "Dutch rule" basically means that you're covered if you pay for the entire meal, drink, or if we're talking years outside the 2018-2025 tax reform blackout, the entire cost of entertainment.

Whether you pay only for yourself, treat the person or group, or pay for both, you can deduct it. So even if you and the person you're with each pay your own tab, you still get a deduction. Same if everyone decides to split the bill equally, instead of quibbling over who ordered the family-size cheesy bread and four drinks while the person who just had an appetizer and water is disintegrating in the corner.

But as mentioned in discerning travel from business meals, don't confuse being able to deduct paying just your own tab with also being able to deduct personal meals and drinks. If you go out by yourself a lot to coffee shops, as indie developers are wont to do to get inspired and avoid cabin fever, you unfortunately don't get any deduction.

Even though as creatives we could argue the merits of needing the social interaction and change of scene to work more efficiently, or even observing something that winds up going in a game later, in the eyes of the law there is no commercial substance to the expense.

But it's a different story if you happen to meet someone helpful in your coffee run like another indie developer, and you offer to buy them a drink in order to get some insight on a business matter, and other forms of talking shop that would transform your personal expense into a deductible business one.

SPECIAL TEMPORARY BONUS FOR RESTAURANT MEALS IN 2021 AND 2022

To subsidize restaurants that were hit incredibly hard during the pandemic, Congress authorized a special tax deduction under the HEALS Act that temporarily expanded business meals to 100% if food or beverage is purchased from a restaurant between January 1, 2021 and December 31, 2022.

Takeout and delivery also counts! So if you're having that team pizza party or don't feel comfortable dining in yet, you can still get a 100% deduction if you bought the food or beverages from a restaurant. The law specifically excludes employer cafeterias and businesses that sell pre-packaged food and beverages not intended to be consumed immediately, so that would encompass grocery stores, convenience stores, vending machines, newsstands, and so on, even if you consume your purchases right away. The 50% limit applies to those items.

For the 100% temporary bonus to apply, you need to have bought your food and drink from a restaurant. This includes coffee shops because the product is meant to be drunk right away, bakeries could be debatable but we know those delicious fruit tarts won't last long.

This means that if you hit up Trader Joe's by the Metreon to get picnic supplies for the first GDC since the shutdown, it would only net you a 50% deduction. But if you went to one of the eateries inside the Metreon or nearby to eat in the park like everyone else, then you would have a 100% deduction.

FOOD AND COFFEE AT HOME AND THE OFFICE

Do you keep up actual office space somewhere, like a dedicated desk at a co-working space or an actual empty office? You have some tricky deductions that can quickly add up.

Think of all the things you have to buy for your home: toilet paper, paper towels, hand soap, and most of all, somewhat shelf-stable food and drinks—snacks, fruit, coffee, tea, and bottled water. Then of course, things like a microwave and coffee maker. A mini-fridge, if you have really fancy digs!

If you buy those things for your home, you can't deduct them, even if you want to argue that a coffee IV drip means you'll get the game out faster. But you can write them off in full if you have an external office, including the snacks and drinks.

Most co-working spaces and flexible space arrangements tend to offer these amenities, like free coffee and tea plus staff who maintain the supply and do the cleaning. So this is more common in areas where you're renting space in a more hands-off fashion, and need to be more proactive in managing your and your guests' comfort.

In order to qualify for these snack and store-bought coffee deductions, you need a traditional rented office or a private suite within a co-working space where you receive mail and regularly work there. The key is really that A) it's not in your home, and B) you regularly have this space.

Since long-term and/or higher-tier subscribers to co-working spaces usually get benefits like storage lockers and being able to use that location as a mailing address, using co-working space instead of a traditional rented office doesn't necessarily disqualify you from being able to deduct these extra expenses. But if these amenities aren't being provided, or the ones provided don't suit your needs, you can deduct expenses that would otherwise be considered personal if you bought them for your home (even if you claimed the home office deduction).

If you're bringing takeout or ordering prepared food and drinks for your external office though, the same rules about meals and entertainment will apply. It needs to have a business purpose, and the temporary 100% business meals deduction will apply if it's from a restaurant, not a catering service or grocery store.

PLANES, TRAINS, AND AUTOMOBILES: OVERNIGHT BUSINESS TRAVEL

Overnight business travel is your freaking Hadouken. You've seen how deductible car expenses really add up, even when limited with a business percentage. But this is where it's about to get real.

Conferences, conventions, and opportunities to showcase your game and connect with publishers and your peers are the dominant form of business travel for indie game developers. This is especially true now that Zoom and Discord have taken over many in-person meetings, although many smaller dev teams still strive to get together in person as often as they can if they feel they collaborate more effectively that way.

Whether it's a conference or a trip in the name of collaboration or research, overnight business travel has more loopholes than local travel where you return home the same day.

Because of these numerous loopholes, it's why the "for-only" test is a cornerstone of defending business travel deductions. **This test basically means that you need to ask yourself whether a rational businessperson would be taking this trip, or if it wouldn't make sense without your personal reasons for going.**

This comes back to three cases you read about: *Peppers, Danville Plywood*, and *R.L.Vitale*. Peppers taking her family members with her and having only vague business reasons for her trips put her in the latter category, that the personal elements superseded any business reason she could've had for the trip. Danville Plywood had a few sparks of being a rational businessperson, but ultimately failed to present this argument because it simply looked like the trip to New Orleans made no sense without the Superbowl. That was the main attraction, not the "sales seminar". While remote meeting and digital event technology was the stuff of sci-fi in 1981, a great deal of business was still conducted by phone at the time and Danville Plywood was no exception. He could've just had a Superbowl party by renting out a local bar or hotel, if not the Danville HQ, to generate productive talk among the customers and staff.

Vitale ironically had the strongest business case of all three: his book's setting was in a far-flung Nevada town and sex work was a major part of the story. The judge let some of his travel deductions stand because they did constitute book research, it was just the brothel visits that didn't because they're still criminalized at the federal level. Vitale otherwise met the for-only test where the other two failed.

If you're flying out to San Francisco for GDC, or Boston for PAX East, and your main purpose for making the trip is to attend or exhibit at the show, then it's pretty cut and dry that you met the for-only test. But if you always wanted to go to Disney World and one of your team members happens to live in Orlando, so you want to find a way to make the trip tax-deductible? You'll have to come up with a way to really substantiate it as a business trip to write off those dinners at Epcot. Going out to the Midwest to see your parents, with only the off chance of dropping by a marketing expert's office a town over? You'll have a very hard time satisfying this test.

The for-only test goes hand-in-hand with the fact that you need a profit motive to make the trip and justify the expense. For most major conventions, they not only provide justification letters on their websites that employees are meant to show their employers to get them to pay for their attendance, but they can also help you mount a good defense. Smaller shows are also the ideal place to network more intimately than the big shows, and just get your game out in front of people. Big or small, games events are business travel deductions in easy mode.

For trips that aren't conferences and expos, that's hard mode. You have a much higher burden of proof to prove that you had a real business purpose for writing that trip off your taxes.

WHAT YOU MUST HAVE IN EVERY OVERNIGHT TRAVEL RECORD

Local travel still has a fairly high burden of proof, as you just saw with having to account for car expenses. But there is a specific statutory requirement, another building puzzle if you will, for trips that involve you going away for at least one night:

- The amounts for each separate expenditure for traveling away from home because the Cohan Rule doesn't protect you here (This means individual transactions backed up with receipts in proper categories. Make detailed expense reports and keep them digital!)

- The departure and return dates for each trip, and the number of days during each trip that you spent on business

- The name of the city or town you visited, if multiple cities then what your purpose was in each one

- The business reason for traveling or the kind of benefit you expected to gain from the trip

You need to do all of this whether you are going to a convention or not. Especially identifying which day was a travel day opposed to a business or personal day, because it makes a *huge* difference in properly computing these deductions.

TRAVEL DAYS, BUSINESS DAYS, AND DEDUCTING LIFE-SUSTAINING COSTS

Let's say GDC starts March 10 and ends March 17, so you decide to make a vacation out of it and come earlier and leave later than the convention dates. Taking note of your departure and arrival dates, you arrive March 7 and depart March 19, making for a 13-day trip.

If you had no other plans to meet dev team members, publishers, associates, or otherwise conduct business outside of GDC, then your only business days would be the days of the convention. Eight days out of the 13 count as business days. You have two travel days as well, so it's 10 out of 13 days that you can take some deductions that add up extremely fast.

You can deduct your airfare, train fare, and so on, plus ground transportation (cabs, shuttles, public transportation) in getting to and from the airport on both those days. If you used frequent flier miles, Amtrak points, and other travel rewards, then you only get to deduct what you actually paid. Not what the ticket price otherwise would've been. But even if you shell out for business or first class seats, you can deduct the fare so long as the trip had a bona fide business purpose.

But the critical hit you can make on your tax bill is your life-sustaining costs: meals and lodging.

You still have a 50% limit on meals, but this time it doesn't matter if you eat them by yourself or have a business purpose or not! Even your airport snacks are deductible, as is that $10 cup of chunky and burnt Starbucks you grabbed once you rolled off the plane to wake up.

Just remember though: **You can only do this if you are going away for at least one night**. If you have a very long drive or train ride from another games event, but are going straight home and definitely weren't going to wait till you got home to eat, you can't deduct the meal unless you were sharing it with someone you have a business relationship with and that fostered the relationship.

But meals add up so fast even if you're trying to stay on a budget, especially if you're going to a high-cost city like San Francisco or Los Angeles for a major event where all the restaurants adjacent to the convention centers tend to gouge attendees. Even with the 50% limit, meals, snacks, bar tabs, and coffee can make for significant deductions. Additionally, if you incurred these expenses at restaurants in 2021 or 2022, then you can claim 100% of the cost instead of 50%.

Keep in mind, you can't do this on your non-travel and non-business days. So in our GDC sojourn example, we have just three days where there's no deduction for meals. Save the splurging at nicer restaurants for the travel and convention days, when those meals will be deductible.

If you're dining solo or with people far removed from your professional life as a game developer, there's also no meal and drink write-off on non-business days. But, if you're meeting up with a colleague incidentally on a personal day, the normal business meal rules apply and you can get a 50% deduction (100% if in 2021 or 2022 at a restaurant).

I HATE TRACKING RECEIPTS: WHAT ABOUT THE STANDARD MEALS ALLOWANCE?

Just like the standard mileage rates, there's a separate standardized rate for travel meals set by the government. Using these standard rates means you're relieved from having to document every single meal, but the trip itself still needs to meet the tests described earlier.

Using the standard allowance could benefit you, if you're a budget diner who has spent far below the standard allowance for the day and region.

Although given inflation and conference hotspot price-gouging, this probably isn't most people.

This alternate gameplay path is also twistier than the direct route of the actual cost method you just read about. You might want to stick to using this method, because simply tallying up your food receipts from the trip can actually be WAY less mentally taxing than the following:

- Consult the General Service Administration (GSA) tables linked below to find the correct local rate for standard meals allowance based on where the meals were eaten (unlike the standard mileage rate, which is universally applied no matter where you travel or live in the US)

- Prorate the amount on your departure and return dates

- Just like how the standard mileage method applies to how you claim car expenses all year, you must use the standard meals allowance for **all** of your overnight business trips throughout the year

- Federal agencies operate on a fiscal year that starts every October, so most people have to choose between which fiscal year to use based on which one has the better rates by location

- You can only use this method for overnight trips; local business meals still use 50% of actual cost (100% for 2021 and 2022 if at a restaurant)

This would bring Zagreus to tears even after you activated God Mode after dying 20,000 times in *Hades*! But depending on how much you travel and your spending habits, this method could wind up netting you a bigger deduction and making the headache worth it. Otherwise, I wouldn't have mentioned it here.

So, the GSA sets these amounts every year, not the IRS. There is a link to the GSA per diem tables on the supplemental webpage you have access to as a result of purchasing this book. Check out their per diem rates (http://www.gsa.gov/portal/content/104877) for the daily allowance based on the zip code of where you will be, it will be the M&IE columns and you can disregard the information on splitting out amounts for meals and incidentals, because that is meant for federal employees.

Just like with using the actual costs for meals, the meal allowance has a 50% limit and no special rules for COVID. Entering my Los Angeles zip code resulted in $74 per day for the 2023 fiscal year. The actual deduction would be half of that, $37 per day.

Interestingly, it was STILL $74 per day with a New York City zip code for the 2016 fiscal year, when this book was first published. Which should tell you how out of touch these agencies are with how much things actually cost. The GSA thinks $18 is a reasonable lunch expense in LA? Oh, you sweet summer children.

If also you're going to be in more than one zip code on a travel day, like taking a road trip to a convention, use the rate for where you will be sleeping that night. This could help you if you leave a low-cost area and sleep in a high-cost one, but hurt you if it's the other way around. How much you'd benefit from the standard meal allowance method also depends on your taste in dining establishments proximal to what is actually nearby, of course.

But then you *also* need to prorate for your departure and return dates using one of two methods. Regardless of which one you'd use, the area that you are departing from to go home is the regional per diem rate that you'd apply. So if you're staying in New York for four days and three nights before going back to Chicago, you'd still be using New York rates on that last day.

The first proration method is the simple federal employee method, which is just to take ¾ of the regional rate for that day. The other method is pretty vague in that you prorate based on a "reasonable business practice and applied consistently." So under the simplified method, you'd have two ¾ days and two full days, for three-and-a-half days to use New York's allowance.

¾ of $74 is $56, two ¾ days and two full days comes out to a total deduction of $260. Looking at the harder proration method, if you look at your arrival and return times on both those days, you could prorate a full day depending on when you arrived or got home. If you arrived in New York midday but didn't get back to Chicago until well after 9PM, it'd be easy enough to say that you had four days instead of three and a half for a $296 deduction.

This hack is pretty difficult, but one that could prove to be worth taking if food prices collapse. But are you still not having fun yet? It's *Five Nights at Freddy's*, but even scarier because he needs multiple per diem rates now, which will send those creepy animatronics running.

If you travel outside the contiguous 48 like Alaska, Hawaii, or a US territory, the Department of Defense sets the rates for those areas, and you'd have to consult their tables (https://www.defensetravel.dod.mil/site/perdiemCalc.cfm). The Department of State sets the per diem rates for foreign travel (https://aoprals.state.gov/web920/per_diem.asp) if you're doing international business, and you'll have to go by the closest region or city on their chart. These tables are linked in the supplemental webpage you gained access to with the purchase of this book.

Some countries, even ones with notoriously lower living costs like Thailand, have extremely high per diem rates that actually could make this headache worth it.

So just like with standard mileage rates for drivers, you might want to keep track of both the per diem rates and the actual costs for your travel meals to see which method is more beneficial for you. Like the mileage method, it also needs to be consistently applied for the year and has the same substantiation requirements.

EXPENSE SUBTRACTION FOR NONBUSINESS GUESTS

People often use conventions and other business travel to supplant family vacations. But you can't deduct the expenses for your family or friends to come with you, you can only deduct what you pay for yourself.

For the airfare, you'd need to examine how much just your share of airfare, taxes, baggage fees, and travel insurance cost out of all the tickets you purchased. This is easier when purchased in separate transactions, but couples and families often opt to book them in one go to get their desired seating. Then for the hotel, you have to find out what they were charging for single-occupancy rooms instead of the rate for families and multiple guests. If the rate at your hotel was $170/night after fees and taxes for one guest, but you paid $250/night for your spouse and child to stay in the room as well, you could only base your travel deduction on the single-occupancy rate of $170.

The same goes for meals; you can only deduct meals for yourself on travel and business days. The meals for your family members are never deductible. Per convention commonalities, if your family decides to dine with another game dev's family, the Dutch rule applies again in that you could only deduct the amounts paid for you and your associate, not your family or theirs.

But now, indie developers often have spouses or travel buddies who are also in the field to save on hotel costs and split the driving. If we switched everything in the example above to a business associate, then all of those travel expenses will become deductible. That person must be your employee, business partner, or industry associate **who would've been able to deduct the expenses on their own, if they took a separate trip from you.**

If you're splitting a room, typically only one person's card will be charged so your buddy will Venmo or PayPal you for their share. Remember to reduce your deduction by that reimbursement.

EXPENSES FOR DEV TEAM MEMBERS WHO ARE INDEPENDENT CONTRACTORS

If you work on your own as an artist, programmer, or other dedicated discipline for various studios, then you might get an offer for incidentals reimbursement depending on the studio's budget. You're considered part of the dev team as a person and valued contributor, but in the eyes of the law you're independent of the studio in question.

Most of the time, this is pretty simple in that they'll ask you to make an expense report, and you'll get paid for whatever your actual costs were. You still have to report the reimbursement as income then just deduct your expenses as usual, including ones that were not reimbursed. However, other studios will just send you a per diem amount without regard to how much you actually paid for things like meals and train tickets. Any overages become taxable income. Whether you're paid on a flat allowance or after submitting an expense report, meals still have the 50% limit (100% temporary boost for 2021 and 2022 if purchased from a restaurant).

On the other side of the fence as the payer, it's a little different in that you might be able to deduct 100% of these costs. If your studio pays someone as a contractor, and they have incidentals expenses on your behalf such as holding your booth for you at a convention you can't make it to, you are subject to the 50% limit on meals that you reimburse them for if you request an expense report or if they documented their expenses without you asking them to. But if they *don't* keep records or account for them separately, you get a 100% deduction.

Let's say your artist comes with you to Indiecade to help promote the game and field press for you, and they're treated as an independent contractor. You offer to pay for their transit card and lunch every day of the show. After Indiecade, they text you some receipts detailing $20 for a transit card and $50 in lunch expenses, so you Zelle them $70. Since the meals were accounted for separately, you can deduct the $20 transit card in full, but you only get a $25 deduction for the $50 in meal expenses. (Although once again, if the $50 worth of lunches were purchased from a restaurant in 2021 or 2022, that $50 could be deducted in full.)

Alternatively, you wait until Indiecade is over then ask them how much they spent the whole trip. They say they totally forgot and threw the receipts out, and can't really tell what's what on their credit card statement. "Dunno, dude. $300?" Grudgingly, you Venmo them $300. And you can deduct all of it because it's just considered part of their total compensation: no differentiating 100% deductible transportation from 50% deductible lunches and bar tabs. It's then on them, not you, to try substantiating those expenses on their own tax return plus reporting that extra $300.

LAUNDRY, DRY-CLEANING, AND COSTUMERY

When I still lived in New York, I'd wait until GDC to have my coat dry-cleaned. After a brutal northeast winter and far too many hours of sleeping on a plane and sitting around a dingy airport terminal, it really needed cleaning by then. Dry-cleaning a winter coat would cost about the same at my old local cleaners as it would to have my hotel do it while I'm at Moscone all day in weather that wouldn't require a coat that heavy, at least not until it was time to go home.

I waited because if I had it cleaned at home, I wouldn't be able to deduct it: but under the business travel rules, I can while I'm at GDC. So...anything you ever wanted dry-cleaned, take it with you on business trips if you can!

For this deduction, it doesn't even have to be dry-cleaning: it can be a wash-and-fold laundry service for both your street clothes and business clothes, or buying detergent and getting quarters to do it yourself.

I wanted to address clothing in this chapter specifically, because it's frequently a thorn in peoples' sides and the travel element is virtually the only time you can get some relief for what can be a very annoying but necessary personal expense. One of the many, many reasons you could not give me a million bucks to go back to the financial industry is that game development is a profession where it's considered an achievement if you left the house wearing pants. I loathed doing battle with polyester suits and flushing at least 10% of my salary down the toilet in business clothes and dry-cleaning, hated it even more that I couldn't deduct it in any way.

Especially since there is no deduction for purchasing those clothes; several Tax Court cases have proven this time and again. There is no deduction for "clothing suitable for personal and private wear." The 1980 case *Hynes v. Commissioner* asserted that just because you don't plan to wear these clothes in your time off the clock, it doesn't mean they're not suitable for wear outside the workplace. But while you can't deduct the actual costs of your street clothes or business suits, you can deduct your laundry and dry-cleaning bills when you have at least one night away from home on business.

For a more recent case citing *Hynes*, *Hamper v. Commissioner* was a blatant case of trying to deduct too many obviously personal expenses. Hynes was a news anchor who had to present a professional and well-groomed image on TV, so he deducted fine clothing, haircuts, and other personal expenses as employee business expenses (professional clothing, for the most part, is held to similar standards for the self-employed as it is for employees). It was a condition of his employment with the TV station that he needed to wear clothes that would properly show up against the background they used for broadcasting, and that were professional and conservative-looking. But he could wear those clothes out to dinner, on the street, and moreover, buy them from standard clothing stores that sell dressy men's clothing.

Hamper is also a news anchor who was subject to similar employer requirements regarding maintaining a clean-cut conservative image with the right clothes and hairstyles. Unlike Hynes, she wasn't even subject to color restrictions. She purchased her clothes from typical women's clothing stores you'd find in any mall or urban shopping district, like Ann Taylor.

You need a bona fide occupational purpose for clothes to deduct them. The most common example is nursing scrubs; both employees and self-employed healthcare workers need them to do their jobs. Sure, you've probably seen an off-duty doctor or nurse at the store or on the subway still in their scrubs. But most people don't wear them as clothing by default and even though you can find scrubs at Wal-Mart, most healthcare workers need to order them from a specialized retailer.

While buying professional clothing isn't a concern for most game developers, it was worth mentioning. But I think most of us are more willing to put on a costume than a business suit. And funnily enough, THAT we can deduct!

You still need a business purpose for the costume or cosplay, but providing that you have one you should have no problem deducting it. For instance, did you put that costume together to try angling for favor with a publisher, if it's from one of the games they've published? Or is it part of your branding strategy to dress up as a character from one of your own games at conventions and while LARPing? If you said yes to any of these, then you can probably deduct the costume. Cleaning and care (like mending, tailoring, and storage) of these costumes is also deductible regardless of whether you're traveling overnight or not. But the costume still has to be something pretty out there for a write-off and not easily mistaken for street clothes; characters that wear "normal" clothes wouldn't fly just like how the news anchors lost their cases, but if you dressed up like one of the cats in *Stray* then you'd have no problems.

TIPS

Tips add up fast even if you're not staying in the fanciest accommodations. Since tips for hotel and airport staff are virtually always in cash, make sure you are diligently recording how much you pay them.

When you tip taxi and rideshare drivers, you don't need to account for the cost separately unless it was a situation where you paid the fare in a separate transaction. For instance, many people buy car services or airport shuttle seats in the same transaction as booking a flight with travel agencies or websites and it's expected you'll tip the driver in cash separately on the day of your trip. Otherwise, the driver's tip is part of the taxi expense if you paid it at the time of the fare.

The same goes for tips on dining out; they're not accounted for separately. The food and drink costs plus sales tax and tip are totaled up and equally subject to the 50% limit, 100% if purchased from a restaurant in 2021 or 2022.

OTHER BUSINESS INCIDENTALS

At some point when you're on the road, you'll likely need to fax or mail documents, or pay outrageous fees for Wi-Fi, because you really need to get your work done and a data connection isn't cutting it. If you're in a foreign country, you may need to pay a translator to help you translate documents or interpret a conversation in real time.

All of these expenses are deductible, regardless of whether it's a business or personal day of your trip.

GIVING YOUR FRIEND TAX-FREE INCOME WHILE YOU CRASH ON THEIR COUCH

Like many indie developers, you're likely a budget traveler. You wind up making friends in other parts of the country after years of knowing each other through Game Dev Twitter, so you can futon-surf your way around.

Most of the lodging discussed in this book pertains to staying at hotels, or perhaps getting an Airbnb. But you'll want to document anything you pay to a friend (or family member, or random stranger you met at the bus stop) for crashing with them; they can get some tax-free income while you still get a deduction.

If you've stayed with a friend or business contact, you've likely chipped in for gas or bought them dinner. Which is a nice gesture, but when you've got business elements like staying for a convention or publisher meeting, you should give them some money and document it by saying that it's rent.

Remember reading about exclusions all the way at the beginning of this book, and how a lot of them are really sneaky? Here's a devious Easter egg for you: if you rent out your primary residence for less than 15 calendar days in the year, the income is completely tax-free.

So if you live in a prime neighborhood and want to give being an Airbnb host a shot for a few nights to help recoup your conference expenses, this is a good way to get some tax-free money. Then when you go to another city and give your friend some money for staying over, have a receipt written up so you can still get a deduction and your friend enjoys some tax-free income. How they decide to use that money is out of your hands. You're giving it to them out of principle: as a friend, for interrupting their daily lives having a guest. But for tax purposes, say it's for lodging. You still have to use comparable local hotel and Airbnb rates instead of treating it like a night at The Plaza. But you'll get a deduction; all you need is a handwritten receipt or that Venmo screencap, and your friend pays no tax assuming they don't rent out that room or couch out for more than two weeks per year. Talk about finding a hidden 1-Up...

INTERNATIONAL TRAVEL

Everything we just went over mostly pertained to domestic travel. There are tighter restrictions on international travel because it's so expensive, requires more advance planning, and subsequently many people attempt to subsidize their dream vacation to Paris with business justification that is shaky at best.

You need to tread carefully with international business trips because there are special separate rules for international conventions, let alone non-event travel like meeting a foreign publisher when Zoom exists. **The whole concept of business, personal, and travel days comes up again when it comes to international trips, but it plays out a little differently than it does for domestic trips.**

This is a time to think of a strategy or arcade game that has bonuses that are very hard to get, or at least just hard to get on the nose–if not having aspects where it's easy to accidentally shoot down an ally or something that's beneficial. *Heroes of Might and Magic* comes to mind again because it was so easy to accidentally smash one of your own troops if their attacks went over multiple spaces on the battlefield.

Except instead of digital goblins, rogues, and swordsmen, you're accidentally nullifying your deductions for that foreign conference or sneaking off to France for the day when that publisher in London insists on your physical presence to decide on whether they'll fund your next project. (Seriously, the Eurostar only takes a little over two hours to take you into Paris. It could absolutely be a day trip with enough planning.)

The conditions for international travel ironically make it easy to take a small international vacation that's tax-deductible, the kicker is that you still need a business purpose for going and you can't get greedy. The following conditions lead to an embarrassment of riches as far as bonuses are concerned, which you don't get with domestic travel. If you meet one of the four following exceptions for your cross-border business trip, you can deduct **ALL** of your travel expenses without having to separate out personal days!

1. No substantial control over the trip: this one really only applies to you if you're an employee.

2. You were outside America for less than a week (seven consecutive days). The days you are still in America or departing American shores don't count, but the day you *return* does.

3. If you were out of the country for more than a week, less than 25% of those days were spent on personal matters.

4. This one is much harder to prove, but if you can establish that getting a subsidized vacation was not a major consideration in taking the trip, you'll get an exception.

So, let's boil it down to the trip length because self-employed people instantly don't qualify for that first exception, and that last one is too nebulous to waste text on.

If you're away from home for less than seven days, *not counting* the days you're still in America on account of layovers and departures, it's the easiest. You can deduct all of your travel, meal, lodging, and incidentals expenses. If you're gone for more than a week, then you need to look at how many personal and travel days there are. Both the days coming into your destination country and heading back to America will count as business days.

Let's say that you're going to Japan for a three-week trip. Two weeks are purely for business with a publisher, talking to contacts at Nintendo, and expediting work in person with one of your dev team members who lives in Tokyo, but you stay an extra five days to live your lifelong dream of seeing Japan.

Travel takes one full day in each direction, so that makes for a total of 21 days to account for. With two travel days and 14 work days, that makes for just five personal days and 16 business days. Just 23.8% of the trip is personal. If your trip was domestic, you ironically wouldn't have been able to take a deduction for the extra five days: but under this international exception you actually can for your basic life-sustaining costs plus incidentals.

If you're going away for more than a week, and you *don't* meet that sub-25% exception, you still get deductions but you're going to have to account for personal days like you would with a domestic trip regardless of length. But even then, there's still some bonus days you'll get with international travel.

The easiest method is to go for a week or less because it eliminates the need to account for personal versus business days, and you get straight deductions for your travel, lodging, and meals. It's assumed that you wouldn't go through the expense and hassle of an international flight for such a short timeframe, but it's honestly the best way to get a mini vacation complete with huge tax deductions. You won't get to see as much in the tourism sense, but if that conference in Milan is only three days and you're in town for six? Get palazzo'd out while you're there!

INTERNATIONAL TRAVEL, PERSONAL, AND STANDBY DAYS

If we turned the sorting out of business days into a card game, international travel has a lot more trump cards than domestic travel does.

You'll want to be mindful of when things like public holidays take place, as well as when your meetings and other events requiring your presence are scheduled. For instance, if you get to your destination on Friday but your meeting isn't until Monday and this trip doesn't meet one of those four exceptions, then you can't deduct the meals and lodging costs for the weekend.

However, if you have a meeting that Friday and your presence is required on Monday, then you can treat the weekend as *standby* days. Standby days count as business days! Standby days like weekends and public holidays are deductible, so long as there are business events going on between them. So if you don't meet that 25% personal time exception for a trip lasting more than a week? Try to save your vacation time for the end of the trip, if you get some standby days!

Travel days are still business days, but now you can also count days when you were supposed to work but couldn't due to circumstances beyond your control, like getting sick, or your client winds up double-booking so you can't come in on the date initially planned.

Days that you devote to your trade are also business days. Even if they don't totally line up with the initial purpose of the trip. Such as going to workshops, taking care of business, working on the game, and so forth, although it has to take up a significant part of the day, at least six to eight hours.

I made the ensuing example very tricky and very plausible. If you're a fan of twisty logic puzzles that tempt you to Google the answers because you just want to get on with the game already, you might want to give figuring out the business days a whirl on your own before reading the answer after it!

You're meeting with a French publisher, and you planned enough vacation days out of your two-week stay that you don't meet the 25% exception. Flying to Paris takes a full day in both directions and you spend your arrival date and the day after it getting acquainted with the city and exploring.

Between meetings with the publisher spread over three days, you find out about a local game jam. After a day exploring, one of the Parisian indies at the event is very impressed with your work and invites you to speak at their studio later that week. Good thing it wasn't until later, because the next day you lose the whole day to a nasty bout of food poisoning that leaves you unable to work on the game or chat with the publisher. After fending off the stomach bug the next day, you manage to get two hours in your hotel room catching up on business email and working on the game. The next day, you spend a whole day going around to coffee shops, working on your game. With your publisher business concluded, the rest of the trip is spent having fun.

So, the two travel days count as business days. The day after your arrival is personal. The three days with the publisher are business days, and so is the day you were unable to work due to unavoidable food poisoning. The day you spent exploring then just going to a game jam would be a personal day, because you didn't spend enough working hours doing things to advance the interests of your business; so the day that you did only two hours of work also counts as a personal day. But since your presence was required for the speaking event you got invited to, that day is a business day, even if it was the same length or shorter than the game jam you just attended where your presence wasn't required. The day you spent working on the game for at least a full work day is also a business day. Since the remaining days were vacation days, eight out of 14 days were for business (about 57%). The trip has enough business elements to be deductible in the first place, and more than half of it was made for a solid business reason. Still, the travel, meals, and lodging expenses for those six personal days can't be deducted.

COVID-INDUCED INTERNATIONAL TRIP DELAYS

If you leave the United States for business or vacation, you need a negative COVID test to return at the time of publishing in late 2022. It must also be one of those RT-PCR or molecular tests; rapid antigen tests are usually not accepted by most major airlines and customs.

But life happens, and even being careful with high-quality masks indoors at all times can result in you testing positive and needing to delay your homecoming until you get a negative PCR. If you made the trip for business purposes, but need to keep shelling out for hotels and food in a foreign land while you're COVID-positive, what happens to your deduction?

The IRS has not issued any formal guidance on whether days lost to COVID count as standby days, including delayed return trips resulting in astronomical lodging costs, or if they are ineligible for such treatment because COVID is a known contagion and foreseeable risk (unlike the food poisoning in the example).

Unless rulings are issued treating such days as standby, when that status is normally reserved for delays of business meetings rather than your trip home, treat COVID-related delay days as personal days and recalculate your personal percentage after the trip concludes.

For instance, you planned to go to Germany for Gamescom and meeting with German publishers to reach their passionate adventure gaming market. You planned for a 10-day trip, with travel taking one full day in each direction, three days dedicated to the conference, and two to meeting with studios and publishers, making it 70% business and 30% personal so you'd need to account for a few personal days.

But you caught COVID at Gamescom, and now you can't get your flight home. You book a hotel for another week, having to keep things on a day-to-day basis with the hotel until after three more days you finally get a negative test, and the earliest flight home you can get is the next day. Your 10-day trip has now stretched to a 21-day one (10 days holed up in the hotel, one more day for traveling home). The hourglass has now flipped, and your trip is just 33% business now.

Unless new rulings or laws dictate otherwise, your extra (and incredibly expensive) days at the hotel after your positive test are not deductible. You'd still be able to deduct your airfare and ground transportation, along with meals and lodging for the seven business days you had. Your incidentals, like Wi-Fi charges and hiring a German interpreter, are deductible regardless of trip length and number of personal days.

Had you gotten your positive test earlier and it caused you to delay your meetings with the studios rather than cancel them or pivot to virtual meetings, you might be able to claim them as standby days, since no formal guidance has been issued declaring that COVID isn't a valid standby reason.

INTERNATIONAL CONVENTION RULES

International business trips for things like publisher and dev team meetups ironically have more loopholes to exploit than domestic business travel. But for conventions, you don't get a reskin. It's like a totally different engine!

International conventions have a lot of strings attached because it's so easy to make a tax-deductible vacation out of a domestic convention even after accounting for personal days, let alone international trips. So of course, an international convention isn't a fast path to a goldmine of deductions. That would be making the difficulty level too easy.

Whenever a convention takes place outside of North America, it has to meet certain requirements in order for you to get a deduction. IRS Publication 463 (https://www.irs.gov/pub/irs-pdf/p463.pdf) defines

"North America," which isn't limited to the contiguous 48; it includes Canada, Mexico, most of the Caribbean, and Central American countries like Panama, Costa Rica, and the Bahamas.

First, you have to establish that the meeting is directly related to your trade as a game developer. Easy enough most of the time. But the next part makes for yet another tough building puzzle; you have to establish that there was a good reason for this event to be held outside of North America and thus, for you to attend. While this wouldn't apply to a convention or conference in Toronto or Cancun, it would for events on every other continent; most notably, events in Europe and Asia although there is also a large Latin American game developer community with presence in South American nations, Australia has many notable industry events, and Africa's games industry is burgeoning. No indie developers have made the brave move to Antarctica to avoid creeping rent costs, though.

Overall, the IRS says that you can only deduct expenses for conventions and other events outside of North America if they're directly related to active conduct of your business, AND it's reasonable to hold the meeting outside of North America.

When you're attending a conference, expo, or other event outside what the IRS deems North America, here's what they want to see to justify deducting your attendance:

- The purpose of the event
- The activities that take place
- Purpose and activities of sponsoring organizations
- Homes of the sponsors
- Other cities/countries this conference has been or will be held in, and that of other conventions that the sponsors put their names on
- Other relevant factors that support your argument

With the indie games world having an international presence and digital events becoming the norm for many industry gatherings, you need to come up with some good justification for why you'd leave America when you've got many major shows in your own backyard (comparatively speaking) plus local and regional events.

On the other hand, game developers also have an upper hand compared to other industries. We have the ability to easily enter foreign markets, work with team members anywhere around the globe, and there are tax incentives and private and public funding for games that exist in other countries which America hasn't caught onto. All of these things make international conventions viable opportunities to get work, find talent, and grow your audience, and thus viable tax deductions as well.

Let's examine our old standby GDC once more, as it's the easiest example. There's the occasional GDC Next in Paris, GDC Europe, and GDC China in addition to the flagship show in San Francisco. We're not going to worry about the purpose and activities too much: we know what it's for.

A cursory look at each event's webpage shows that there's a few main sponsors and partners in common, but each one has unique sponsors that won't be at the other events. Virtually all of the sponsors are part of the industry: you'd have a harder time proving an international conference is related to your field when totally random companies comprise a majority of the sponsors and offer things that are unrelated to game development. For the major conventions like GDC, Casual Connect, and Gamescom, you wouldn't have to worry about this too much.

But do these companies also sponsor a lot of American conventions or just ones in their own country or continent? If they frequently sponsor American events, that could put you in jeopardy. It's not likely to be the defining factor in losing the deduction, but it would get factored in if you don't meet the other criteria.

Moreover, what about the partner organizations? They are more likely to kill you than the sponsoring companies. If IGDA is hosting the event then you're covered because of the international presence, but if you have a local collective that only has American members which decides to convene in Europe or Asia, you'll be dead faster than falling off a stair in a Sierra game.

As for "other relevant factors," you really need to get a leg up on the business side of your niche to justify the deduction. You're likely to have two major factors to mount a good defense, and that's the talent and the market in those countries. Case in point, Adventure X in London. If you make adventure games or games that heavily emphasize narratives, are one of the OG Adventure Game Studio (AGS) developers, and want to get a better foothold in the European and UK markets, that's the event you need to attend. A significant portion of AGS developers are in the

UK or continental Europe, and for an extremely long time it was almost impossible to meet other AGS-ers in America. It only helps our cause that point-and-click adventures sell more in the UK and western Europe than in America, so reaching a convention full of foreign peers and fans would be crucial for making a profit.

Whereas you'd have a harder time proving that your deduction has merit if you attended Adventure X but you aren't speaking, aren't showing your games there, create in different genres so a leap to adventure games is more speculation, and lack a clear intent to reach UK and western European markets.

* * *

With diligent planning, you can basically get a tax-deductible vacation providing that you mix it up with enough business travel, and local travel can also give you some relief along with the actual costs of attending events. Some of these expenses are obvious, and others are hidden more deviously than that one pixel you need to click to go to the next room already.

And the more fellow indies you surround yourself with, the more fun games you will make, and the more you can prove that these expenses had an actual business purpose!

But now it's time to leave the bonus-heavy games like *Donkey Kong Country* behind and move onto turn-based games like *Heroes of Might and Magic*.

Turn-Based Strategy

Depreciation of Big-Ticket Items

IT'S IMPORTANT THAT YOU know what to do with big-ticket items as depreciation methods are insanely complex, not to mention so boring that it would make an afternoon of those dollar bin PGA tour 3DO titles look fun.

Ergo, I'm not going to go into as much detail on big-ticket items as I did for travel expenses, given that the average indie developer doesn't tend to heavily invest in hundreds of thousands of dollars' worth of equipment that requires complex depreciation schedules and paying attention to tax code changes that affect them. But you should have an idea of how depreciation works, because so many game developers use starting their own studio as a good reason to get that fast and powerful Maingear tower. Once your studio grows, you may also consider buying other equipment if you use it frequently, like filming and motion capture equipment.

There are multiple methods of depreciation, and this book concentrates solely on **MACRS (Modified Accelerated Cost Recovery System)** because it's the system you are going to be using 99.9% of the time given the types of equipment indie developers are most likely to purchase and how long you will have these items.

Your tax professional should have a good handle on depreciation. Most tax software intended for the general public is honestly a crapshoot when it comes to inputting depreciation, and the more equipment you have the

DOI: 10.1201/9781003335733-13

bigger mechanical pain it's going to be if you change software packages or tax pros. All in all though, depreciation has some trickiness to it, but it's a lot like those boss battle vectors that look scary and intimidating at first then it's all a matter of knowing where to make that appendage hit.

There's some key concepts you need to get familiar with in order to determine which depreciation strategy makes the most sense for you in terms of both your tax bills and mental energy. And I'd strongly recommend doing a quick playthrough or watching some gameplay videos of *Heroes of Might and Magic* (I and II), because this game's mechanics are definitely coming up again.

DEPRECIATION = TURN-BASED

Remember when you read about amortizing your start-up and organizational costs, and how it utilized both direct hits and those spells that sapped away at enemy health points for several turns? The exact same concept is at play here. Amortization refers to deducting something intangible, like your start-up expenditures or buying a copyright from another studio, while depreciation is the term for deducting a physical asset over a fixed time period.

Depreciation is the wear and tear of vehicles, furniture, real estate, and equipment meant to last you more than one year. These things are called **fixed assets** (or depreciable assets).

Because game developers tend to tie up their capital into labor and their intellectual property rather than equipment, depreciating equipment isn't a huge concern if you keep your games simple hardware-wise, and your only tool of trade is the computer you're using. But if you're going into console development, you're definitely investing in more equipment. Sound designers need good microphones, mixers, and keyboards, while most game artists swear by their Wacom tablets. Whether or not you exclusively develop for mobile and need native devices for testing, you're going to need a cell phone and/or tablet simply to take care of business at home and on the go. All of these items are depreciable, although you can expense them in full which is discussed later in the chapter.

When you play *Heroes of Might and Magic*, you can only build one structure in a town per day (turn) until you can build no more. Depreciation works similarly in that you deduct part of that fixed asset every year (one turn) until you can't anymore.

Compare this to when you buy things like art supplies that have to constantly be replenished, meals and drinks with your dev team that are enjoyed in the moment, and one-time expenses like convention passes. Just like how meals are meant to be eaten right away, that pass is meant to be used in an incredibly limited timeframe. You just deduct these expenses in the current year and you're done. Depreciable assets are more like building those *Heroes of Might and Magic* towns: you need multiple turns to get them to the point where there's nothing left to build. Depending on what your income and other expenses each year/turn are like, this can be helpful or hurtful.

BASIS, REPAIRS, AND CAPITAL IMPROVEMENTS

Basis is an extremely complicated subject, as you saw in the breakdown of business entities. When it comes to depreciable property, basis is usually just your purchase price but other things can get tacked onto it. Because depreciation wears down on the basis, the number after you subtract depreciation is **book value**.

Repairs and maintenance for your equipment are deductible expenses that have no impact on basis. But if you send your computer tower in for repairs, and you get substantially more memory and other upgrades that made it better rather than just restoring it to a usable state, you'd have to treat that cost as a capital improvement. Capital improvements then make for an **adjusted basis**.

For example, you spent $500 on a tablet. You buy a $10 case and pay $50 to fix a cracked screen. It initially had a 16GB capacity, but the repairman offers to upgrade the capacity to 32GB for $100. The case and screen repair are deductible supplies and repair expenses, but your basis in the tablet is now $600 because that improvement is a capital expenditure. The original basis was $500; the adjusted basis is $600.

Now let's say you bought a high-end computer secondhand for relatively cheaply because it was under a payment plan with the store, and you assumed that payment plan as part of the deal. Assumed liabilities also add to the depreciable asset's basis: if you paid $500 cash for the computer and assumed a $1,500 loan as a condition of that purchase, your basis is $2,000. It's not that much different than if the computer was new, cost $2,000, and you put the whole thing on your credit card. You'd still have a $2,000 basis. But because you can often find cut-rate prices on secondhand equipment this way, it's important to know that assuming a liability like that will add to the basis as if you paid for the whole thing on credit.

Knowing exactly what that item's basis is not only helps you properly figure out tax deductions but also what happens if you sell that item.

Often, the average indie developer will use a computer or mobile device until it packs it in. With planned obsolescence and overall device quality not being as robust as it could be in the name of quarterly profits, these items usually aren't sold at a profit and the proceeds aren't significant enough to create a taxable event. If you do have a gain on the sale, it is taxable.

However, you should always note when you've sold or disposed of devices used in your business, even if you expensed rather than depreciated them.

HOW MANY ROUNDS OF DEPRECIATION?

Computers, tablets, and so forth are what's called "five-year property" in the tax profession, in that you depreciate them over five years/turns.

A vast majority of equipment you'll use is five-year property, furniture and fixtures get seven years if you're going to buy them for an office or convention gear. Since it's doubtful that most game developers are going to use fruit-bearing trees (10 turns) or race horses (three turns) in making a game, we're going to stick with five turns when discussing equipment. Things that get far more than five turns, such as real estate, are beyond the scope of this book, although we will touch upon real estate depreciation just a little in the home office chapter.

LISTED PROPERTY

The term listed property is one you're going to have to get familiar with. Items that have a personal and/or recreational element to them constitute listed property. In other words, virtually everything that we work with:

- Desktop and laptop computers
- Related peripherals like printers, hard drives, and scanners
- Tablets
- Game consoles
- Cameras (video and photographic)

- TV screens

- Microphones

- Instruments

- Cars

And the list goes on. If you can use it to take pictures, record, play, or even communicate, then it's listed property.

So, what's in store for you? You need to carefully note where and how much this item is used. Listed property requires more sensitive record-keeping than other depreciable assets, especially cars. Then the depreciation deduction can be limited and more complicated if you don't have at least a 50% business usage on these items. Even if you use something 100% for business, you *still* have to substantiate it, such as keeping logs and/or photographic evidence. Listed property can be a real killjoy in that way, although it has become easier for the social media addicts out there who also talk at length about their recording and editing rigs. It not only helps put your name out there, it substantiates your business use of many listed property items!

The only exception to this is cell phones. Thanks to the Small Business Jobs Act of 2010, cell phones are no longer listed property. While they're still subject to a business percentage if you don't get a separate phone just for business, you don't need to go through the hassle of declaring your personal phone listed property. You also don't need to use it for at least 50% for business, but you'd honestly be hard pressed to find an indie developer in the 2020s where they weren't already using their phones at least halfway for work.

Then there was an exception for computers and peripherals that are exclusively used in a dedicated external office or home office. You had to take the home office deduction in order to meet this listed property exception if you don't have an external office. Which was a big deal if you didn't use your computer, printer, and so forth at least halfway for business reasons. Laptops don't meet the exception if you take them around with you, so this exception would really only apply to desktop towers and other peripherals that aren't very portable like printers.

However, the 2018 tax reform also removed computers and peripherals from listed property status, providing that they were placed into service after 2017 regardless of whether you use them at a dedicated office or your home office.

The listed property restrictions shouldn't be a problem for most indie developers because it's easy enough to use one of these devices primarily for business. It's substantiation that can be the hard part if you don't use it primarily for business: if you use your TV screen at home all the time and only drag it out with you four or five times a year for conventions and playtests, you're not likely to get a deduction for it. Whereas showing gameplay and testing videos on social media and documenting the process in a dev diary, demonstrating how much you use your TV for non-leisure purposes, might be a better choice for proving that you do in fact use an Xbox for business 50-80% of the time.

Nevertheless, if you placed that computer or other item into service PRIOR TO 2017, you do have to be concerned about listed property restrictions. Game consoles also don't fall under the "computers and peripherals" exception, the IRS considers listed property to be "Property generally used for entertainment, recreation, or amusement (including photographic, phonographic, communication, and video recording equipment)" which a PlayStation or Nintendo Switch would definitely fall under. As industry professionals, we'll also have an easier time claiming them for business use than say, an insurance company. Still, listed property restrictions will apply to some common purchases for indie game developers.

KEY DATES FOR BIG-TICKET ITEMS

The most important thing to note is the date the computer or other piece of equipment is placed into service.

More often than not, it's the same day of the purchase or the day after. But things will happen such as trying to squeeze that last bit of life out of a tower before retiring it. Or you're faced with a sudden relocation, and it takes a month or two to locate and unbox that new dual-monitor setup. Hence, it's important to make that distinction because the *service date* is when you start depreciating that item. So the turn in this turn-based RPG doesn't necessarily begin on the purchase date.

The other date you need to note is when you dispose of it (retirement date). Disposal can be from selling it, charitable donation, getting destroyed in an accident, or just plain throwing it away if it doesn't work anymore. Other forms of retirement are scrapping it for parts or using it personally and not for business anymore.

Depreciation starts the day you start using that item, and ends when there's no more left to deduct (fully recovered the cost) or the date you dispose of that item, whichever comes first.

Also, don't confuse idleness with the service and retirement dates; you start depreciating on the service date then if you stop using that item but still have it, you still take a depreciation deduction as usual. Things only change when you dispose of it in some way.

USING CONVENTIONS: SPLITTING TURNS INTO SMALLER TURNS

Going back to *Heroes of Might and Magic* yet again, combat in that series is also turn-based. Each troop of creatures attacks once and if your Hero can cast spells, it could be done once every turn after all of the troops had a chance to attack. Each main turn then had a bunch of micro turns, depending on how many troops you had.

Some enemy troops will fall like stones, and others need several hits from all your troops plus a spell from the Hero to go down. Using the five-year property guideline, let's say that your Hero casts a spell so in the first turn, all of your troops do a lot of damage plus there's magical damage from the Hero. The enemy wears on them a little. Now they fight back consistently for three more turns, then in the fifth and final turn you only need to do a miniscule amount of damage to get the enemy to go down.

And that's basically how depreciation works in terms of what time of year you placed the item into service: depending on the convention and method used, you could do a *lot* of damage in the first year, a middling amount in the next few years, then you take down those remaining bits of enemy hit points in the last year.

You might be wondering what the significance of the service date is if virtually everything else you spend money on just gets deducted in full, regardless of what *time of year* it was purchased. This is because depreciation goes by the *number of months* that equipment or furniture is being used in both the year you start using it, and the year you dispose of it.

Then you must apply the **mid-quarter convention**. MACRS has a few different conventions, and indie developers will virtually always use mid-quarter for common major purchases like computers, tablets, cameras, motion capture equipment, and other tools of the trade. You'll see an example of this convention very soon.

DEPRECIATION METHODS: DOUBLE-DECLINING BALANCE AND STRAIGHT-LINE

Once you know that fixed asset's basis and class (we're assuming five-year class here), followed by the convention, you need to pick a method. Sounds more and more like an intense strategy game, doesn't it?

Depreciation methods are used in both the bookkeeping and tax code versions of your overall recordkeeping, but have some stark differences. Bookkeeping depreciation is virtually always straight-line for very small businesses that don't have much in the way of equipment. But tax code depreciation works differently, because there's incentives in our ever-changing laws that entice you to do things like buy more equipment. Congresscritters want happy donors, so of course, you're going to see different tax incentives every election cycle where they want you to spring for tens of thousands of dollars' worth of furniture and computers intended to grow a game studio from a garage operation to a stable presence in your city.

Assuming no special circumstances like the inevitable 2018 tax reform changes to depreciation you'll read about soon, you have three options under MACRS. You can use 150% or 200% double-declining balance (DDB) or straight-line like your books (S/L). DDB is more beneficial in those early years right after an expensive equipment purchase because that balance is simply bigger. Whether you'll opt for 150% or 200% depends on how much you think you should deduct now, opposed to future years.

Yet again referencing *Heroes of Might and Magic*, particularly the third and fourth installments, using DDB is a lot like summoning a temporary but powerful troop, like faerie dragons, to supplement some permanent Level 2 troops like tigers or gargoyles. That summoned powerful troop will inflict a great deal of damage in the first three combat turns before disappearing, then your less powerful permanent troops will finish the job in just two turns for a victory.

Choosing S/L for the asset's entire recovery period would be more like casting a consistent duration-based spell such as Poison. You'd take the five years and split 20% of the cost equally over those five years, except the first and last years will be smaller because of having only partial years of depreciation deductions for both, since it's based on the number of months.

To clearly illustrate this concept: You pay $2,000 for a new computer tower on April 1 and place it into service the same day. For simplicity's sake, you use this computer solely for work in your dedicated home office. It's a quality tower built to last, you use it well past that five-year recovery point.

Under S/L, you'd get a consistent $400 depreciation deduction for five years. But since you placed the computer into service in April, that mid-quarter convention for the second quarter only lets you deduct just 12.5% of the $2,000 basis ($250) in the year of purchase. *You can deduct $400 in the ensuing four years consistently, then that leftover $150 in the sixth year.*

If you opted for 200% DDB instead, the way it works is that you would use 40% of the computer's basis or book value every year since DDB is essentially twice the straight line rate (20% for five years).

There is a MACRS chart to consult for the correct mid-quarter convention, and it says to use 25% for depreciable assets placed into service April-June. 25% of $2,000 is $500, so that's your depreciation deduction for the first year, which then makes the new book value $1,500.

For the second year, 40% of $1,500 is $600, so you'd deduct $600 that year. You'd repeat this process for the third year, deducting 40% of the $900 book value ($360). However, now that you're down to a $540 book value and two years of life remaining as far as the IRS is concerned, it's no longer worth it to do DDB because 40% of that is $216. Why deduct $216 when you can deduct $227 by switching to S/L?

The reason you can take $227 is that the MACRS table says S/L deductions for the fourth and fifth years can be 11.368% of the original basis, which is $227. You'd deduct $227 for those two years, then have $85 left over which would get deducted in the sixth year.

Yes, it's rather confusing with more steps than assembling your idyllic *Minecraft* village. Software that keeps track of depreciable assets can expedite this for you, but you can't always trust that they'll get it right. Dates matter for depreciation deductions even more than your travel deductions and other expenses!

The citations section in the back of the book have links and instructions for locating the correct convention tables. There are also many solid depreciation calculators published by schools and small accounting firms that you can use for free before investing in tax software that can handle tougher transactions like depreciation.

Just remember to seek a calculator that has *tax* depreciation, not book-keeping depreciation, because there's stark differences between the two which is why most indie developers eventually seek out a tax professional.

ONE APPENDAGE HIT: EXPENSING EQUIPMENT (§179 DEDUCTION)

You might wonder why you just bothered reading through all of this information on depreciation, and the constant New World Computing references when you might not even play or work on games like it, all to have it turn out that yes, you CAN just expense your new computer and other equipment.

It's because sometimes it pays to depreciate and other times it doesn't. §179 also has some special conditions attached to it.

Obviously, the §179 deduction is named after the section of the tax code and it's the ubiquitous name thrown around in tax offices nationwide for expensing those big-ticket items.

After all, despite the chip shortages that caused PC, card, and other component prices to sharply rise during the pandemic, electronics are overall much more accessible compared to yesteryear. There's plenty of indie developers working with high-fidelity engines and cinematic story-telling on the same $400 laptops they used to attend college. With the rise of influencer culture and Internet videos becoming integral for large and small businesses alike, digital filming equipment has also attained more accessible price points.

Thus, it's incredibly common that depreciating items too durable to be considered supplies won't make sense. If you spend $50 on a new keyboard, it seems pointless to do all this additional recordkeeping and calculations when you'll only deduct about $10 every year. It makes sense to deduct it all in one go.

You can do this for up to **$1,050,000** worth of eligible depreciable equipment per tax year, so even that $2,000 computer from the detailed example above could be expensed.

Thanks to the 2018 tax reform, this limit was $500,000 then it was raised to $1 million with a phaseout range of $2.5 million (formerly $2 million) and both of these numbers will be adjusted for inflation for every year after 2018. At the time of publishing, the limit for qualifying property is $1,050,000.

Even for items with a higher price tag like that computer, §179 might appeal to you more because it also means you're not tediously keeping track of usage, service and disposal dates, and so forth. And it just calls to most game developers because §179 is particularly appealing for electronics prone to insanely fast obsolescence, like tablets and phones. It's reasonable to expect that you would have a quality microphone or desktop computer for five or more years, but how long does a phone or tablet last when you're using it constantly? Pick up a few tablets for your PAX booth and if you get lots of foot traffic, you're lucky if any of them turn back on within a year!

Here's the big caveat: §179 cannot create a NOL if you have no other personal income.

Remember our old friend, the NOL? The friendly NOL that can eat into your other personal income, and even your spouse's as well? Time to nerf it!

There's another reason why I taught you all about depreciation and its numerous steps when you're purchasing computers and other expensive items in your studio's name; it's because expensing these items under §179 can't create a NOL.

You won't be forced to depreciate those items, although depreciation can create and deepen a NOL while §179 deductions can't! But if you want to expense that new computer or furniture, and you're running in the red, your deduction will be suspended until you post a profit.

Ergo, if you don't have much revenue right now, the §179 deduction won't be too helpful for your big-ticket purchases. Aside from the flat dollar limit of $1,050,000 indexed to inflation, you must post a profit to use that deduction.

For C corps, this principle is pretty straightforward: if all of your other business expenses exceed your revenues, you have to suspend the deduction until you post a profit.

But if your business isn't a C corp, other items on your personal tax return might affect your §179 deduction if your studio isn't bringing much money in yet. If you're still receiving wages from a job or driving for Uber to help with the bills while you work on the game, these types of income will help you take that §179 deduction without having to suspend it.

For instance, your single-member LLC studio brought in $5,000 of royalties, but you had $10,000 in dev costs for the next game. If this was your only income, you wouldn't be able to take a §179 deduction for the $500 you spent on a new laptop and would have to suspend it or opt to depreciate. However, if you have a job that paid $35,000 in wages, it will help offset that loss so you don't have to suspend your §179 deduction.

The deduction functions independently of NOLs, but if you have enough other income, you can claim them even if you have a business loss.

A common myth about §179 is that it's all or nothing when it's actually pretty flexible. For virtually all of the asset classes that a game dev is most likely to use, you can take normal depreciation, a full §179 deduction to expense it all, or split the two some way.

Let's say that this year was very fruitful, and you just started a new game that you think will take all of next year to finish. Subsequently, you don't want to fully expense your new custom computer that cost $3,000, because you want those deductions two years from now in anticipation of your next title selling well based on Steam wishlist data so far and all the email sign-ups you collected at shows. You could take a §179 deduction for $1,000 and depreciate the remaining $2,000 if you started getting significant preorder revenue or fan donations. Or, expense $500 and depreciate $1,500. The possibilities are endless, but the same rules would apply regarding §179 functioning independently of NOLs and being unable to deepen one if you have no other personal income (or operate as a C corp).

PERSONAL AND BUSINESS PERCENTAGES

Using a business percent on a turn-based deduction like depreciation isn't that dissimilar to when you'd put a business percent on an expense that's easier to calculate such as your Internet. In all of these examples so far, they also assumed 100% business usage.

If something is listed property, it MUST be used at least 50% to qualify for §179 treatment. While computers, peripherals, and phones no longer fall in this category, this restriction still applies to game consoles and a lot of film equipment. It could be fairly cut and dry that you're using it all for business or maybe 80% of the time for business usage. But if your primary purpose for owning a console is to play games instead of study them, or testing your own versions so you can distribute on that console, you would need to depreciate instead of expense that business percentage.

Going back to the $2,000 computer purchase once more, if you use it for business 70% of the time then you could take a §179 deduction for $1,400 to expense it completely, or you could depreciate the $1,400 using S/L, or DDB then S/L. Depreciation comes out to $280/year under S/L.

If you bought a Nintendo Switch for $300, but use it about 30% for play-testing your own games so you can sell through Nintendo, the comparatively lower price point would make you think that a §179 deduction for

$90 wouldn't be that big of a deal. But since consoles and game-centric devices aren't freed from listed property restrictions, like computers and tablets, you must depreciate it even though it's only $90, about $18 per year.

SPECIAL RULES FOR VEHICLES

Passenger cars have extra limits imposed on them, even more than the ones already in place on other listed property. (Passenger cars are the most probable vehicle. There's special rules and limits for vans, trucks, and SUVs that are beyond the scope of this book.)

When you read about deducting your car expenses, you saw there's a more methodical way of determining your business percentage compared to how you approximate your device usage. There's apps that can monitor the latter, but it's far more straightforward for car trips. You can also deduct a surprising amount of auto expenses like a percentage of your lease or car note.

Depreciation is writing off an actual chunk of what you paid for your car, just like all those arcane methods you read about with deducting the cost of a new computer. Cars just have their own rules.

There is a maximum depreciation for cars that changes every year based on when you placed the car in service. Cars also use a **half-year convention**, unlike all the other equipment that uses mid-quarter.

There is a chart to consult in Publication 463: Travel, Car, and Gift Expenses (https://www.irs.gov/publications/p463#en_US_2021_publink100033959) for the passenger car depreciation deductions based on the year you put it in service, and the IRS updates it every year. At the time of publishing, the maximum depreciation chart covers cars placed into service between 2003 and 2017, and a separate chart for 2018-2021 since the 2018 tax reform provided more incentive to purchase cars and now allows luxury vehicles to be used as business property. Prior years also distinguished personal cars from trucks and vans; from 2018 onward they're included in the same category.

Let's say that you bought your passenger car and placed it into service in 2016. Per the chart in Publication 463, the maximum depreciation deduction for the first year is $3,160 since it is a personal car, not a company car used strictly for business. In the second year, the maximum is $5,100, $3,050 for the third year, and $1,875 for fourth and later years (usually up to six, given the half-year convention).

Going back to our original example of an indie developer using their car for business reasons 10% of the time, their depreciation deduction is limited to $316 for that first year of using their car for their business needs like driving to conferences and local events.

Per the car expense options already discussed, if you take the standard mileage rate consistently then you don't have to worry about computing a depreciation deduction for your car. But if you use the actual cost method, then you do.

You also must use S/L method if you use the car for less than 50% business during the year. Cars are five-year property just like computers, so that comes to about $63 per year maximum. This is based on the actual cost of the car, so if you paid $25,000 for the car and depreciated it S/L for $5,000 a year over five years, you don't apply your business percentage first. You see if that S/L figure exceeds the maximum, and it does. Your deduction is still 10% of that maximum. But if you bought an older car for $8,000 instead, with S/L depreciation of $1,600 per year, then you would use this baseline since it's the lesser of the actual car's basis or that maximum from the table. In that case, your depreciation deduction for your car would be $160 given a 10% business percentage.

Had you gotten a new vehicle after the 2018 tax reform, the max depreciation limit is significantly higher: over $10,000 for the first year, $16,000 for the second year. These numbers will also index with future legislative changes and inflation, so it's crucial to keep this publication in mind if you frequently drive for conferences, expos, meeting your dev team members and other games industry business plus you are considering a new car.

LEGIONS OF ENEMIES: RECAPTURE

We've been having so much fun discussing depreciation methods, turn-based strategy games, and socking your enemies (well, your tax bill) in one hit opposed to several rounds. But now we're facing depreciation's Wario counterpart: recapture.

If you indeed grew up playing *Heroes of Might and Magic*, this is the part where you're going to fight those big purple magic-resistant dragons—the most powerful monster in the game. Just when you thought you beat the baddies with your spells, legions of gargoyles, and hordes of hydras, these zounds of dragons had to appear and torch your hard-won deductions with their blue flame breath. Where just like those dial-up tournaments of yore as you watched your trolls and druids get vaporized, you're now swearing at the computer.

Recapture generally refers to disposing of a depreciable asset before the recovery period is over and having to claim the depreciation you previously deducted as income. But recaptures aren't limited to disposals before those five years are up, since the five-year class is what we primarily deal with. As indie developers whose tools of trade sometimes have listed property restrictions on them, and they *always* did in the past, you need to be especially careful with how much you use these items and documenting it in some way. This part has gotten easier if you document your life and work on social media frequently, but we get it. Some of us are completely uninterested in the whole industry influencer thing and just want to make games, keeping things secret sauce until release like in the Wild West days of the games industry.

For most normal equipment, you only need to worry about recapture if you sell or otherwise dispose of it before its predetermined recovery period is up. Listed property is *really* sensitive to recapture, since it can happen at any time. Any time that your business use falls below 50%! The same rules true of anything you took a $179 deduction for, and the law states that the listed property rules trump the $179 ones.

Fortunately, mobile devices, computers, and peripherals aren't listed property anymore as of the 2018 tax reform. This was a huge concern when that was the case. But as previously mentioned, this could be an issue with tools like game consoles and certain filming and motion capture equipment, since many game developers rely on these tools if they're not working strictly with phones, tablets, computers, and pen and paper.

We need to first examine a more "normal" disposal before getting into the nebula of business usage causing a premature recapture. Here's a very likely scenario that is often the basis for $179 deductions—obsolescence making you scrap electronics.

You paid $500 for a console that you used entirely for development and testing purposes (100% business). It was purchased and placed into service February 15, 2021. A new console and operating system rolled out which made most of your alpha build completely unusable, so you had to cut your losses on a new console. Subsequently, you decide to sell the old console on eBay. On May 2, 2023 you got a buyer and netted $50 after fees and postage.

Using DDB, you deducted $175 in 2021 and $130 in 2022. Your 2023 deduction would've been $78 had you kept the console, but you could only deduct $39 since it was sold in the second quarter (half the year). Thus, the total *allowable* depreciation is $344 (the $175 and $130 depreciation deductions you already took, plus the $39 for 2023).

After deducting the allowable depreciation from the original purchase price of $500, your new adjusted basis for the console is $156. Subtracting this from the sale price of $50 **results in a $106 loss that you can deduct**. Whereas if you sold that console for closer to what you paid, or even more if it became one of those obsolete items with a cult following on eBay, it'd result in a recapture gain which is also called a $1250 gain, referring to the tax code section for recapture income.

In this simplified example, there was no question of the item being used solely for business so we didn't have to worry about this next part. It was pretty cut and dry in that the console was solely used for work. But it's going to be harder if you don't use that item for more than 50% business reasons. Because even if you didn't sell that console, the year that you dip below 50% business usage is the year you'll be subject to recapture of the depreciation you'd already taken! Luckily, this isn't a concern for computers and phones anymore.

Don't get toasted to a crisp by dragon breath, or by recapture. If you're in serious doubt that you're going to use listed property for less than 50% of the year, very carefully note how you'll use it. If it looks like you'll only occasionally use it for business, you might want to play it safe and keep it a personal purchase just to avoid the headaches, and keep your business devices strictly for business.

CONVERTING PERSONAL ITEMS TO BUSINESS PROPERTY

You already had your computer for a few years before you decided to seriously go indie. It may shock you that you can actually take a deduction! This is called converted property.

While you can't claim a $179 deduction for converted property, you can claim depreciation for the year that you started to use it for business. If you bought your computer in 2018 and used it solely for personal use up until 2020, 2020 is when it'd be considered to have been placed into service.

Assuming you don't have a home or external office, you're subject to the listed property restrictions and would also have to use a business percentage. Now that computers and peripherals are no longer listed property, this is less of a concern but you still need to apply a business percentage if that device isn't strictly for game-making.

No depreciation is allowable for the years it was personal use, but in 2020 onward you'd still be able to deduct something and this is one of the few instances of being able to take what's essentially a retroactive deduction. It's totally like one of those mutant zombies from *Heroes of Might and Magic II* slopping around the map!

* * *

Depreciation is definitely like a very tricky turn-based game. Unlike a totally fixed combat map in *Heroes of Might and Magic*, you don't know how well you'll do in future years just yet. You just have to make a reasonable forecast and work with your tax pro on what you both think makes sense. I didn't want to bore you with the super-fine details of depreciation, because there's a very strong chance you'll either be trusting tax software to handle it or your tax pro, but there's tomes on depreciation that could outweigh all the code from every single *Civilization* game ever made if you printed it all out on a dot matrix machine. We'd be here until we both could've gotten at least six more games out.

Onward and upward to your home office!

Gone Home

The Deal with Home Office Deductions

W HEN THIS BOOK WAS initially published, it was long before "work-at-home space" was frequently plastered across ads and "COVID" was nowhere near our vocabulary. Because working at home has become such a necessity and no longer an aberration, the IRS wasn't examining this particular area as hard as they have in the past.

Although now that there has been a stronger public policy push to send people back to offices as millions of new home-based businesses sprang up during the pandemic, it could be up for re-evaluation.

Because in the beginning, taking a home office deduction came with a fairly high burden of proof that was a lot like one of those building puzzles or strategy games. It was like being drawn in by the cool box art of old Nintendo games, or liking the cartoon it was based on but you open it up and sit there aghast at the execution fail: how could the *Teenage Mutant Ninja Turtles* not be able to swim?!

For the most part, this aspect of the tax code hasn't changed much since the pandemic except one key aspect: employees could claim the home office deduction provided that the home office was for the convenience of the employer, not the employee's request. But now that doesn't matter because the 2018 tax reform killed employee business expenses for a vast majority of people and you won't get them back until 2025.

DOI: 10.1201/9781003335733-14

It isn't the *concept* of the home office itself, like how proving business usage of game consoles or your car could get nebulous before the age of Big Data and mobile devices simplifying the process. Or, that in spite of how much data we can easily get on our travels, business trip deductions are just a common audit target because as you read, many people try to deduct obviously personal trips.

Rather, it's the sheer fact that people live in their abodes, even if they also work in them. And it's harder to separate the business from the personal elements when you're in a small home or have roommates.

Now that working at home has become a fact of life rather than the kind of thing people would give you weird looks for as late as 2015, the laws still haven't caught up yet so you need to strap in for some more precedent and how to IRS-proof your house.

THE SOLIMAN CASE AND THE HELIX NEBULA: IS YOUR HOME YOUR PRINCIPAL PLACE OF BUSINESS?

To defend a home office deduction, there's three factors the IRS and Tax Court look for:

- Whether a home office is essential to your business

- The amount of time you spend there

- Having no other place to do office kind of stuff

To expand upon these factors, let's look at the different ways indie developers tend to get things done and where we fall on the spectrum. So many of us work from home, but home also isn't the only place where we work. Especially now that COVID completely reshaped the way people look at workplaces, and the portability of many careers.

Some game developers strictly prefer to work at home, others are digitally nomadic. Those random observations in one's jaunts can frequently inspire your work: coffee shops, the bus, the library, the park, the list goes on. Co-working spaces also offer a change of scene, with some offering occasional day or week passes with others require a long-term rental contract. Game developer collectives also form when multiple developers to band together and split the rent on a dedicated office they can customize to their needs and also host events there.

If you're going the long-term rental contract route or renting a desk at a game developer collective while trying to claim a home office deduction, then

I'd worry more about defending this deduction in comparison to the coffee fiends who need a steady supply of Verve and home-brewed beans won't cut it.

Before we delve into case law concerning home office deductions, here's the questions you should be asking yourself:

1. Approximately how many days out of a given week do you work from home? How many hours in those days?

2. Does anyone make work space available to you as a condition of your work and not because you're offering money? This would be situations like a business partner who has a spare desk at their day job, a game dev collective you frequently patronize offers you a hot seat, or a major client provides you with a place to work.

3. If you are still working a regular job, are you sneaking in significant amounts of game development on company time and thus making use of their resources?

4. If you said no to all the above, do you voluntarily rent co-working space, or a desk through a flexible arrangement? How often are you there working on the game or providing services? Do you also handle management and administrative tasks from there, or at home due to security reasons?

5. Where do you receive business mail? Is it your home address, registered agent or PO box, or a rented office, co-working space, or game dev collective?

6. For office errands like preparing mailings, sending faxes, writing checks, scheduling, making and taking calls, and having a place to sort and store business records, how are you taking care of these things most of the time? Do you do them yourself at home? Virtual assistant? Patronize Staples or FedEx Office type establishments, or perhaps your lawyer's or accountant's office?

7. If you buy office supplies, where do you store and use them?

8. In what capacity do you work in the industry? If you have a dev team of at least two people, what is your primary role? Secondary roles?

9. How many people are on your dev team? Where do all of you live and/or work? How do you convene and communicate?

In answering these questions, how does your work situation look?

If you really don't spend a lot of time at home for game development and/or business management purposes, you could have a hard time proving you really need a home office. It all really depends on the circumstances. If someone is making workspace available to you or you choose to go elsewhere regularly, like entering a contract with a co-working space, it could jettison your whole deduction. Particularly if you spend more time at the co-working space than your home, especially if you are receiving mail there and using their amenities and services, you definitely could lose the home office deduction.

Then the nature of the games business is key after looking at the time spent at home, especially depending on what your role is: what are you doing there and how important is it to keeping your studio going? As you're about to see, game developers are actually pretty fortunate in this aspect.

Soliman v. Commissioner was a landmark case that set some of the most-cited precedent in defending home office deductions in audits and Tax Court. His case is what ultimately established the necessity of having a home office.

Soliman was an anesthesiologist who provided pre-op and post-op care at three different area hospitals for about 30-35 hours a week. He didn't have an office at any of the hospitals, nor did he share or have his own external medical office. So he converted a bedroom in his home into an office and spent about two or three hours a day doing administrative and research tasks in this home office. The IRS initially struck down his home office deduction because while the work he did there was relevant to his medical practice, they proclaimed that Soliman's home wasn't his principal place of doing business. The hospitals were.

Going back to those three basic factors the IRS and Tax Court frequently scrutinize, the only one Soliman really satisfied was the third bullet point on the list. He just didn't really have anywhere else but home to do these things.

The time he spent in his home office was fairly miniscule relative to the time he spent at hospitals. The IRS initially used that fact to deny the deduction because of the nature of his work as a medical professional. It involved going to the hospitals to take care of his patients, so the home office was deemed nonessential for the medical care he provided. So when he challenged this in Tax Court, the judge agreed with him. The Court stated that given Soliman's profession, the home office didn't provide the kind of *specialized* setting for his work that you would see at a hospital. He didn't have gurneys and heart monitors in there to dole out anesthesia but moreover, he wasn't seeing patients there. However, Soliman used his home office to research treatments, prepare medications, call doctors and hospitals, and all of the same administrative tasks you do as game devs such as read this book, talk to your lawyer and accountant, and so on.

THE FOCAL POINT TEST

Soliman fought the law and he won. Thanks to him, Congress clarified this section of the tax code regarding home offices being your principal place of business. If a home office is the ONLY place where you can get management and administrative tasks done, then you can make a stronger case for your deduction.

But with countless professions now only requiring a computer to build a multi-million dollar business, the rise of co-working spaces, virtual assistants, and the ability to even do your books on the phone? It's a cause for concern because these things were not readily available when the case was adjourned in 1992, yet Soliman is still cited to this day. Work-at-home space wasn't even further legislatively clarified during a global pandemic that made working at home an utter necessity!

Enter the focal point test. This is what the judges deployed when Soliman appealed the IRS' decision.

The dissenting judges admonished the upholding judges for not really looking at the fact that Soliman just didn't have anywhere else to take care of the business aspects of his anesthesiology practice. No one made space available to him. Yes, he took care of his patients at the hospitals. But in his home office, he was taking care of the business: calling surgeons and patients, preparing treatments, billing hospitals, researching procedures, and doing his continuing education to keep his license. The dissent cited the law for traveling salesmen that permits them to take a home office deduction because despite doing most of their business on the road, the time they spend at home is spent on paperwork and calls relating to their business. With his case calling for a clarification of the law, the Court declared Soliman's focal point was his home office and therefore entitled to a home office deduction.

Let's quit *Surgeon Simulator* for a minute and switch to one of those food stand games with *Baie v. Commissioner*. Baie owned a hot dog stand

and like *Soliman*, she converted a bedroom into an office to use for book-keeping and administrative tasks like keeping track of health department permits and vendor orders. She also used her own kitchen to do prep work and cooking the night before for all of the food she sold.

There was no room in her food stand for all of the cooking equipment and ingredients, so she kept them all at home. But the Court zapped her deduction, saying that while preparing and pre-cooking food at home was definitely helpful to her business, this activity wasn't substantial enough. Her focal point was deemed to be the hot dog stand because that's where the food was put together, packaged up, and purchased by the customers.

Well, we as indie developers have a situation more nebulous than either *Soliman* or *Baie*. Both of them had to be physically present somewhere to make money: Soliman at the hospitals, Baie at the hot dog stand. Soliman billed from his home office and had checks sent there. Baie had to get cash in person to sell hot dogs. Where does that leave game developers? We're literally in the ether! In terms of when we get paid for our work, that is.

Once the hard work making the game is done, we can make money in our sleep. People from around the world buy our games on Steam, the Epic Store, the App Store, through bundles, and many more digital portals at all hours of the day. If I'm making the game here in California and tell someone at a convention in Toronto to buy a copy and they immediately do so on Steam, I don't get the money instantaneously. It's sent out to cyberspace and isn't received until a royalty report is generated along with payment based on how many copies were sold that month.

Publishers and distributors rarely send checks anymore either, almost everything is done through PayPal, Stripe, or ACH bank transfer unless they're very small companies.

Moreover, we can make the game and handle management duties from virtually anywhere thanks to modern technology.

These attributes actually strengthen your case for choosing your home as your focal point. But what about the actual work you do at home? If you spend a lot of time working on the game there, it also helps your case just as much as doing the admin and management work. After all, there's things you'll want to do at home rather than a place with public Wi-Fi such as going over your online banking and transmitting confidential documents. (Even though VPNs took a huge bite out of those concerns.) But if you still do those things in co-working spaces or a teammate's home anyway, it could throw off your focal point and hurt you.

If you're occasionally renting a desk at a co-working space due to renovations or just needing a change of scene, you shouldn't have trouble defending your home office deduction. But if you're claiming both the home office and a dedicated space with a rental contract, which one is your focal point? Do you have a business reason for claiming both of them, like your rented space having quiet areas to record content if it's too noisy at home?

"But wait!" you shout. "I strictly do art, audio, or writing for games and don't deal with the business of getting the end product sold on Steam and the like. I just get paid for my services. What about me?"

Artists, composers, and sound designers in particular can rejoice. You're more likely to work solely from home and not have your dedicated space get challenged, and also not have simultaneous long-term rentals get challenged either. There's certain things you can do in a rented workspace dedicated to your craft that you just can't do at home because of background noise, other inhabitants, and having proper support services on deck. If you live in a tiny studio apartment that doesn't have room for a drafting desk, chances are you might intermittently or long-term rent studio space where you can fit those museum-size canvases or sound mixing equipment.

Whereas programmers and writers who can take their laptops anywhere have more gray areas to contend with: how can you justify claiming the two simultaneously when you must prove that you use that space regularly and exclusively for business?

THE TURTLES THAT CAN'T SWIM: EXCLUSIVE AND REGULAR USE

Exclusive use doesn't refer to the "I also rent a co-working space" aspect, it pertains to how you use your actual home. It means that you use the space allotted for literally nothing but work. Yes, literally nothing but work.

Not even getting 10 seconds of enjoyment out of *Overwatch* when you really claimed your subscription as a business expense to examine the mechanics. Looking back at *Baie*, she didn't have exclusive use of her kitchen. It was still used to make meals for her family. So even if the Court recognized her home as the focal point instead of the hot dog stand, she still couldn't deduct even partial use of her kitchen because it failed the "exclusive" side of the equation.

It's this insidious notion of exclusive use that makes appealing a home office denial almost unwinnable by design, especially if you have a small abode. Although it isn't impossible to win: I listed a few more court cases in the citation section for you showing what kinds of spaces have been defended, but there's a very interesting case where the petitioner won using a fraction of a bedroom.

Huang v. Commissioner is fascinating because part of his home office deduction was denied, then another part of it was sustained citing a 1991 Tax Court case that was just shy of the *Soliman* precedent. Huang was a musician and composer who taught an after-school program, gave private violin lessons, and composed and recorded music. He shared a three-bedroom and two-bath apartment in Pasadena with his brother.

Huang claimed part of his personal bedroom as office space along with part of the spare bedroom he used as rehearsal space and a recording studio. When he had to supply pictures of the rooms in Court, the judge found that the bedroom furnishings didn't depict a workspace. It was 2002, so it was expected he'd have a massive clunker for a computer and a phone on a desk, but the main piece of furniture in the room was a fold-out couch that he also slept on. He used the closet for personal belongings but also equipment he used in the after-school program, and some instruments. The second bedroom had a more distinct boundary with soundproofing, chairs for students, and the walk-in closet containing his keyboard. Huang and his brother stored some personal items in this spare bedroom, but the business purpose was more apparent. He was also required to rent a room at a local public school to run his after-school program there, but the school didn't give him an office or any place to handle the administrative aspects of the program. He just taught music lessons to students whose parents paid the fees, and handled the business tasks at home like preparing bank deposits, calling schools and parents, and creating flyers to advertise the program in the neighborhood.

Based on this information, the court ruled that Huang was indeed entitled to a home office deduction even if it wasn't for an entire bedroom. While you can use multiple rooms for this deduction, as upheld in *Williams v. Commissioner* in 1991, you can also use just part of a room or a tiny studio apartment: even a closet!

Putting up a partition like a hollow wall also helps, or something like a curtain, dressing screen, or the old indie standby of just putting duct tape on the floor to help measure your square footage. Whether you constrain or go big, you can take a home office deduction so long as it meets the regular and exclusive use requirements.

But make no bones about it, it WILL be harder to prove if you don't have at least an area sectioned off solely for work. Personal stuff can't be thrown in your exclusive area. If you have kids, they can't be using your desk to do their homework. For a majority of urbanite indies, exclusivity is harder to prove when you're making games in the same exact place where you take most of your meals and watch your favorite shows.

Devs in areas that don't clamor for space as much frequently have a steadier leg to stand on because having a separate room or even separate structure is less likely to get challenged. Who wouldn't want a game development hut in a backyard? But it could still fail the exclusive use test for some reason or another. It's all too easy for your personal and business spaces to overlap when you live there, and thus wind up not meeting the exclusive use test.

The regularity portion of this is easier. You have to use the place regularly to do business. Given how hard it is to drag one of us away from the computer when you're really making progress, the regularity part isn't hard to prove. Just because you might take care of business from the road or a coffee shop doesn't mean you'll lose the deduction. So long as you are in your home office frequently, you're good. But if someone else does make space readily available to you and you're using it just as much or *more* than your home, it could be a problem.

It's really that exclusivity part that can make your life miserable if you wind up getting audited. Depending on both your life and work set-ups, this is something you can just easily make unwinnable without even being aware of it. Given that homes are well, lived in, it's definitely like wondering why the turtles can't swim in the NES adaptation of *TNMT*. Obviously, if a friend traipsed in there at some point the IRS has no way of knowing. But if an agent sees something that belongs in a bedroom or living room in there, you'd be met with some side-eye. Don't be too scared of these rules, so long as the personal intrusions on your home office are no worse than something that would go on in a real office building, you should be fine.

MAPPING YOUR BUSINESS PERCENTAGE

Okay, we're done with the masochistically difficult old NES games. Now that you've been given the strategy guide for beating their metaphorical tax counterparts, let's say that from this point forward you've determined you meet the exclusive and regular requirements and your home is undeniably your focal point.

Before we get to what you can deduct, we have to look at *how* you can deduct it. There's two ways to map out your business percentage of your home: the number of rooms, or square footage.

Let's say that you rent a 1,200 square foot two-bedroom apartment and use one of the 13 × 10 bedrooms for an office (130 square feet). There are a total of five rooms in the apartment.

The number of rooms method is usually only used when the rooms are all somewhat the same size and you're using up an entire room. If your business area doesn't take up the whole room like in the Huang case, and/or uses an amount of space where it's hard to figure out how equally-sized all the rooms are, the square footage method is better. In this example, taking a deduction for a room is more beneficial because it's 20% of the whole place while 130 square feet is barely 11%. For simplicity's sake, we'll say the rooms in the apartment are all similarly sized so you're going to use 20% to prorate your home expenses.

Indirect expenses will use that 20% rate. This would be rent or mortgage interest, real estate taxes, insurance, security systems, and utilities that cover your entire home. Any unrelated expenses for things that *only affect the personal portion* of your home don't count, such as lawn care or having the kitchen painted. It has to affect the entire home to be partially deductible. **Direct** expenses are 100% deductible because they only affect your business area, like having your home office painted, cleaned, or repairs that were done in this room only.

HIERARCHY OF HOME EXPENSES

We're not in *Donkey Kong Country* anymore, where the deductible expenses were plentiful and in most cases, could easily offset your other income to give you a loss: the following are some mechanics straight out of *Doki Doki Literature Club*. You think you're in for this fun ride, but it's straight up horror!

The home office deduction is limited to the income after your other business expenses, your **tentative profit**. It's a little like how expensing your equipment functioned separately of NOLs, except that home office deductions also can't create a NOL so they work a little differently than your other business expenses.

If you're running in the red, the only items that can add to a NOL are mortgage interest and real estate taxes. Although you're not entirely screwed if you're a renter because whatever you can't deduct in the current year can be carried forward indefinitely to future tax years, but still be subject to that tentative profit limit.

So let's say that your studio is taxed as a sole proprietorship and it made $30,000 last year. You had $10,000 in eligible business expenses, so your tentative profit is $20,000. For your home expenses, you paid $18,000 for a year's rent, $1,000 for a year's utilities, $200 for tenant insurance, and $500 to have the office painted. $19,200 are indirect expenses and taking 20% of them results in $3,840 and the $500 paint job is a direct expense so all of it is deductible. Your total home office deduction is $4,340 and since you have more than enough tentative profit, you can deduct all of it and not have to worry about carryovers. Deducting that $4,340 from the $20,000 gives you a total net income of $15,660 and this is what you'd use to figure your self-employment tax plus other personal items like the Earned Income Tax Credit.

To illustrate the tentative profit limit, let's say the game didn't sell as well as anticipated. We'll reduce your income to $12,000 but still have $10,000 in business expenses and that same $4,340 in home office deductions. Home expenses are considered in two tiers:

- Real estate taxes*

- Mortgage insurance premiums

- Mortgage interest*

- Casualty losses

  - Depreciation (of the actual home, for homeowners)

  - Rent

  - Insurance

  - Repairs

  - Utilities

The first tier is primarily relevant to homeowners. All of those items are deductible on some level regardless of whether you use your home for business or not, while items in the second tier are only deductible if you do.

Casualty losses are losses caused by natural disasters, fires, and other unforeseen catastrophic events. While usually the realm of homeowners, renters may also face casualty losses of personal and business belongings if a disaster strikes.

Regardless, casualty losses and mortgage insurance premiums can't add to a business NOL like real estate taxes and mortgage interest can (which is why those two were starred). Since this example is for a renter, we don't have to configure those just yet.

If you had $12,000 in revenue and $10,000 in expenses, that leaves a $2,000 tentative profit. But since the home office expenses exceed $2,000, only $2,000 can be deducted this year. The remaining $2,340 has to be carried into next year where the tentative profit limit will come into play again. Because your self-employment income is also down to zero, you at least won't have to pay self-employment tax.

Now if you owned this apartment instead of renting it, we'd have a different story. Your mortgage payments were $12,000 for the year, of which $5,000 was interest. Real estate taxes were $2,000 and condo insurance was $400. Utilities were still $1,000 and painting the office also cost $500. After consulting the charts, depreciation is $590.

The paint job would still be deducted in full because it's only for the office. Depreciation is calculated separately, explained below. All the other expenses are subject to the 20% business rate but deducted in a certain order:

Tentative Profit: $2,000
Mortgage Interest (20%): $1,000
Real Estate Taxes (20%): $400
Subtotal: $600

Direct Expenses: $500
Subtotal: $100

Indirect Expenses:
Insurance (20%): $80
Utilities (20%): $20
Subtotal: $0, you can only use $20 of the full $200 worth of utilities. Everything else gets carried forward.

Remaining Indirect Expenses:
Remaining Utilities: $180

Depreciation: $590
Home Office Deduction to be Carried Forward: $770

But what if your mortgage interest and taxes were higher? Leaving the other expenses alone, here's how it would look:

Tentative Profit: $2,000
Mortgage Interest (20%): $2,000
Real Estate Taxes (20%): $800
Subtotal: −$800

Direct Expenses: $500
Subtotal: −$800, need to carry over

Indirect Expenses to Carry Over:
Insurance (20%): $80
Utilities (20%): $200
Depreciation: $590
Home Office Deduction to be Carried Forward: $1,370

You'd have a business NOL of $800 that you could use to offset personal income, and $1,370 in home office expenses to carry forward to the next year. If your game suddenly gets a new audience because of a streamer who picked it up or you land that dream publishing contract, you'll be glad you had this in your back pocket and that the IRS really loves homeowners.

DEPRECIATING YOUR HOME

If you own your home, you can deduct depreciation based on the purchase price with some adjustments. Business real estate is depreciated over a 39-year period, and your home is considered to be business real estate once you start taking the home office deduction.

Last chapter, I didn't get into real estate depreciation because it's pretty rare that an indie developer will own commercial real estate. But even with the US real estate market in total fracas, it's not out of the ordinary for indie developers to become homeowners.

Depreciation for your home works a lot differently than depreciation for equipment. You have to consult a table beyond the first year you start taking this deduction, and for that first year you need to know what the value of the land is. Property tax records should tell you if you have a house.

If you own an apartment or other housing on a shared lot, you can usually get this from the building's financial package prepared by the management where it'll be calculated for you. This is standard practice in New York City, plus the City also sends you an annual land value statement if you have a condo or house. But if you can't easily find this information where you live, you can usually find your condo association or building through your local tax assessor and a land value will be listed for your lot. If you can't find the land value for your individual unit, you can compute your portion by dividing the total land value by the number of units on the lot (usually, the number of residential apartments in the building).

The reason for this is that land can't be depreciated so it must be removed for this calculation. For the condo in the last example, here's how depreciation was determined assuming that this wasn't your first year of having a home office.

You paid $120,000 for the condo a few years ago and started using the second bedroom as an office last year, so it's your second year of depreciation. Comparable apartments in your building are now selling for $140,000 so you're going to use your purchase price since you have to take the lower of actual cost or market value to figure out this deduction. The building's financials say your portion of the land is worth $5,000 so your depreciable base for the whole condo is $115,000. The home office is worth 20%, or $23,000. Since you've been using the home office for a full year from here on out, you can use January's percentage on the depreciation chart which is 2.564% for every year until the 40th one. Depreciation comes out to $590.

Had this been the first year of using the second bedroom as a home office, you'd have to go by the *month* you started doing that.

SIMPLIFIED BUT SMALLER HOME OFFICE DEDUCTION

Starting in 2013, the IRS instituted a simplified way of deducting your home office similarly to those standard meal and mileage allowances: you can deduct $5 per square foot with a maximum of 300 square feet, and don't need to substantiate the expenses. Just that you used this square footage for business purposes. This deduction began at $5 per square foot and is still $5 per square foot at the time of publication.

The IRS has a chart (https://www.irs.gov/businesses/small-businesses-self-employed/simplified-option-for-home-office-deduction) explaining the differences between choosing the simplified method versus the normal method with all those lengthy calculations you just read about. So let's examine the pros and cons of this simplified method which has a maximum value of $1,500–a far cry from the numbers you saw even with fairly modest examples for a homeowner and a renter.

You still have to meet that regular and exclusive test, and take a square footage calculation. You can't use the room number method or claim the full 300 if you only have 130 square feet like in the example.

Like the standard meal and mileage allowances, you'd still have to account for properly using your home office but you're relieved from having to substantiate those expenses. But since 130 square feet only equals a $650 deduction, the simplified method is really only worth it if you have absurdly low housing expenses resulting from several generations of rent control or you get to live somewhere for free. For most people, the actual costs will virtually always yield a bigger deduction.

Another major downer with this method is that you have the same limitation with your tentative profit like you do with the standard method. But unlike the standard method, where you can carry your unused home office expenses forward if they exceed your tentative profit, you can't do that. You can't import your save file to use in the next installment. You have to use it or lose it, and it has a max value of $1,500 to begin with.

The only real benefit is if you own your home, and you use this simplified option to avoid a recapture when you sell. It's up to you to make an informed choice, but when I still practiced, many people still opted for the standard method because the recapture you're going to read about next was still worth the vast tax savings at the federal and state levels.

KARTING WITH BOWSER: HOMEOWNERS BEWARE

As you can see, homeowners have several extra benefits that renters do not, aside from being able to take a loss with their real estate taxes and mortgage interest. But renters get off easy if they move. Homeowners don't when they sell.

The "excluded gain" rules are a bit beyond the scope of this book, but I will provide the 5 Second Movie version. If you sell your home for more money than what you paid for it, which definitely happened to many homeowners during the suburban bidding wars in the early days of COVID, then you have a gain. You can shimmy out of paying capital gains tax on up to $250,000 ($500,000 if married filing jointly) of that gain provided that you used it as your primary residence for *two out of the last five years preceding the sale* and did not use it for business. Home offices count as using it for business!

So yes, this feels like you just went Karting with Bowser. You thought you were getting all these incredible write-offs but you sat next to the enemy boss all along!

But even if you met the time guidelines for the excluded gain, those generous depreciation deductions could have a steep price: the aforementioned recapture tax, which is definitely deadlier with a six-figure home than a $2,000 computer. Whatever your depreciation deductions were over the years, you need to recapture them when you sell.

Let's say that the condo you bought for $120,000 ends up selling for $200,000. In the years that you owned it, you deducted $5,000 of depreciation. The $80,000 profit on the sale leaves you well below the $250,000 threshold for not having to pay capital gains tax, assuming you only used it as a home office for two years or less out of the past five years. But you still have to pay taxes on that $5,000 recapture. And not at that soft capital gains rate.

Still, the taxes you pay on the recapture–or even capital gain, which tends to be lower than the rate on statutory income–might be worth it considering how much home office deductions save you on self-employment tax alone, plus state and local taxes if your jurisdiction is liberal with business deductions.

Compare this to renters who break or ride out their leases and don't need to go through all this. You just deduct the rent then you don't have to recapture anything when you leave. But if you value ownership and want to go that path, this is just what you need to be aware of to minimize the damage Bowser is going to inflict on you so you can make an informed decision.

* * *

It's not the home office deduction in and of itself that's impossibly difficult, but rather the conditions that allow you to claim it that make you feel like you're under sadistic crunch at a poorly-managed studio that wants to get a game out in time for that holiday shopping rush.

But now you're getting a break from the sadism: the 2018 tax reform gave small business owners a little gift that was supposed to make up for nerfing our NOLs.

Late Game Content

Minding Your QBI

T HE 2018 TAX REFORM was the largest and most material change to the tax code in several decades. It got its share of praise and criticism from all sides of the political spectrum, with the most notable annoyance coming from the beleaguered tax professionals who were socked with the largest change some of them had seen in their lives literally overnight. After they already had end of year advisory sessions with their clients on what last-minute decisions they should make versus things that should wait until the new year.

One of the most notable changes is a deduction that is structured so strangely that it deserved its own chapter. This deduction's setup is unorthodox but a great deal of indie developers will certainly benefit from it whether they're aware or not.

It is called the Qualified Business Income Deduction, or QBI for short. In the field, it's called the 199(A) deduction for its tax code section. QBI was meant to phase out the Bush-era Domestic Production Activities Deduction (DPAD) that was supposed to entice American manufacturers to come back to shore and get new entrepreneurs to create manufacturing businesses, but neither really happened and it wasn't claimed often. DPAD was folded into QBI by encouraging *all* kinds of businesses, even things like gig work and freelance hustles if you have a day job. QBI is

DOI: 10.1201/9781003335733-15

for small regional businesses and non-employers alike, which definitely encompasses indie game developers!

The best way to describe QBI as far as tax functionality goes is that it's a lot like striving for Mr. Qi's perfection rating in *Stardew Valley* where you caught every fish, found every Stardrop and golden walnut, and have every achievement. Ginger Island and Mr. Qi's walnut room are late game content if the player already upgraded the farm, got married, and rebuilt the community center. But while you can find the walnut room soon enough, it's tough and rare to attain Perfection. Most players give up and move on to other games or the need for human interaction.

It's similar with QBI. It's special endgame content that you only get to unlock if you survived everything this book threw at you so far, like being able to choose the best entity for your needs, properly substantiate and defend all of your business expenses, claim that home office deduction, and still post a profit.

It's something only a die-hard completionist would strategize far in advance, while the average player focuses more on the meat of those business deductions.

GOLDEN WALNUTS AND QI GEMS: THE EASY AND HARD MODES OF QBI

So, let's begin with who is eligible for the QBI deduction. If you haven't played *Stardew Valley* before, or you haven't worked on a game that utilizes multiple currencies in late game content like it does, these additional currencies open up to trade them for upgrades and very special items. Think of the Qi quests: Some of them are fairly simple like giving 50 loved gifts in a week, then you have the nigh-impossible quest to grow 1,000 units of Qi Fruit.

There's two tiers of QBI deduction that operate similarly. You can embark on the easy quest tier or the really hard quest that only three people ever solved before they rage-quit. The tiers are based on your income level.

Regardless of which tier you fall into, QBI is a deduction that is based on your business profits but it gets posted on your personal tax return. This means that C corporations are not eligible, and ineligible business-derived personal income items that are reported on your personal tax return such as dividend payments, distributions, and your officer salary. You can still have these items and claim the QBI deduction, provided that your income is under the tier limits and you have other eligible QBI. However, these items on their own wouldn't be considered QBI.

QBI-eligible business profits must be taxed as a sole proprietorship, a partner in a partnership or a multiple-member LLC, or the shareholder of an S corporation. What makes this deduction different from the others isn't just its odd location on your personal tax return, but it also examines your *personal adjusted gross income*. Not just your business profits, as you've read about so far.

If you own multiple businesses, or in the more probable case for game developers you have some freelance or gig work income on top of what you earn as an indie developer, the aggregate of those profits is used to calculate your QBI deduction.

As previously mentioned, there's three tiers of the QBI deduction: one easy, one that's tougher, then one as hard to get as Qi Fruit. Naturally, we'll begin with the easy tier. It is based on total personal income and allows most lines of work, including specified service trades or businesses (SSTBs), which you'll read about in the next section.

Here's a simple and realistic example: you're an indie developer who made $60,000 in wages at a marketing job in 2021. You also make games on the side and netted $20,000 in royalties that year. These were your only two income sources, making your gross income $80,000. You're a single filer who didn't have any additional adjustments except for 50% of your self-employment tax, which comes to $1,413. This makes your adjusted gross income (AGI) $78,587.

Because your AGI is below the phase-in range and hard limit for your filing status, you qualify for the maximum amount of the QBI deduction. The maximum is 20% of your eligible business profits, and $4,000 is 20% of your $20,000 studio profits. That $4,000 is then deducted *after* your itemized or standard deduction on your personal tax return, making it a BELOW below-the-line deduction.

The following amounts are based on the 2021 tax year and are pegged to annual inflation:

Threshold before Phase-In Begins	Filing Status
$164,900	Single, head of household, qualifying widow(er), estate or trust
$164,925	Married filing separately
$329,800	Married filing jointly

If your AGI is below these amounts, you're in the clear for a nice and easy deduction! But there is one caveat: investment income like capital gains and dividends can mess this up. This deduction is meant to primarily benefit entrepreneurs who have most of their assets tied up in their businesses rather than the market.

So let's revisit our simple example and make it a little harder. You still have $60,000 in wages and $20,000 in studio profits, filing as single, and your only adjustment is 50% of your self-employment tax. This time, you made some investments and received $250 in qualified dividends and $3,000 in long-term capital gains from stock you forgot about then cashed out to help pay for your next game. Your gross income is $83,250, AGI is $81,837, so you're still under that threshold.

Your deduction is unaffected because these were relatively modest amounts. But based on the computation process for QBI, having more investment income and a great deal of capital gains can put a crimp in how much QBI you're allowed to deduct.

This is still easy mode. Once your AGI is past the threshold for your filing status and tax year, you'll go from Qi's Kindness to that dreaded Qi Fruit. This happens with the phase-in range and SSTB designation.

WHAT IS A SSTB?

SSTBs are primarily professional services, meaning that your work is the chief product. The exclusion list the IRS provides encompasses the following:

- Healthcare

- Law

- Accounting

- Actuarial science

- The performing arts

- Consulting

- Athletics

- Financial services

- Brokerage services

- Investing and investment management

- Securities dealers

A vast majority of these SSTB flags aren't concerns to indie game developers. But there's one more I left off intentionally, and "performing arts" and "consulting" are the two big ones to think about.

Performing arts refers to theater, bands and musicians, dance, and other types of live entertainment. Game composers who play or conduct live shows may need to be careful with this. Although if you conduct an orchestra once a year at a local awards show while your main source of income is making music for use in games and other projects, you should be able to avoid getting hit with this SSTB label as a performance artist. But if live shows are a major part of your income, you could miss out on this deduction.

Consulting is also one that many indie developers and tech experts could hit a gray area. Is your chief source of revenue consulting on projects, the industry, or a specific discipline if it's not game royalties or work for hire? That could land you the SSTB label.

There's one more exception category and that is "any trade or business where the principal asset is the reputation or skill of one or more employees or owners."

That is a giant word salad to basically mean "influencer."

While one could argue that most established small businesses are based on reputation and/or skill, it's not a total catch-all. When there was a great deal of confusion about this exception in 2018, the IRS had to clarify that this is demonstrated by being compensated to endorse products, receiving appearance fees for media like TV and podcasts, and any kind of branding, licensing, or trademark of your name, likeness, signature, or other aspects of your identity.

This applies mainly to influencers, streamers, and other content creators. But there's athletes who have sports gear with their name branded on it, and that would also fall into this category. So if you become a game development celebrity where mousepad companies pay to use your name or autograph, chances are you could miss out on this late game bonus.

202 ■ The Definitive Guide to Taxes for Indie Game Developers

Under easy mode, you don't need to worry about this. But if your total personal income puts you in the zone for hard mode, you'll be disqualified if you're a SSTB.

But for the upcoming hard mode, we're going to assume that your primary source of income is game royalties and work for hire, where you're not hit with that SSTB distinction.

QI'S COOKING: QBI IN SLIGHTLY HARDER MODE

The Qi's Cooking quest is a good example for this calculation, because it's a harder quest than Qi's Kindness. You might run out of key ingredients before the week is up, but it's certainly not an impossible quest late in the game. This is where you'll still get a QBI deduction, it just won't be a full 20% of your business profits.

QBI has the following hard limits for the 2021 tax year, pegged to annual inflation:

Hard Limit	Filing Status
$214,900	Single, head of household, qualifying widow(er), estate or trust
$214,925	Married filing separately
$429,800	Married filing jointly

What this means is that if your personal AGI falls between that initial threshold and the hard limit, your QBI deduction is subject to a phaseout range. Staying consistent with our simple example, the phaseout range for a single taxpayer with eligible business income is $164,900-$214,900.

In the last example, your AGI fell below that $164,900 threshold. So let's see what happens when you have to do this the hard way, because you sold enough copies or got enough Patreon subscriptions to make it into this phaseout range.

You're a single filer whose only source of income is your game studio. You netted $200,000 in profits in 2021 with a single-member LLC taxed as a sole proprietorship. Half of your self-employment tax comes to $11,532 which makes your AGI $188,468, squarely putting you in the phaseout range. You haven't totally lost the deduction, but it will definitely be less than that straight 20% of the profits you saw earlier.

Taken from IRS Form 8995-A, the complex version of computing the QBI deduction, there's a multi-step calculation best explained with a picture instead of just words:

Form 8995-A (2021)						Page **2**
Part III	**Phased-in Reduction**					
Complete Part III only if your taxable income is more than $164,900 but not $214,900 ($164,925 and $214,925 if married filing separately; $329,800 and $429,800 if married filing jointly) and line 10 is less than line 3. Otherwise, skip Part III.						
				A	**B**	**C**
17	Enter the amounts from line 3		**17**	40,000		
18	Enter the amounts from line 10		**18**	250		
19	Subtract line 18 from line 17		**19**	39,750		
20	Taxable income before qualified business income deduction	**20**	188,468			
21	Threshold. Enter $164,900 ($164,925 if married filing separately; $329,800 if married filing jointly)	**21**	164,900			
22	Subtract line 21 from line 20	**22**	23,568			
23	Phase-in range. Enter $50,000 ($100,000 if married filing jointly)	**23**	50,000			
24	Phase-in percentage. Divide line 22 by line 23	**24**	47 %			
25	Total phase-in reduction. Multiply line 19 by line 24		**25**	18,683		
26	Qualified business income after phase-in reduction. Subtract line 25 from line 17. Enter this amount here and on line 12, for the corresponding trade or business		**26**	21,317		

Disregard Line 18 for now, because this comes up in the Qi Fruit difficulty level if your total personal income exceeds the hard limit. Although you will need to use this number here as well, it has to do with how much property you have.

Just like how the easy mode used 20% of your business profits, you'll start with that amount here as well (20% of $200,000=$40,000) and reduce it by 2.5% of your eligible property's basis. Then you need to consider your AGI against the threshold for your filing status, and this difference is taken as a percentage of the prescribed phase-in range. It came to 47% for this example, with the total QBI deduction being $21,317.

It's a little over 10% of the studio's profits, which is certainly nothing to sneeze at.

QI FRUIT: QBI IN HARD MODE

If your profits really hurtled into the stratosphere, this is where the upper hard limit comes in. If you also have that SSTB designation because you're a consultant, influencer, or other professional on that list, then you don't qualify for QBI at all by this point. The rest of this section doesn't apply to you, you're only allowed up until the end of that phaseout range.

This is the part that benefits highly successful indie developers far less than the easy version of this deduction. Because very small game studios generally aren't capital-intensive, and tend to be non-employers forever (or at least for protracted timeframes), we tend to lose out on this piece of late game content because your QBI deduction becomes limited by wages and how much business property you have.

If your AGI is more than $214,900 using single filing status, then you need to nerf your deduction base by the greater of 50% of W-2 wages, or 25% of W-2 wages plus 2.5% of your qualifying property's basis.

The wages part is easy, it's based on how much you paid out in wages reported on W-2s for the year. Then you have UBIA, unadjusted basis immediately after acquisition. This is for literally ALL of the property that your studio owns, no matter when it was acquired, and without those pesky depreciation calculations. If you've been using that $5,000 custom PC for a few years, then $5,000 is part of your UBIA. So long as you didn't dispose of it that year, you're good.

To make this go faster, you're still a non-employer who paid $0 in W-2 wages but your UBIA is $10,000 after accounting for computers, furniture, and other equipment. There's no wages to consider, but 2.5% of $10,000 comes to $250.

We'll repeat the same scenario as last time, but double your profits to $400,000. With 50% of self-employment tax being your only adjustment for $14,210 total, your AGI comes to $385,790, which is definitely past that hard limit.

Your deduction is just that $250 for all of the property you own.

Part IV	Determine Your Qualified Business Income Deduction				
27	Total qualified business income component from all qualified trades, businesses, or aggregations. Enter the amount from line 16	**27**	250		
28	Qualified REIT dividends and publicly traded partnership (PTP) income or (loss). See instructions	**28**			
29	Qualified REIT dividends and PTP (loss) carryforward from prior years	**29** (	)		
30	Total qualified REIT dividends and PTP income. Combine lines 28 and 29. If less than zero, enter -0-	**30**			
31	REIT and PTP component. Multiply line 30 by 20% (0.20)	**31**			
32	Qualified business income deduction before the income limitation. Add lines 27 and 31 ▶	**32**		250	
33	Taxable income before qualified business income deduction	**33**	385,790		
34	Net capital gain. See instructions	**34**			
35	Subtract line 34 from line 33. If zero or less, enter -0-			**35**	385,790
36	Income limitation. Multiply line 35 by 20% (0.20)			**36**	77,158
37	Qualified business income deduction before the domestic production activities deduction (DPAD) under section 199A(g). Enter the smaller of line 32 or line 36 ▶			**37**	250
38	DPAD under section 199A(g) allocated from an agricultural or horticultural cooperative. Don't enter more than line 33 minus line 37			**38**	
39	Total qualified business income deduction. Add lines 37 and 38 ▶			**39**	250
40	Total qualified REIT dividends and PTP (loss) carryforward. Combine lines 28 and 29. If zero or greater, enter -0-			**40** (	)

Form **8995-A** (2021)

There's no phaseout calculation like in the last example, because your total income puts you well past the phaseout's upper threshold so you have to use the greater of 50% of wages or 25% of wages plus 2.5% of UBIA versus a phaseout calculation.

Still, at least you got a $250 deduction. It's not like how you don't even get partial Qi Gems for those blasted blue melons that barely spawn.

* * *

It's uncertain whether this deduction will live past 2025, as there has been no major push to let it sunset or get extended. But if you're reading this book for an eligible tax year, enjoy that late game content if you made it this far. Because now we're going to talk about meta content, which is the various concepts that happen around your studio's tax matters and business decisions.

Why Your Fiscal Year Is Like Dinosaurs Living with Humans

READY TO DELVE INTO *Chrono Trigger*, or perhaps the aforementioned *Steins;Gate*? Where you have to do some time travel in order to progress in the game, and the past is just blown up into the present like dinosaurs living in the Middle Ages? Figuring out what accounting method to use and whether you should rely on a calendar or fiscal year isn't that much different!

Let's put on our programmer hats for a minute. Think about defining parameters that are used in game design, particularly a room or certain areas of a room. When you're figuring out the timing aspects of your cash flows using both a **method** and a **year** as global variables, you have a few different parameters that come into play here.

1. How often do get you paid, in the business sense?

2. Do you have some degree of control over the amounts (i.e. hours billed) or no control (your game sales are at the mercy of the distributor)?

3. How much is the business earning?

DOI: 10.1201/9781003335733-16

4. When do you (reasonably) expect to release your game?

5. How often do you pay people and companies?

6. How much do you pay them?

7. Does your studio have other sources of income aside from game royalties?

8. Do you value your mental energy over potentially saving on your tax bill?

If you haven't released a game yet and are completely pre-revenue, the timing of your first dollar proximal to when you officially opened for business is important because that's how you differentiate your start-up and organizational costs from your other deductible expenses. But when you reasonably expect to release your next game or receive a major payout is equally important, because if it's going to be in the next year or so, then you'll want to consider the pros and cons of a calendar year or a fiscal year. The same goes for which accounting method to use.

Your taxes can vary wildly depending on how much revenue you're bringing in, how many people owe you, and vice versa. Deciding how to time your income might not be that crucial in the early years when you're probably not making or spending much money yet. But depending on how you structure your business, deciding which time flux to use can wind up costing or saving you thousands. Now let's switch gears and think about designing a board game!

CALENDAR VS. FISCAL YEARS

Imagine a board game that has a looping structure like *Monopoly*. You start at Go and move around the board where it's just a square loop. Passing Go means that you completed the loop and you collect $200 to signify that. That's basically how a calendar year is: the year begins January 1 and once December 31 passes, we just change the year on our calendars rather than collect $200.

Most individuals are calendar-year taxpayers. So are a lot of small businesses. Many freelancers and small companies opt for the calendar year just for the sheer fact that it's easier to keep track of. There's no additional paperwork required to use a calendar year, it's the default setting for small businesses.

Fiscal years can be 52 or 53 weeks and are good for businesses with pre-dictable cycles or seasonal aspects, such as resorts and those Halloween stores that seek out vacant lots every fall then they're gone when November comes. A calendar year might not accurately represent a business like those which would depend highly on vacation months and peak costume-buying season but be vacant most of the year. Thus, a fiscal year is a more popular choice.

An ice cream shop in a temperate zone like the East Coast would be likely to open in the spring and shut down by Halloween. A fiscal year starting April 1, 2023 and ending April 2, 2024 would be more helpful than a calendar year in terms of income accuracy and being able to get the most deductions, which leads to another fun and wacky tax fact: A fiscal year that is exactly 12 months is actually considered an improper tax year, hence the 53rd week in a lot of fiscal years. The example above is exactly one year and two days, or 52 weeks and four days. So even though 2024 will be a leap year, it wouldn't hit 12 months on the nose in the future.

Alas, game studios are not ice cream shops or ski resorts. Because every indie developer has different timelines plus business and personal con-straints, it's difficult to say if sticking with the calendar year for ease is bet-ter than the recordkeeping challenge of a fiscal year that could potentially save money.

It ultimately depends on if you're already generating royalty income, how much of your income comes from publisher agreements or work-for-hire, the length and type of games you make, and the timing of other events that would cause surges or drops in income. The latter is the hard-est to predict because you honestly have no clue when a Twitter firestorm is going to bless you with thousands of sales. Or if you'll have protracted timeframes of very little or no income because you're just not getting eyes on your Steam and Epic pages.

Choosing a fiscal year over a calendar year will also depend on your business entity, and how your personal income will shore up with that of the business. Having served clients of all income levels, here's how I see it: How do you want your tax return data to look if personal taxes are a factor for your business structure?

Namely, are you more concerned about paying less taxes or having your income appear a certain way? It almost always boils down to housing, healthcare, or student debt. If a fiscal year posts bigger profits, it means paying more taxes but also helps you get approved for a mortgage since your tax returns are how most self-employed people prove that they have sufficient income to buy or rent.

Inversely, if a fiscal year posts *smaller* profits and you're in income-restricted housing, need subsidized healthcare, or you are on an income-based repayment plan for your student debt, you often need to submit your tax returns to qualify for these programs if you're self-employed and it's in your best interest to keep your profit lower if these needs shape your decision-making.

It can be hard to tell in the beginning. You're calendar year by default, and you can always change to a fiscal year down the road once you have some historical data for comparison.

But in the name of just not wanting to expend further mental energy on it when tax matters are already so complex, most people just stick to the calendar year. Recordkeeping sure can get confusing under a fiscal year. Virtually every example in this book relied on a calendar year to avoid further confusion! If you plan to use a fiscal year, you should definitely run it by a tax and accounting professional first. Especially since if you want to change it, you have to file for a change of year and the IRS only grants this *once every 10 years* unless you have an extremely bizarre case.

CUMULATIVE BOOSTERS AND ENEMIES IN ACCOUNTING METHODS

Accounting methods are a different animal than tax years, but they manipulate transactions rather than time specifically. When you think of a game that has a stage-specific scoring mechanism plus boosters that you can store for future use like *Angry Birds*, accounting methods will make a little more sense. **We will also assume that we're using a calendar year for all of these examples.**

You have a publisher-funded game, so you're not manually dealing with numerous distributor accounts. Rather than waiting for your Steam, Itch, and other monthly reports, the publisher issues quarterly royalty reports and typically pays you a month after you receive them. This means you don't see your fourth quarter report until January of the following year, and you aren't paid until February. How do you handle this under the two main accounting methods?

CASH METHOD AND CONSTRUCTIVE RECEIPT

Cash accounting means that you recognize income and expenses as they happen throughout your calendar or fiscal year. Just like opting for the calendar year, this is the method most small and solo business owners opt for to avoid wasting mental energy. But while it obviously makes more sense for indie developers to use the calendar year, it isn't always true of cash accounting.

Thinking of *Angry Birds*, you have your score for each stage. How well you play in stages that precede or come after it will have no effect on that stage's score. And basically, that's how cash method business taxes work. Not barring having any carryovers from the prior year like §179 deductions or excess home office expenses, it's essentially the same concept. If you didn't pay for a business expense in that year, you don't deduct it. If you didn't receive that payment in that year, you don't recognize it until you actually get paid.

So as for the money that the publisher owes you for your game sales between October and December, it's going to go on the *following year's* tax return even though the sales took place in the prior year. By the notion of **constructive receipt**, you didn't get the report until January and the money wasn't in your hands until February. It's off the hook for the prior year's tax return because it wasn't made available to you in that year.

Confusion with royalty reports is a common situation for game developers. The report could be quarterly or monthly, some publishers and distributors like GOG require you to invoice them once the report is generated instead of paying you automatically, and sometimes there are minimum dollar amounts you must meet in order to get paid. But it's about to get murkier than an *Angry Birds* level, because constructive receipt is all about when the money becomes available to you without restriction. This is a concept that definitely feels like channeling that annoying green boomerang bird.

When I handled taxes for more traditional businesses that accepted checks, some people would have a check dated for the end of the year but hold onto it and not deposit it until January because they thought they could defer income that way. *That strategy is made of fail.*

If you receive a check for royalties or work-for-hire towards the end of the year and aren't sure what year to report it in, look at the date on the check. If it's the new year but the check still has last year's date, you have to report the income with your last year's taxes even if you didn't receive and deposit the check until after the new year. The money was made available to you in the old year.

And if you ask a client or publisher to just postpone the date on a payment, it's also not going to work. Constructive receipt took place simply because *they made the money available to you* beforehand and said it was yours for the taking. But since indie developers have to contend with primarily digital payments, especially in an age when the sales and payment processes have been outsourced to algorithms rather than accounting departments, things can get confusing.

Many publishers and distributors often don't issue royalty reports until well over a month after royalties have been accrued, and sometimes there are minimum thresholds that you have to meet in order to get paid. The most ubiquitous example is Steam. Steam pays out monthly but you don't actually gain access to your money until you've generated at least $100 in net royalties. With hundreds of thousands of payments that need to be processed every month, this is their threshold to make processing yours worth it. If you didn't earn enough on Steam that month, the royalties will accrue in the ensuing months until you reach $100, then automatically pay out.

Until you reached the $100 threshold, Steam didn't make the money available to you yet. You don't recognize those unpaid accrued royalties as income under the cash accounting method until you reach that minimum and your payment gets processed. Whereas in the publisher-funded game example, even if you don't actually get paid until January, you still have to include those Q4 royalties in the prior year's income because they did make the funds available to you that were earned in that same year.

Despite the confusion that constructive receipt can cause, most small businesses like the cash method because they just find it easier. When you're a small business, you also have the choice whether or not to use the cash method. Once you start pulling in at least $5 million a year, you'll be mandated to use the **accrual method**. And if you have inventory, you also have to go accrual unless you pull in less than a million per year.

If your studio is a C corp, you can't use the cash method regardless of how much profit it generates.

PREPAID EXPENSES

If you use the cash method, there's one exception to this notion of "deduct it if you paid for it now" and that would be prepaid expenses. This wouldn't encompass paying retainers for lawyers and other professionals, because a retainer can be returned to you at any time if you cease working together or you're broke and need development funds. This treatment applies to prepaying for hosting, insurance, extended warranties, office rent, and other expenses that cover a long timeframe.

You're subject to one of two rules when it comes to prepaid expenses. There's the 12-month rule and the general rule.

The 12-month rule is the easiest. If the benefit doesn't stretch beyond 12 months from when it starts, you can deduct it in full. If you spend $100 on a 12-month device insurance policy for your computer where the coverage kicks in on October 1 of this year and expires September 30 of the next year, then you can deduct it in full under the 12-month rule.

The general rule comes into play when you prepay for more than 12 months. Let's say that you paid $500 for a hosting package to save money on your network of websites over two years, because the host offered a significant discount compared to paying for just one year. You have to prorate the costs to the years that they cover, and like depreciation, this is calculated by the month.

Your hosting service starts April 1 and ends March 31 of two years from now. The 24 months are $21 each, and your first year is nine months of coverage for $189. The second year's website expense deduction is for the full year of $252, and the third year gets the remaining three months at $63. You get a $4 bonus deduction based on IRS rounding conventions since $500 / 24 months = $20.83.

Whether you use cash or accrual accounting, you need to do this for all prepaid expenses that don't meet that 12-month exception.

ACCRUAL ACCOUNTING

Think about games where you can rack up things like potions, power-ups, and other items to save them for later. Even if your score changes every level, those goodies stay with you until you use them but recognized as being in your possession you obtain them. And accrual accounting is sort of like that: expenses are deducted when they're *incurred*, not necessarily paid while income is recognized when it's earned and not necessarily received.

So let's use two major indie game distributors in this example since they have different royalty payment processes—Steam and GOG. First with the cash method, then with accrual.

GOG sends you a report in December showing that you netted $300 in November. Their payments aren't automated so you have to invoice them;

life gets busy, and you don't get around it until December so the payment arrives in the middle of January. Steam's $100 minimum payout is preventing you from getting that $50 you're owed for November. You make $40 in royalties in December, making it JUST under that threshold so you aren't getting paid until February assuming you netted at least $10 in game sales in January.

Starting with the cash method, the $300 GOG payment would be part of the current tax year's income. They made it available to you that year, even though you had to invoice them first. You also made the effort to chase that payment in December. The Steam royalties on the other hand don't have to be recognized as income yet, because they're still not making the money available to you.

Under the accrual method, the treatment for the GOG royalties would be unchanged. You made the sales and invoiced them that year. But you would need to report the Steam payment as well, even though they haven't paid you. If your game really gets ignored in January and doesn't result in enough sales to reach the $100 threshold, you might not even know when you'll reach the minimum. So even though you didn't actually use that superpowered slingshot until several stages after you received it, you still picked it up much earlier.

When it comes to income, you recognize it as the earlier of when "required performance" occurred, when payment is due, or when you get paid. Since Steam has an automated system and only a $100 minimum to get a payout, there's no due dates you are enforcing and performance would be selling copies of the game. And that definitely happened before you got paid. Payment from GOG would be due when you sent them the invoice they requested. But your required performance already happened before you did so, you sold copies of a finished game.

For fan patronage like running a Patreon account, if you have a low tier that just thanks them for their support, your required performance is just existing. But if you have higher tier that promises patrons early access to content, patron-only perks, and so on, your required performance would come after you've fulfilled those obligations even though you were paid beforehand. If you use accrual accounting and it takes a while to give out those patron-only perks, some of your Patreon earnings could be deferred while the rest would be recognized that year.

If you offer services that require invoicing such as doing web design work, then you'd have to recognize the income upon billing that client after doing the work. Even though they haven't paid you yet, you did your required performance first so that's when you'd recognize the income.

What if you get money for a game that HASN'T been finished?

WHAT ACCRUAL ACCOUNTING REALLY MEANS FOR CROWDFUNDED GAMES

While many gamers and studios alike have experienced crowdfunding fatigue after the Kickstarter gold rush of the early 2010s, and the first liability cases for crowdfunded products and delivery failures have begun appearing in courts, the IRS has also clarified treatment of crowdfunding campaigns. They're definitely taxable when you're raising the funds for a game, art project, or other business or creative venture.

At the time of publishing, however, the Supreme Court has not yet ruled on whether crowdfunding proceeds are pre-orders or just a large sum of fan donations collected in a brief timeframe. No such cases have escalated to the Supreme Court yet. The creator and backer alike take a risk that the game won't get released. Even if they are backing a project with a very well-known development team who has a history of always delivering, there is still the risk that it won't get delivered.

Timing is of utmost importance if you plan on crowdfunding your game, as is choosing the right tax year and method to help time your income and expenses. This is because of that required performance concept; it's fairly straightforward when you're selling a finished game. You're done once you get the royalty report, no matter how long it takes to get paid.

Kickstarter and Indiegogo now release tax forms for processing your crowdfunding payments. But how do you account for them, and are you better off with the cash or accrual method?

If the campaign is just for finishing funds and you reasonably expect to finish by the end of the year, you'll probably be fine with the cash method. But if you're just at the demo stage and anticipate needing significantly more financial support to reach alpha stage, it can literally take years as many prominent Kickstarters have demonstrated by now. I was at the helm of a project that took six years to deliver, *Spaceventure* took a decade, and sadly there were many other games that completely failed to deliver at all.

Even after the legendary Tim Schafer kicked off the Kickstarter gold rush when Double Fine raised over $3 million to make a point-and-click adventure game and a documentary of the development process? They had plenty of hands on deck, but took two years just to get part of the game released. The second half of *Broken Age* didn't come out until 2015, three years after the funds were raised.

Crowdfunding is a situation that definitely calls for the accrual method most of the time. Accrual accounting can bite you at times, but Kickstarter campaigns are when they come in handy because even legends with lots of financial and human resources always need more than a year.

Many indie developers have been utterly burnt by the cash method when running a Kickstarter in the middle or the end of the year. They don't actually incur the largest relevant expenses a year or two after receiving the funds, all while the project isn't in a finished state making money yet (the prime reason to use accrual accounting to defer your taxes).

Even though lower circuit courts, Tax Court, and the Supreme Court have not officially ruled crowdfunding to be pre-orders, the eyes of the law still regard crowdfunding proceeds as prepayment as far as your tax and accounting treatment goes. Prepayment means that while you'd have to recognize the income right away under the cash method, you could defer the income under accrual on the date that you deliver the product. Your required performance doesn't occur until the product is delivered.

So, where does this leave you if you want to go the rewards-based crowdfunding route? Take a look at the timing of your deliverables and what seems like a realistic date for them. Not just when you think you'll release the game, but how many other promises you'll fulfill in your campaign. Then think about expenses and when you'll be most likely to pay them.

Some project creators will start sending out digital and/or physical rewards before the game is complete to keep their backers happy since most people now know that it takes a very, very long time to get to release. In-game rewards such as having a character modeled after you or having your own voice or dialog in the game also count as deliverables. So, this can muddy up the concept of required performance where you'll need to recognize bits of revenue as you go (luckily, those pledges are identifiable).

When planning a crowdfunding campaign, it's best to look at what you plan to offer as well as when you plan to deliver those things aside from the game itself. If you're offering physical rewards, how much do they cost and do you plan on fulfilling them to backers right away or waiting until the game gets released? Delays will happen no matter how much you plan in advance: life happens as indie developers frequently need to work an outside job on top of working on the game itself. Scope and feature creep are virtually always inevitable if you substantially exceeded your goal. But if you think that some of your deliverables are going to be completed and sent to backers in a tax year prior to the release date, then the accrual method doesn't necessarily mean that you'll be recognizing the income in the year of release. It will be recognized gradually.

To illustrate this with an example, let's say that you raised $30,000 on Kickstarter for your game. Kickstarter takes 5% and payment processing fees are another 5%, so you net $27,000. You're using the accrual accounting method so you don't recognize the entire payment upfront. One of your backers paid $500 for a custom character portrait and you provide this later in the year. While the game still isn't out yet, you've fulfilled one of your required performance aspects of recognizing $500 worth of revenue. Fortunately, that's not the case for the rest of the funds because nothing else has been fulfilled yet.

It's like a very painful RTS with shoddy mechanics for sure. Accrual doesn't always mean a total complete deferral, just mostly deferred depending on what you offered and when you sent it to the backers. Try to best guess when your most major expenses will happen relative to when you will collect the funds if your crowdfunding campaign is successful, and take note of whether you fulfilled anything before the game got released.

DEDUCTING BUSINESS EXPENSES UNDER THE ACCRUAL METHOD

Deducting business expenses when using the accrual method is a similar concept to the revenue recognition side of things, but a little inverted. All of the events that confirm incurring that liability must have occurred, the liability must be easily quantified, and economic performance took place.

An example that explains these concepts in English, not legalese: you hire a freelance social media manager to help you reach players and grow your digital presence. They provide a detailed consultation as well as reference materials, then actively manage your studio's social media accounts for a month. At the end of the month, they send you a clearly-itemized bill.

Under the cash method, you wouldn't deduct this marketing expense until you pay that bill. But under the accrual method, you'd be able to take a deduction *once you are billed*. Accrual taxpayers take a deduction once the expense has been incurred, not necessarily paid.

In this example, it's easily quantified with a bill and the economic performance—the consultation and active managing of your accounts—overlaps with the events that confirm incurring the liability.

Whereas to make this like yet another round of *Heroes of Might and Magic*, you can't see what enemy players are doing on the unexplored side of the map and that hurts your deduction. If someone has been doing work for you but hasn't sent you time logs or invoices, anything that could provide you with a reasonable estimate for what they're charging, you can't take a deduction until they provide you with at least one of those things.

BADDEST BADDIES: BAD DEBTS

Accrual taxpayers get a benefit that cash taxpayers don't—the ability to write off bad debts. If a client or publisher doesn't pay you, and it becomes hopeless that they ever will pay you because the company declared bankruptcy or they just vanished, you can deduct what they owe you. But the catch is that you had to recognize the unreceived payments as income at some point before. You can't just take a deduction for what didn't happen.

So if you worked with a publisher who owed you $500 in back catalog royalties then they close up shop without ever paying you, you can deduct that $500 you never received but had to recognize as income when you got your royalty report. You'd still need to sufficiently document efforts you made to collect on the amount like email chains, phone records, and if it was for a pretty big amount, hiring lawyers or collection agencies. If the publisher went bankrupt, it's easier to prove you had no hope of ever collecting that money.

Some smaller companies that are barely breathing but not quite dead yet may want to honor their agreement with you by offering a settlement or partial payment if they can't pay the full amount owed. If this happens, you just get a bad debt deduction for the part you don't collect.

EXPENSES YOU PAID WITH A CREDIT CARD

If you pay your business expenses with a credit card and don't pay it until the next month or carry a balance, it doesn't matter if you use the cash or accrual method. Expenses paid with credit cards are treated just like you paid in cash. What really matters is *what* the credit card paid for and the nature of each expense, not the fact that you used one. That and keeping it separate from your personal credit and debit cards.

*   *   *

You'll indeed feel like you're playing with the forces of time trying to figure out which year type and accounting method to use. For crowdfunded projects in particular, it reveals many gray areas based on the current regulatory environment as well as deliverable timelines. You also run the risk that a crowdfunded project might not deliver, all while the laws are stuck in the past.

How You Treat Development Costs and All the Gamasutra Content That Filled You ·with False Hope about the R&D Credit

W HERE MOST OF THE chapters so far have been centered around excit-
edly finding treasures you didn't even know existed, this chapter is
the opposite. It's actually a complete letdown. Not just in light of how this
existing tax benefit is structured, but the fact that legislative changes are
now even pulling indie developers into the mix in a bad way.

We've gone over how to deduct your plethora of expenses from your
simple recurring ones like website hosting to more complex expenses
requiring additional records like travel. But I left development costs out of
the previous chapters, because we've now hit a fork in the road: until the
2018 tax reform, you had a couple options for how to treat your research

DOI: 10.1201/9781003335733-17

and development (R&D) expenses (which is how dev costs often get classified).

It's akin to an endless runner game, because that's exactly what game development frequently feels like. You think you're finally making traction and then things backslide because a team member isn't able to commit to the project anymore, an engine upgrade changes the best practices and it completely upends your work, or you lose some health points in real life and have to focus on getting better. Ergo, when things stop feeling like an endless runner, which could be years down the road depending on the size of the game you'll need to assess how much the game cost you and what you can reasonably expect to earn from it.

You are standing in an open field west of a white house, with a boarded front door. You open the mailbox and a postcard says that the most direct route is to simply expense all of your dev costs as they happen. To your left, there is a sign pointing to a craggy valley where you can capitalize your dev costs over a 10-year period. A sign pointing south indicates that the steep mountain ahead is the R&D credit.

Wasn't the road to the south impassable? And wouldn't it be great to just whack a tree to get zorkmids instead of all this paperwork? (Younger readers may not get this paragraph's reference, but older fans of Infocom adventure games will.)

ARE YOU JUST STARTING OUT?

Remember going over the load screen, your start-up costs? You might have some research and experimentation expenses that can be expensed in full, or amortized like your start-up costs but with a much shorter period under the creative safe harbor.

Unlike the start-up costs that have an option for you to expense up to $5,000 then amortize the rest over 180 months, development costs for your game have the option to get expensed in their entirety in the year they are paid, or recover them over five years if they are not experimental.

If they *are* considered experimental, then you can amortize these costs over 10 years, separate from your start-up costs, but you cannot expense these items in the same year. This option is there for you for projects further down the road, but has a unique aspect in that it has to be treated this way whether your business is brand new or long-established. You cannot lump your development costs in with your start-up costs, even if you have a brand new company. You have to expense them in full when they occur, or amortize them over 5 years, 10 years, if experimental.

Game development IS often rife with experimentation. For most businesses, this 10-year election wouldn't apply, because methods and processes in product development either don't apply to them or they are utilizing proven processes. But many game developers are also doing this now, what with using universal game engines like Unity plus plug-ins, templates, and asset packages designed for their chosen genres.

As game developers, we fall into a unique category: both technological and artistic loopholes will apply to you, such as the high-tech maneuver to treat development costs differently. These costs are actually referred to as **research and experimentation costs**, because you take some uncertainty in developing a new product or process, even if it's using an engine countless developers have already used.

You're trying to perfect your design even if it's a proven engine and genre that's already established. You could be trying to improve upon mechanics you saw elsewhere or invent totally new mechanics, completely subverting players' expectations the way *Doki Doki Literature Club* did, where it looked like another anime-style dating sim or visual novel then it turned out to be a horror game.

There's that old adage proclaiming that only seven stories exist in the world, that anything you could possibly create has already been done before. This rule is fairly consistent for games, even the ones that revolutionize genres and stretch the medium's capability: EVERY game was inspired by something else. There's tens of thousands match-3 games out there; *Stardew Valley* was inspired by a farm sim, then an explosion of farm sims with backstories sprang from the furor, and even large corporate brands jumped on the dating sim bandwagon. But each game is still unique in some way, whether it's in the storyline, the art assets, how the narrative was implemented, employing mechanics from a different kind of game, or maybe doing an unprecedented genre merge.

No matter how experimental your game could be considered though, your other option is to skip the deduction and opt for the R&D Credit.

THE R&D CREDIT IS A WAGE-BASED CREDIT

As the chapter's title implies, you probably read some nice accountant's article on Gamasutra that got your hopes up: it proclaimed your studio could get MILLIONS OF DOLLARS from the government by filing this one tax form.

They show up every tax season like clockwork. I get a consultation request from a garage indie developer who read it, we discuss their business plans, then I have to deliver the bad news that they are not going to get $20,000 in finishing funds from the federal government in the form of this powerful orb of a tax credit.

It's because the R&D tax credit is structured to benefit very large companies with thousands of employees, who put years of research and millions in expenditures towards the rollout of new products. And as you can surmise from reading past chapters: not being capital-intensive and relying on our own labor and that of dev team members who work on a freelance basis means we're not going to get a smaller version of what the Fortune 100 companies receive in R&D incentives.

Small employers in tech, manufacturing, and games can still somewhat benefit from this credit, non-employers far less so. Hence, accounting firms specializing in R&D matters are simply trying to reach part of this audience. They're marketing to the finance departments of AAA studios and AA/III owners and managers who have a headcount of 5-20 rather than the average indie developer. Even if they use the term "indie developer," they're not referring to the vast majority of indies who are non-employers with annual revenue below $150,000.

If this revelation made you angry, don't shoot the messenger. After all, your state might have something for you to take advantage of in conjunction with the federal R&D credit or in lieu of it. But this messenger is telling you not to get your hopes up on the federal level if you're a non-employer with relatively low revenue, since you will see little or no benefit from the R&D credit.

The Research and Experimentation Tax Credit, simply known as the R&D credit, encourages businesses to invest in new products, processes, and take risks by giving them a tax credit for certain expenses in taking these risks. Because these ventures majorly fuel economic growth and innovation, even when initiated on a small level regardless of the projects' success rates, lobbyists in tech, pharma, and manufacturing fought for years to make this credit a permanent part of the tax code.

They got their wish in 2015 with the passage of the Protecting Americans against Tax Hikes Act (PATH Act). The R&D credit is now a permanent part of the tax code, providing that businesses don't double-dip in getting both a credit and a deduction for eligible R&D expenses.

If you're not paying yourself yet and are primarily hiring talent on a freelance basis, you won't really benefit. But if you plan on growing your studio to the point you have at least one employee who isn't a corporate officer, the R&D credit just might shower you with some Sonic rings.

WHAT IS CONSIDERED AN ELIGIBLE R&D EXPENSE?

Even if you're not claiming the R&D credit, which is the case for most small indie studios who are non-employers, you need to know what is and isn't considered an R&D expense because of some unfortunate law changes that have come up which you're going to read about after seeing how the credit works.

Remember, these items are not treated as start-up costs! They need special labels in your recordkeeping system:

- Licensing an engine, or any other software and subscriptions need to make the game

- Paying people whose work is an integral part of the game:

  - Producers

  - Project managers

  - Programmers

  - Narrative designers

  - Game writers

  - Artists

  - Animators

  - Sound designers

  - Composers

  - UX and accessibility consultants

- Alpha testing

- Licensing or commission of art, sound effects, music, and other game assets

These expenses usually constitute the majority of game development costs, but there's others that didn't make it onto this list. That's because while items deserve their credit and respect in the games industry, they are NOT considered R&D costs as far as tax law goes:

- Quality assurance

- Paid beta testers

- Marketing expenses at any stage of the game's development

- Survey development and administration for players

This is true of both the R&D credit and deduction.

OVERVIEW OF HOW THE R&D CREDIT WORKS

As previously stated, indie developers who are small non-employers are more likely going to benefit more from the R&D deduction than the credit. You could still qualify using freelancer payments and asset license purchases (and your own compensation if using a corporate structure), but the benefits are slashed compared to what the credit is worth when you're claiming employees' wages.

That's how AAA studios get millions off their tax bills. Take Activision where they have both external and internal development, and more employees than the populations of entire towns. Even if you only looked at the relevant internal departments, there are enough bodies to form the Republic of Warcraft. Compare that to the average indie who faces a long period before they can pay themselves consistently, let alone other people. The former has thousands upon thousands of salaries that are eligible for the credit.

The next factor goes back to the basics at the very beginning of the book: the fact that the R&D credit is non-refundable. If you recall from earlier, this means that you can only use the credit to the extent that you have taxable income. Although it is worth mentioning that unlike most refundable credits, the R&D credit doesn't have a "use it or lose it" policy. You can carry the credit forward up to 20 years! If you deduct all of your R&D expenses and it creates a loss, you can also carry that NOL forward, but it's pretty unique for a business credit to do this.

But let's say that your studio is at a stage where you're hiring employees and paying yourself a regular salary (an actual salary reported on a W-2 form that meets reasonable compensation rules if your studio is an S corp). It's worth weighing the benefits of taking the R&D credit.

There's a four-part test to determine if you're eligible for it:

1. Does your studio intend to develop a new product or development process?

2. Technical in nature?

3. Is your studio's activity out to eliminate technological uncertainty, whether it's in terms of feasibility or the uncertainty of the design?

4. In doing all this, are you following some process of experimentation to overcome the uncertainty?

Let's go through this list. All of the conditions must be satisfied in order to take the R&D credit, otherwise you must take the R&D deduction instead.

In the first test, this means you must be making a brand new game. While it's common for Indie developers to re-release old titles that have revamped graphics, voice acting, and other improvements, those expenses don't qualify. It must be a new game.

Games are technical in nature, so the second test is an easy A.

The third and fourth tests are the ones more subject to interpretation by the IRS and the courts. Genre-bending games and pure experimentation have more leeway. But even if you're making a game in a proven genre, your studio's technological feasibility will vary wildly from another's! Overcoming uncertainty can be anything from "if I fill this screen with soft-bodied objects, how long will it take the game to crash" and "Can you get *Doom* to run on a Dream Phone from 1992" to "will even the pickiest FPS fan stop dead in their tracks to play my murder mystery dating sim about sentient blocks of cheese forming a polycule in Cleveland?" (Give me credit if you end up making this game).

Game developers certainly have these factors on our side. It's the implementation that's the hard part.

Going back to the first two tests, the following projects would be **ineligible** for the R&D credit:

- R&D funded by an individual, a publisher, grant program, or any other third party

- DLC, add-on purchases, and expansions if they were not part of the original game's release

- Adaptation or duplication of existing business components, such as updating a game you already have for sale

- Research that you conduct after development has kicked off

- Reverse engineering

- Surveys, studies, market research, data testing, and quality control

- Software developed for internal use

- Research related to arts, humanities, and social sciences (games still fall under computer science, fortunately)

- Foreign research conducted outside of the US

The first item on this list already eliminates publisher-funded games, anything using grant funds, work for hire, and crowdfunded games. It has to be an original game using different sources of funding like your own money, prior profits, bank loans, or raising funds through an investor for the general growth of the company.

If you make DLC and expansion packs for a game that's already been released, you cannot use it for R&D credit purposes *unless it's part of the original release*. A great example of this is *Graveyard Keeper*—a successful game in the vein of *Stardew Valley* but with a hefty dose of mortuary science and a leftist donkey.

Graveyard Keeper was released as a standalone title then the fanbase grew and demanded more content and features. ConcernedApe released various official expansions and quality of life updates for *Stardew Valley* but made them available for free since the game sold millions of copies before moving on to other projects. Unable to offer free updates, Lazy Bear Games took a different approach that avoided the longer, riskier, and exponentially more expensive process of creating a second game. They simply expanded the world and gameplay of *Graveyard Keeper* over the years with DLC. *Stranger Sins* added a pub and new quests to the game, and *Better Save Soul* introduced new characters alongside quality of life updates.

Expanding a game with DLC is an intriguing topic from both business and game development perspectives. But as far as tax law is concerned, DLC initiatives unfortunately wouldn't qualify for the R&D credit.

Graveyard Keeper was publisher-funded and wouldn't have qualified for the credit anyhow. But let's say it was self-funded. The original game would've qualified, but the DLCs wouldn't. If these expansions were planned out ahead of time however, then offered for sale alongside the game at initial release, then the development costs for that DLC would also qualify.

If you're offering free updates, patches, mods, and other aspects of version control, you'll be able to deduct the costs associated with them but can't use them to claim the R&D credit.

The same goes for reskinning and reverse engineering your own games. Doing this kind of experimentation and selling the results is all fine and well. It just won't qualify for the R&D credit.

If you work with foreign studios to outsource assets and support functions, projects that would otherwise qualify for the R&D credit will not actually qualify at all, if a significant amount of development-related work is offshored.

ELIGIBLE EXPENSES AND HOW THE R&D CREDIT IS CALCULATED

This is primarily a wage-based credit. Wages to employees directly engaging in, supporting, or supervising the R&D activity (read: making the game or helping get it shipped) are what make up the bulk of the credit.

If your studio is an S or C corporation, and you pay yourself a salary while being an instrumental part in making the game as is the case for a vast majority of indies, you can use your own wages as well.

100% of the wages paid to employees in development roles like project managers, programmers, and narrative designers can be used to figure out the credit. It must be people who you pay as employees and the credit is computed with just their wages, not payroll taxes.

Only 65% of independent contractor pay can be used to calculate the credit.

Supplies that were used to make the game can also be figured into the credit at 100% of their cost. For most game developers, this would include art supplies and office supplies used in paper prototyping, design meetings, and printing hard copies of game design documents. So long as you can prove that these supplies were linked to the game's development, it should hold up for the calculation.

However, equipment does not count for the credit. This namely encompasses electronics like computers, tablets, and consoles, but filming and motion capture equipment used by more well-funded indies would not go into your R&D credit calculation.

Interestingly, if you're renting or leasing computers outside of where you normally work then that would count. But since most indie developers use their own computers for their own games, we're primarily looking at whether your project is eligible, and how much the credit is worth relative to the tax benefits you'd get from the R&D deduction instead.

All of the costs outlined above are the qualified base costs. There are a couple complex ways that the R&D credit is calculated once you've determined all your base costs (which is virtually always certain employees' salaries and independent contractor pay).

We have yet another one of those building puzzles here, and this one is definitely 1980s NES games degrees of unforgiving. There's a fixed base percentage calculation that depends on how many years your company has been in the trenches making games.

Since it's typically more established studios that take advantage of the R&D credit, let's say you started your studio as an S corp in 2015 and you paid yourself a $60,000 salary for the first time in 2021. You contracted a sound designer for $5,000 and an animator for $10,000 while you did all the programming and writing, and spent $100 on art supplies to do your own concept art and experimentation. 100% of your salary and supplies will count, but only $9,750 (65% of $15,000) will count for the people you worked with on a freelance basis.

This would bring your total qualified R&D expenses to $69,850.

Here's where it's about to get more obnoxious than that dreaded Qi Fruit quest in *Stardew Valley*: you now must figure out what your **fixed base percentage** is, and this depends on how many years you've been making games, and what your qualified R&D costs were in those past years. (This is why precise recordkeeping is so direly important!)

We're going to use the alternative simplified credit formula where you have to take those qualified costs for the past three years. If you had none at all in prior years because you weren't paying yourself a salary yet, or hiring freelancers to help you and took a DIY approach, then your credit would just be 14% of the current year's costs, $9,779 (14% of $69,850).

If you did have qualified R&D costs in prior years, even if you didn't actually claim the credit, it's more complicated. Let's say that your qualified R&D costs were $35,000 in 2018, $20,000 in 2019, and $8,000 in 2020, which makes your total qualified R&D costs for the past three years $63,000. You have to take 1/6 of that based on how many years you've been in business, which comes to $10,500, and deduct it from this year's qualified R&D costs ($69,850, which makes your fixed base $52,500). Then you take 14% of your fixed base for your final credit: $7,350.

Remember, this is $7,350 that gets shaved directly off your tax bill and can be suspended if you don't want to use it now! But how does it stack up to deducting almost $70,000? This is why the credit usually doesn't benefit indie developers at all, especially not in the early years where you're not paying yourself a salary like in this realistic scenario that was actually based on one of my clients.

There are two other R&D credit calculation methods that are more complicated, particularly if your studio has been around for more than three years. Because the audience for this book is primarily indie developers just starting out or looking to build upon the business aspects after a few years in operation, it's out of the book's scope. Even so, a vast majority of tax professionals are likely to direct you to this simplified alternative method based on both your dev costs and how long you've been in the business.

CHANGES TO HOW R&D IS TREATED IN 2022 AND BEYOND: EVEN THE NON-EMPLOYERS!

Based on conversations with other indie developers and the accountants who serve them, the general consensus is that it benefits most indies to expense their development costs whether they're working on their first commercial release or have been in the industry for some time. When you start drawing a salary, that's when you need to do that calculation above and see if you'd benefit more from the tax credit or just taking a straight deduction.

There's just one problem. Making the R&D credit a permanent part of the tax code came with a price. Regardless of how much or little revenue your studio is bringing in, you're about to lose your ability to do a straight deduction of your R&D expenses.

While the professional sector knew this was coming in 2020, tax professionals and corporate interest groups have lambasted this incoming change because they see it as punitive to small businesses and discouraging innovation. While a large corporation can still claim millions of dollars in R&D credits while enjoying a permanently reduced corporate income tax rate, deducting your R&D costs if that credit isn't as beneficial won't be an option anymore.

I will not sugarcoat it: this proposed change could definitely screw a significant number of indie developers.

For tax years beginning after December 31, 2021, meaning 2022 and onward, companies of any size cannot immediately expense R&D costs for software development and other activities anywhere. Instead, you now have to amortize these expenses over a five-year period starting with the midpoint of the year that these expenses were paid or incurred (increased to 15 years for expenses incurred outside the US, like if you're subcontracting with foreign studios).

This is irrespective of the R&D credit. This move takes away an extremely powerful deduction and could even force indie developers to use the accrual method instead of cash method by default since you're now forced to amortize. The "experimental" language has also been stricken from the tax code, meaning that this restriction applies whether your dev costs would be considered experimental or not.

If we round up our calculation example to $70,000 for simplicity, that would equate to a $14,000 deduction over the course of five years instead of a straight $70,000 deduction. Which if you have a pass-through entity and it leads to a NOL, will definitely affect your personal taxes as well.

With the 2018 tax reform instituting those limits on NOLs, the only advantage of this new mandate is that it could benefit you if you have long stretches of time with little or no income. While this is common for indie developers, stretching those costs over five years would provide you with a more even deduction if the game sells better than expected after finding an audience. But if the game has *Among Us* degrees of taking a very long time to find its audience or it just never goes over, this enforced longer recovery period disproportionately impacts small studios and will definitely cause many to spend less on R&D.

At the time of publishing, this is the current legislative reality and many individuals and businesses have expressed discontent with lawmakers regarding this matter. Since readers have access to a webpage where I will post annual tax law updates every December, you can stay posted through the Taylor & Francis team and if any changes come to the treatment of development costs after the next election cycle, you'll be made aware.

* * *

So, that wraps up the infamous R&D credit. Knowing how to treat your R&D costs is important even if you don't claim the credit. You can't use it for games that aren't new, funded by a publisher or grant program, and whether you'll benefit depends on how your pay structure is set up and how much revenue your studio is raking in.

Now it's time to switch gears to inventory, because while our space is predominantly digital there's still a physical element with boxed editions and swag.

Rubber Chickens with Pulleys in the Middle (Inventory)

IF YOU'RE A DIE-HARD adventure gamer like myself, you'll likely think of that ubiquitous red satchel from *King's Quest V* when it comes to the word "inventory". Or the random gathering of nonsensical objects like moldy bits of cheese, ladders that can be jammed down your pants, and real actual red herrings. Those descriptions range from poetic to whimsical!

Unfortunately, inventories in this context are something of a snore. You're likely to have thousands of items that look exactly alike. If you're keeping goods on hand or in a fulfillment center hundreds of miles away to sell them online, your recordkeeping burden significantly increases.

You need to keep tabs on what's coming in and out, and depending on what you sell, this can be very daunting and frequently requires extra pairs of hands. Most accounting software also usually needs a third party add-on to tackle complex inventory systems, which luckily most game developers don't have to contend with although the more items you have on hand the harder it will be.

While keeping active inventory is usually more of a concern for the tabletop games space, it can come up with indie developers as well. Some older gamers prefer the nostalgic feel of boxed games and the awareness

DOI: 10.1201/9781003335733-18

that they always have a copy in case your digital catalog gets pulled from a distributor.

Selling swag like T-shirts, plushies, keychains, and figurines has also been through some evolutions: studios had to take the risk on buying limited runs of these items then see if they sold. Now that print-on-demand services like RedBubble and Printful are on the scene, studios can upload their designs and have another company handle the printing, storage, and fulfillment of these items and all without needing to keep inventory on hand, and subsequently do tedious inventory accounting!

Generally, when you use these print-on-demand services, you collect a royalty payment for the merchandise you sell and don't need to keep an inventory for tax or accounting purposes. But if you have significant control over the process and are in a situation where you need to collect sales tax, you might need to do some degree of inventory accounting after all.

But whether you take the DIY approach or hire a company to manage all of your physical goods production, you will need to keep track of inventory if it's in your hands. If you bought a lot of swag for a crowdfunding campaign and keep the extras on hand to sell at conventions, you need to be aware of inventory accounting and how it works.

If you have no plans to sell boxed games or merchandise at all, you can skip this level since none of this applies to you.

TYPES OF INVENTORIES

There are three kinds of inventories: raw materials, work-in-process, and finished goods.

You need not take "**raw materials**" too literally; if you're making a special edition box set and ordering various components such as cases, outer boxes, old school manuals, and whatnot, those all count as raw materials even if they're finished goods in the concrete sense. A half-finished set would be **work-in-process**, while the completed sets ready for sale would be **finished goods**.

To make your life easier, we'll just work with finished goods inventory for the examples. But if you sell items made by hand, or that have several manufactured components, you'll want to look into those other inventory types more closely.

INVENTORIABLE COSTS

It's not just the actual per-unit price that you have to pay. The following costs get factored into your inventory:

- Printer or factory setup charges

- Freight/shipping

- Sales taxes

- Customs duties

- Any other fees set by the manufacturer for extras, or going below the minimum order quantity

- Inventoriable overhead like storage and insurance

You want to order a set of 500 figurines for your crowdfunding campaign and to sell the extras at conventions. It costs $4/unit for a total of $2,000 plus $800 in setup charges. After production, you're billed for $1,000 in freight and $50 in duty.

It's not just that $2,000 unit cost that gets allocated to inventory. Adding those other charges results in $3,850 of inventory, coming down to $7.70/ unit. You would record this expense as an asset, rather than a deduction.

NON-SALE TRANSACTIONS TO KEEP TRACK OF

Inventories have quirks to them that can lead to a migraine faster than trying to find more of those Qi beans to grow those godforsaken melons you'll never get enough of. (Serious question: Did ANYONE ever successfully finish that *Stardew* quest?)

Obviously, you'll want to keep track of whenever items sell and how much you have left, because if you have insurance on your inventory, manual counts are usually required to keep your coverage. But you still need to record the following:

- Items taken out for personal use

- Units that break from everyday handling

- Damaged units from unplanned disasters like fire or zombie apocalypse

- Any units you set aside for promotions, giveaways, or marketing samples

- Inventory donated to charity

These inventory transactions are treated a little differently than simply selling them.

COST OF GOODS SOLD (COGS)

Inventory is an asset, like your cash and receivables. What you pay for inventory doesn't get deducted right away. Not until it's sold, or something else happens to it.

When it comes to bookkeeping, cost of goods sold (COGS) is normally equal to your beginning inventory after deducting your ending inventory. For tax reporting, it's a little more complicated.

If you take out items for personal use, like giving gifts to friends and displaying them in your home, you have to report it but can't take a deduction. Swag that you set aside for promotional giveaways gets deducted as a marketing expense, not COGS. Then charity giveaways are treated differently, because it depends on what you're giving away, how the organization will use it, and how you set up your studio.

C corps tend to get a bigger benefit for charity deductions than the other entities do primarily because they just have a flat 10% of income limit on donations with an option to carry any overage forward, whereas you personally might not itemize on your personal tax return and thus lose out on any tax benefits from donating. Your donation will be worth the smaller of its market value or the actual cost. For our figurines, we'd have to deduct $7.70 per unit donated instead of the $20 sale price. It has to be kept out of COGS.

So we have the figurines you purchased for $3,850 total and cost $7.70/unit. Let's say that you bought them in May this year and sold 100 figurines for $20 each by year end, making $2,000 in sales and $770 in COGS. Assuming there's no other inventoriable overhead, your profit from swag sales is $1,230. The remaining $3,080 in inventory sits there as an asset. You can't take a deduction for that $3,080 yet.

Then some other things happen like you accidentally break five figurines when moving boxes, use 50 of them for promotional samples and giveaways, and donate 10 to Extra Life. The five that broke cost $38.50

which you can write off as damage, while the $385 for 50 figurines is deducted as a marketing expense. Then assuming that your studio doesn't operate as a C corp, you have to remove the $77 in donated figurines from your inventory count to be transferred to your personal taxes.

You can still get deductions when you have inventory, it's just not as straightforward and you have to report them in different places. It's important to bear this in mind because it will affect things like your ability to take the $179 and home office deductions, since COGS "comes first" compared to your other expenses.

So if you have the $2,000 in swag sales leading to a $1,230 profit plus another $5,000 in royalty income, $6,230 would be considered your total revenue before your other expenses: *not* the full $7,000 of royalties plus sales before accounting for COGS. This is because COGS would create a loss if too many non-sale deductions got up there, that's why it's structured the way it is.

To briefly revisit home offices as well: if you store a significant amount of inventory at home and want to take the home office deduction, that pesky exclusive use test doesn't come into play if it's just for inventory storage. If you use your linen closet to store game boxes, figures, T-shirts, and the like, the IRS won't care that there's also clean fluffy towels for you and your housemates in there. But tread carefully if you have both a regular home office plus dedicated external storage, the exclusive use test comes back to bite.

*   *   *

I didn't want to spend much time on inventories, because many people gravitate to game development purely for dealing with as few physical goods as possible. Especially now that most studios both large and small outsource their merchandising and box production to print-on-demand services and third party shops like Fangamer that solely focus on selling merchandise, so you don't need to be bothered with inventory accounting, sales tax, fulfillment, and all the headaches.

But I figured you should be aware of how inventories work, because some indie developers like to build up their brand with swag. We come from a variety of backgrounds and some see T-shirt sales as just part of the game, others get extremely engaged in the process and want to control as many of the creative aspects as possible while turning it into a major revenue stream. Third party merchandisers can put a severe crimp in those plans, and inventory accounting is just going to become an unfortunate reality of your business processes.

Other studios just want control over how their physical copies turn out. If you make board and card games, you need to know what's in this chapter! It's also good to know if you want to do a crowdfunding campaign and you bought inventory but haven't delivered it yet.

To stay on topic with inventory, it's now time to discuss the most annoying baddies since getting blindsided by ghosts in *Pac Man*: sales taxes!

Sales Tax: Torment

E VEN IF YOU DON'T plan on selling swag like T-shirts, boxed games, and other goods, sales tax could still be of concern to you because some states and cities started charging sales tax for digital downloads. Washington, D.C. is one of them, in that the District explicitly names "canned and custom software" in its edict so that means game developers are definitely impacted.

Some third-party merchandising sites, like your own Redbubble store, will collect and administer the sales tax for you if you sell swag through them. But if you're building your own storefront through a service like Shopify or just putting PayPal and Apple Pay buttons on a basic webpage, then sales tax administration is definitely going to be a concern for you.

All of the major digital distributors like Steam, the App Store, Epic, and Itch will also handle sales tax since they are the point of sale, not you directly. The same goes for third-party marketplace behemoths like eBay, Etsy, and Amazon. If that's where the buyer completes the sale, that's who handles the sales tax.

But if you're going to go Web 1.0 and offer players an option to just buy your game from your own server without needing to make a Steam account and sundry, that is not only an awesome old school approach but also one where you will be on the hook for sales tax and thus need to be aware of the responsibilities.

DOI: 10.1201/9781003335733-19

Even if you choose to absorb the sales tax from customers, you still need to report and pay sales taxes.

If you use a digital or physical fulfillment service, or a print-on-demand service, you will also need to check the fine print to determine what the actual point of sale is and whether you need to administer the sales tax or they will.

If you sell merchandise at conventions outside of the state, county, and city that you live and operate in, you could be on the hook for temporary sales tax obligations if you make sales there.

There are over **9,600** sales tax jurisdictions in the US. 9,600! Individual towns, cities, and counties can charge sales tax on whatever items they want, in addition to what the state collects. There's no federal sales tax mechanism. Unlike in smaller countries, where there is a federal GST (general sales tax) or VAT (value-added tax) on certain purchases that is uniformly applied, this is a matter left entirely up to state and local governments. The only federal law that applies is the Dormant Commerce Clause from Article I of the Constitution: it means that no state may pass laws that discriminates against, or places an undue burden upon, interstate or international commerce.

That "undue burden" part could be widely interpreted. One could argue that having literally almost 10,000 sales tax jurisdictions for a country with just 50 states is an undue burden in and of itself. Only Alaska, New Hampshire, Montana, Delaware, and Oregon don't charge sales tax at all on the state level (with the exception of a few Alaskan boroughs). If you don't live in those states, you'll have to find out which jurisdiction(s) you're liable for and get a schedule of taxable items.

Since the first edition of this book was published, a landmark sales tax case was overturned and the new law of the land is the outcome of the Wayfair sales tax case that escalated to the Supreme Court. *Wayfair* has removed many of the "Wild West" elements of Internet sales now that e-commerce basically runs the planet.

THE UNHOLY TRINITY OF NEXUS, QUILL, AND WAYFAIR

One of the foremost concerns in sales tax matters is where you have **nexus**. When *Quill* was still law of the land, the way it worked was that businesses only had to worry about charging sales tax in jurisdictions where they have nexus.

Nexus refers to having a significant physical presence in that location. The state, county, and city where you incorporated and operate count.

As indie developers who tend to work from home and use their home office as their main business address, your residence would be that first nexus. If you have multiple owner-operators of your studio, and they live in a different jurisdiction than you, it could also be considered nexus although it's usually the address listed on your tax returns. But if you have an office, even a home office, in that location, it could be considered nexus.

However, server location has been considered to establish nexus for digitally-based companies. If you sell swag and store items for your own storefront (opposed to using a service like Printful where the merchandise isn't yours until an order is placed) or use a fulfillment house in another jurisdiction, that might be considered nexus as well.

Once you've determined where your studio has nexus, you would need to apply for a sales tax license for *each* jurisdiction and collect it at the proper rates for that jurisdiction's items. To invoke this chapter's name, it sounds like many planes to cross. Except that this time, you'll totally want to repress each memory as you come across it!

Even as e-commerce infrastructure has changed the way that nexus has been viewed by tax authorities and the courts, this is an important concept to know. It's also what has made many small businesses and studios gravitate to large distribution platforms that have dedicated staff and external support for handling sales tax for thousands of jurisdictions.

So, with a lack of federal infrastructure for sales tax and an ever-changing landscape for how we sell physical and digital goods and services, how has this been handled in the courts—and enforced?

The 1992 Supreme Court case *Quill Corp v. North Dakota* is a landmark case that was used as precedent for almost 30 years. Prior to *Quill*, *National Bellas Hess v. Department of Revenue of Illinois* was decided by the Supreme Court in 1967 that mail-order businesses didn't need to collect sales tax in states where they didn't have significant physical contact.

It's obvious that the way people shop and sell drastically changed between 1967 and 1992, then 1992 and the 2020s. *Quill* was the real gamechanger, until *Wayfair*.

Quill Corp was a Delaware corporation with offices in Illinois that sold office supplies and boxed software. Their sales were made mostly through mail-order and by phone. The North Dakota tax department smacked them with a sales tax notice saying that they owed three years of unpaid sales taxes on office equipment and supplies sold in North Dakota. Quill Corp got their North Dakota clients through magazine ads, telemarketing, catalogs, and promotional flyers. They had no employees, warehouses, fulfillment centers, or offices in North Dakota.

North Dakota argued that under due process, Quill Corp had a physical presence in North Dakota because of floppy disks. You read that right: a physical copy of software, since digital distribution just wasn't there yet in the late 1980s, supposedly entitled the state to collect sales tax. "Floppy disks and copy machines constitute physical presence under due process" was literally the argument the tax commissioner of North Dakota used.

This prompted the Supreme Court to reexamine *Bellas Hess*, which was just a 25-year-old case at the time, since it also dealt with mail-order sales. *Complete Auto Transit v. Mississippi* came up as well: Complete Auto was a Michigan-based car transporter service that moved General Motors vehicles from the railhead in Jackson, Mississippi to dealerships throughout the state, but the GM cars were assembled back in Michigan. The Mississippi state tax authority sent Complete Auto a bill for the privilege of doing business in the state.

When challenged in Mississippi State Supreme Court, it was referred to as a sales tax since it was based on Complete Auto's in-state gross receipts. The case escalated to the Supreme Court because Complete Auto felt it was unconstitutional taxation of interstate business that violated the Commerce Clause. But the Supreme Court went in Mississippi's favor, holding that it wasn't a sales tax but a "privilege tax" for doing business within the state. If the dealerships were still ordering from GM and needed their orders delivered, it did not discourage interstate commerce, because those orders were still being fulfilled after the tax was paid. Complete Auto had a sustained physical presence in Mississippi, where they benefited from local resources like police and roads. Moreover, their customers were not paying the tax; they were.

Quill Corp had absolutely no physical presence in North Dakota and thus did not benefit from the state's resources funded by sales taxes. Citing both *Bellas Hess* and *Complete Auto*, the Supreme Court ruled that Quill Corp was not obligated to collect and remit sales tax from North Dakota customers. The ruling clarified that mail-order businesses needed to have a physical presence in that state in order for a state government to declare nexus and require sales tax to be collected.

As the Internet went from a Wild West with small shops creating websites to massive marketplaces like eBay and Etsy, it was Amazon that first posed a major challenge to this idea as the company grew from a small bookstore to the utter behemoth it is today. Until 2012, Amazon cited *Quill* not to charge sales tax on its online sales if they didn't have a fulfillment center or office in that state. But retail associations and state lawmakers felt that this gave large online businesses an unfair competitive advantage over local retailers that collected and paid their sales taxes, and so began the push for state courts to send "Kill Quill" arguments to the Supreme Court.

They got their wish in 2018 when furniture retailer Wayfair went up against South Dakota. There was a tiny tear in the burgeoning e-commerce landscape that became a gaping hole when *Quill* was decided, because it was based on the Dormant Commerce Clause but Congress can override it by granting authority to states who want to interfere with interstate commerce. Which basically describes the entire Internet. Thanks to the *Wayfair* ruling, state tax authorities now have authority they lacked under *Bellas Hess* and *Quill*.

In 2016, South Dakota passed a law requiring online sellers to collect and remit sales tax if they delivered more than $100,000 worth of goods or services into the state, or had 200 or more in-state transactions regardless of the amount. Wayfair sued South Dakota citing *Quill* and the Dormant Commerce Clause.

But our laws are slowly catching up with technology: the Supreme Court sided with South Dakota and overturned *Quill*. Most states now follow the South Dakota model, where if you have $100,000 in sales from that state, you must collect and remit sales tax. Some impose a transaction threshold that may or may not be lower than 200 transactions as well.

Since most indie developers strive to see that much global revenue in a year, and rely more on distributors like Steam than the shareware pioneers did, this is less of a concern for us. But if you want to sell merchandise or you're in the tabletop space and want to build direct sales channels instead of relying strictly on marketplaces like Amazon, then this is absolutely a concern for you.

If you only sell your games through a third party, which is now the dominant form of digital game sales, you have no reason to worry. Steam, Epic, Apple, and all of the other giants have tax departments; you get your royalty statements and that's it.

But if you'd like to open up direct sales channels, or sell merchandise without relying on third-party print-on-demand services, periodically take a look at where your sales are coming from. If it looks like you're going to pass a significant number of transactions and/or that \$100,000 point with a state you don't live or operate in, it's worth looking into a sales tax specialty administrator like Avalara.

Not all states and jurisdictions charge sales tax on digital downloads, but some do like aforementioned Washington D.C. If a customer orders a boxed game and a T-shirt from your website, some jurisdictions don't tax clothing but others do. Because no one wants to manually research almost 10,000 jurisdictions, most e-commerce frontends like Square and Shopify have adapted to a post-*Wayfair* world. They usually have automated sales tax assistants designed to alert you when your sales are approaching the threshold in a certain state.

It indeed sucks that you aren't going to know you've passed that threshold until the machine has combed through all of your transactions, and you're not going back and billing those customers for unpaid sales tax: you're definitely absorbing it then charging sales tax to customers in that state from that point on.

Nevertheless, this is how sales tax administration drastically changed and made the Internet far less of a Wild West since the first edition of this book was published. Merchandising is often a crucial and reliable income stream for content creators, as well as indie developers who built up a fanbase, so you must know what you'll be up against.

RESALE CERTIFICATES

If you're buying goods in bulk for selling on your website or using as rewards in a crowdfunding campaign, you can fill out a resale certificate to avoid paying sales tax on those goods. To do this, you usually at least need an EIN but some jurisdictions will require a sales tax permit as well.

If you're buying goods for promotional purposes, like the infamous Sonic Toad chip clips, you usually can't avoid the sales tax.

REMITTING SALES TAX

If you have direct sales outside of the big distributors and marketplaces, such as selling swag at conventions or your own website, you will need to file sales tax returns in the appropriate jurisdictions. Depending on the jurisdiction, sales tax returns are due annually or quarterly.

This is why good recordkeeping is very important, because the sales tax reports usually want to know what your *total sales* were compared to the taxable sales. Some will also want to know what kind of items were sold, and now that e-commerce is the norm, what percentage of your overall sales are allocated to their jurisdiction.

Even though we now have automated sales tax assistants with e-commerce platforms and digital recordkeeping makes everyone's jobs easier, don't do what many unfortunate cash register audit victims do and accidentally spend the money that was supposed to be sent to the sales tax authorities. Keep track of how much you've collected and now owe that jurisdiction, and remember to earmark this money separately from the rest of your business funds so that you don't get totally shellshocked when the sales tax return is due.

DO I OWE SALES TAX ON MY CROWDFUNDING CAMPAIGN?

You might. As the Wild West of the digital world is long gone, rewards-based crowdfunding campaigns do trigger sales tax in some states. The state of Washington has a whole comprehensive guide on when you would collect sales tax on pledges (https://dor.wa.gov/forms-publications/publications-subject/tax-topics/crowdfunding), which you can find a link to on the supplemental webpage for this book.

Washington requires project creators to register for a business license to collect sales tax if the campaign raises $12,000 or more.

However, most states do not have comprehensive guides like theirs. Some would consider crowdfunding a preorder while others don't see crowdfunding campaigns as finished products or services that would merit sales tax collection.

If you are planning on running a crowdfunding campaign and offering physical rewards, you should contact your state revenue department to find out if there's a digital download tax and if so, if games (software) are included. If you're offering other rewards like digital books and soundtracks, those may also be subject to the digital download tax. Planning a successful crowdfunding campaign is an incredibly difficult endeavor as it is, and income taxes require enough consideration!

The last thing you want is a revenue-hungry state tax department chasing after you because unlike the IRS, those guys don't have to follow a taxpayer bill of rights and due process.

* * *

For most indie developers who plan to rely on the major distributors, at least for the foreseeable future, sales tax might not be a major concern out of the gate. But if you'd like to offer players more options, these are the risks you need to think about alongside the benefits now that the legal system is slowly catching up with technology.

Classification Quest

Do I Issue a W-2 or 1099?

MOST INDIE DEVELOPERS TREAT the people outside of themselves and their business partners who work on the games as independent contractors. Sometimes this treatment is correct, but not always.

For a lot of small businesses regardless of industry, owners don't want the ongoing cost or administrative burdens of having employees. For a vast majority of indie developers, there's also the concern of not even being able to pay yourself, let alone regularly pay other people. Ergo, the use of freelancers who are treated as independent contractors. Even in AAA studios and large software companies, the use of contingent labor is very common.

As flexible work arrangements become more prevalent, freelancing continues to see explosive growth whether it was by choice or out or circumstance, and fed-up workers "quiet quit" into new careers in the wake of multiple pandemics, there have been countless attempts at the federal and state levels to come up with a solution that works for everyone. While some companies blatantly flout labor and tax laws by misclassifying a worker as an independent contractor when they should be an employee, there are also several legal gray areas where it can be genuinely difficult to determine someone's status.

When you have employees, it's not just a matter of being able to regularly pay them but payroll taxes and administering them add at least 15%

DOI: 10.1201/9781003335733-20

to their gross pay. You also need to file quarterly payroll tax returns as well as buy workers comp insurance. Whereas with an independent contractor, all you need to do is file 1099s for each person who received $600 or more during the tax year. As of 2020, you now need to file Form 1099-NEC, which stands for non-employee compensation, while royalty payments would go on 1099-MISC.

Confusion over worker status where they receive the wrong forms and no taxes taken out of their pay (or too many taxes, if they were really an independent contractor and not an employee) is called **worker misclassification**. This is an area that bleeds into labor law since status calls on worker protection laws concerning things like overtime and the Fair Labor Standards Act (FLSA) among others. But we're going to concentrate on the tax aspects, which are onerous enough.

There's a lot of gray areas in determining who should get a W-2 (employee) or 1099 (contractor). Just because you don't want to be burdened with the expense of workers comp and payroll taxes doesn't mean that you can just declare the people who work for you to be 1099 freelancers, and be done with it! The same is true for just saying that you can't afford to make someone your employee.

BE MINDFUL OF DEPARTMENT OF LABOR RULINGS

In the original edition of this book, it delved right into the 20-factor test that is typically employed by the IRS. But since executive orders override the IRS, the Trump administration's 2021 ruling loosened the definition of "independent contractor" to instead employ an "economic reality test".

Literally at the time the manuscript of this second edition was getting ready for publishing, the Biden administration has proposed a more stringent set of criteria to classify a worker as an independent contractor. The FLSA already defines who is an employee and employer, but does not define an independent contractor.

In short, the proposed ruling wouldn't really affect the 20-factor test traditionally enforced by the IRS but would use the FLSA to determine employees' rights if they have been misclassified as an independent contractor under the 2021 independent contractor rules that are far more relaxed. If this proposal passes, it would rescind the Trump administration economic reality test and focus more on the behavioral factors you're going to read about.

Labor laws are outside of this book's scope, but the courts have used both the IRS test and FLSA definitions in worker misclassification suits. We're going to focus primarily on the IRS test, since it's the tax aspects most entrepreneurs worry about.

WHAT SETS AN EMPLOYEE APART FROM AN INDEPENDENT CONTRACTOR?

What the IRS' 20-factor test, and even Department of Labor rulings to some extent, really boils down to is CONTROL.

How much control do you have over that coder, artist, sound designer, web developer, and so on? Not just their time but also in how they do the work? Does your arrangement look like an employee-employer relationship or like you're just hiring them for a single gig or project?

Successful freelancers know that happy repeat clients, some of which we've retained for longer than we've had traditional employment, are the key to a strong bank account. So, how does the law view a long-term arrangement as one of an independent contractor rather than an employee?

There are three main concepts that umbrella over the 20-factor test: behavioral control, financial control, and the type of relationship your business has with this person.

BEHAVIORAL CONTROL

Do your expectations of this person working on the game line up with a client-freelancer relationship or employee-employer relationship?

While this also would fall under the relationships concept, behavioral control is really what determines the *kind* of relationship. An employee-employer relationship means that you have control over not just the results of work accomplished, but also how that person is doing it. You're telling them when and where to come to work, what programs and tools to use, and other little details.

Do you provide a place for them to work on a regular basis, along with tools like software subscriptions? Are you telling them how to get the job done beyond giving them specs, such as "this music needs more tension" or "Can you make this character taller"? Beyond giving deadlines, are you telling them what days and hours they have to work? Do you regularly evaluate their work aside from just looking at the end results?

If you answered yes to these questions, it definitely points more to an employer-employee relationship than that of an independent contractor.

Timing is also a major focal point in determining whether or not you've got an employee. Do you request a certain amount of hours per week, or do you just want the work done? Are they active in the day-to-day management of your studio, or just there for certain tasks and projects? While long-term relationships don't necessarily make someone your employee, as every successful freelancer is well aware, it's not likely that someone who's truly freelance would stick around after the game's released or their tasks are done. You'll still talk on social media and keep up in person after the game's out, but they're not picking up the slack on your other business tasks and projects.

FINANCIAL CONTROL

How someone gets paid is a factor that is frequently considered in misclassification examinations and suits. Does the artist that you hired for sprite work do this kind of work for other studios, or are you the only one in the picture? Do they have a website, social media presence, business cards, and other means of advertising their services? If not, are you paying this person like an employee by the hour, week, or month, or are you paying them per milestone or flat fee? Employees don't send invoices, they just expect a paycheck.

Business expenses are another one. Do you offer reimbursement or do they take care of expenses themselves? While not a be-all end-all in figuring out if that person is really an independent contractor, courts still look at it.

Let's say a major convention is coming up and your studio asks the freelance artist who's been working on your game to come help with your booth, and talk about the game at panels and to the press. You Venmo them some funds to help with gas, give them one of the passes the convention organizer gave you, and share the costs for the hotel suite you booked. An employee or independent contractor could easily fit in that scenario, although an employee would expect an employer to cover the hotel while an independent contractor wouldn't.

Compare this to the artist having to buy their own supplies or asking you to reimburse them for supplies specially bought for your game. As an independent contractor, they're unlikely to ask for a reimbursement and will instead factor their estimated supplies expense into their quote.

Artists and composers have a classification advantage over writers and programmers in this sense, because they often have what the courts refer to as "significant investment" in their tools, equipment, and skills. Game developers in general fall into a gray area on this aspect, because so many game-making tools are now totally accessible: all we need to invest in is a computer that doesn't die every five minutes nowadays, and you don't need a game design or computer science degree to have a successful games career.

Whereas high-quality synthesizers are also more accessible compared to yesteryear, composers and sound designers will invest thousands of dollars in professional-grade recording rigs if they want to keep landing AA and AAA gigs with leeway for the occasional indie game, plus their own projects.

In the construction industry, bringing a basic tool set to work that you could find on Amazon for $50 wouldn't be considered a significant investment. But having your own forklift would be.

The significant investment factor also involves considering whether or not you'll make a profit on the gig. Employees just look at getting paid while independent contractors factor in the opportunity cost ("Would I miss out on a better client or project if I accept this? Is it worth giving up time for my own projects?") and the expenses associated with each gig to determine if it's worth their time. While someone seeking employment would probably pick the job that pays more than the other while considering commuting expenses, profit-seeking is still considered an independent contractor realm and based on significant investment.

RELATIONSHIP

Do you plan on having this person around for the long haul and not just one game or task? And are their services *instrumental* to your studio?

Just because you hire someone to work on multiple games or help you out with some non-game stuff won't automatically make them your employee, but you need to be mindful of these other behavioral and financial aspects. They all tie together if that person thinks they've been misclassified and requests the IRS to step in and take a look, or the IRS looks at the 1099s you've issued over the years and examines you themselves.

Contracts are a major relationship aspect. In the US, employees don't typically sign contracts before employment begins. Professional freelancers usually have their own contracts that they use for their clients in addition to what companies they work with ask them to sign. Just because you gave someone a contract with the terms of work that says they're independent contractors doesn't automatically make it so under the law of the land.

What kind of services are being provided to you? Game developers who need programmers, artists, and so on can be hurt in this area, because those services are pretty integral to making a game. While it won't entirely kill being able to claim that person is an independent contractor, it still gets looked at. You're far more in the clear when you hire someone for a non-game aspect like marketing, website back-end maintenance, or business consulting.

OF CODE AND COAL, OR HOW THE LAW WAS FOUGHT

One of the most infamous and relevant misclassification cases was Microsoft's brobdingnagian settlement that had to be paid at the height of the dot-com era. In *Vizcaino v. Microsoft*, a class action was filed by several independent contractors who worked for Microsoft but were actually treated just like they were employees in all but name and benefits. They were repeatedly called back for several projects between 1989-1990 and often paid more than the employees, but received none of their benefits like 401(k) contributions and employee stock options.

They had to sign independent contractor agreements stating they weren't entitled to these benefits. Microsoft utterly failed to treat these "freelancers" like freelancers. How? They required these workers to work onsite side by side with the employees, doing the same exact job duties, working the same hours, and were given equipment and supplies. Upon the appeal, Microsoft had to pay a $97M settlement for back pay and benefits, since these workers were obviously misclassified. And that's not even counting those non-deductible fines!

In contrast, one of the first landmark misclassification suits took place in the 1940s and demonstrated more of the gray areas to come in ensuing decades. In *Silk v. United States*, a coal retailer called Silk paid workers to unload coal in his railyard. The workers showed up whenever they pleased and brought their own tools for the work. Silk didn't own any trucks, so he paid drivers with their own trucks for coal deliveries at a set price per ton. These truckers also did the hauling at their own discretion and did similar work for other coal companies.

The Supreme Court decided that the truckers were independent contractors, but the unloaders were employees. The reasoning behind this was that the unloaders only supplied picks and shovels, the basic tools to do the job, so this was seen as lacking significant investment. The fact that they didn't work regularly at Silk's facilities was insignificant, since Silk had a *detrimental reliance* on their labor (remember our old friend from the hobby loss cases, detrimental reliance?)

The precedent that this case set was that even though Silk didn't really control the unloaders in terms of how often they showed up for work and how many hours they put in, he still *retained the right* to exercise supervision over these workers. Silk couldn't really have a business without them, unless he'd be hauling coal out of rail cars all day himself.

While *Silk* is a more appropriate comparison to gig app labor like Uber drivers, we need to liken *Silk* to a game developer as best as we can. The unloaders would be programmers and artists, while the truckers would be marketing managers. Silk needed both services for sure to make a living, but if we set this in modern times, he could always call a trucking company instead of individuals with their own trucks.

Whereas he just doesn't have a business without people to unload coal even if they choose their own hours. The same could essentially be said of game developers who aren't doing every single thing by themselves or in-house, though it would depend on the scope of the projects. But once the game's released (the coal's ready for transport) and you hire some extra pairs of hands to help you get word out, just like how Silk didn't tell the truckers what routes to take or how to unload the coal at the destination, you're also probably not going to tell your social media manager or publicist how to do their jobs. Just so long as they drive people to that Steam page!

HOW YOU CAN GET SMACKED FOR 1099 ABUSE

It's not just the payroll taxes and mandated benefits like worker's compensation policies that cause intentional 1099 abuse, but also imminent and potential liability that make unscrupulous business owners intentionally misclassify workers. You're held legally and financially responsible for any damage your employees inflict on other peoples' property and well-being, while this would not be the case for independent contractors (even though assaults and thefts in gig work, both to and by customers, have raised many interesting principal-agent legal arguments).

Behold the following awful but probable scenario: your community manager gets rip-roaring drunk at a convention and hurls a TV out of a hotel room window, it lands in the pool where your chief designer was hanging out and they wind up in the hospital. The hotel bills your studio for the damage, so you pay it then file a claim with your insurance provider who has to jack your rate now. Your workers comp policy takes a beating as well. Shortly after that, your artist blatantly sexually harasses and threatens your programmer, who files a suit. Then after you fire your community manager and artist for reckless behavior and they file for unemployment, your unemployment insurance rate goes up for each employee too.

Terrible situations like those examples unfortunately happen in every industry. And that's precisely what makes intentional misclassification so tempting to lots of cash-strapped new businesses: they need bodies but risk cutting paychecks more rubbery than an eraser factory. And who wants to be held liable for collateral damage?

Well, the price to pay for trying to skirt the law is even higher. Starting with the IRS, there are really steep fines if you misclassify workers in addition to the payroll taxes you were supposed to pay. They will either catch onto you when they examine how many 1099s you issue and the amounts and consistency over the years, or if a worker files a request with the IRS to investigate your studio and determine if they're really an independent contractor or employee.

You're also getting the Department of Labor involved, because you can be fined for failure to buy a workers comp policy (or buying one then adding employees to it only after they get injured on the job). You'll be fined for every year that you don't have a workers comp policy but were supposed to. These fines can be well into six figures.

You're getting your state involved as well. State labor departments may come down really hard on you if there are additional restrictions concerning whether an independent contractor is actually independent, such as California's restrictive AB5 legislation that went so far with relinquishing independent contractors' flexibility that it required a clean-up bill after actual freelancers with their own LLCs raised hell about losing clients when they weren't, and had no desire to be, their employees.

Play it safe. If you want to remain a non-employer, carefully look at how you pay and treat the people you're non-employing. Don't do what Microsoft did and treat them like employees you're just giving the wrong tax form to.

SAFE HARBOR FOR UNINTENTIONAL MISCLASSIFICATION

If you grew up in the 1990s, remember all those PSAs and lectures about the difference between drug abuse and misuse? It comes up with tax evasion versus tax avoidance as well.

It's the same idea when it comes to worker classification. Intentional 1099 abuse means that you are willfully misclassifying workers just because you want to skirt liability, workers' compensation, and payroll tax expenses. Let's face it, these costs ARE bigger than zounds of Ancient Behemoths, but failing to play by the rules and paying the damages is like facing off against a throng of Archangels. (Did you really think you'd make it to nearly the end of this book without another *Heroes of Might and Magic III* reference?) Whereas 1099 *misuse*, unintentional misclassification, is where you have some penalty relief because you're using the IRS' voluntary settlement program and not intentionally trying to skirt the law.

Providing that you had a reasonable basis for treating a worker as an independent contractor, the IRS will work with you to make your penalties not as horrific as they could be. You don't get any protection if you just blatantly give out 1099s when you shouldn't and say, "Hey, I can't afford to have you as an employee, but I'm going to treat you like one anyway." The "I can't afford it" defense won't hold up. Nor does the remote work defense. Even before COVID, plenty of companies offered telecommuting options but instituted time reporting, hour caps, monitoring for your device or home, and other restrictions that spell employment instead of a client-provider relationship.

A reasonable basis for fighting a misclassification notice would be something like that worker lacking freelance experience and treating the gig like a regular job while you don't ask for time logs, tell them that they're free to work on other projects, and so on. Another reasonable basis would be one of those games that gets trapped in development hell where you are billed so much throughout the years that it looks like this person *could* be your employee, but they work on other projects and showcase your game on their website alongside others.

I NEED EMPLOYEES BUT CAN'T AFFORD THEM FOR THE LONG RUN. NOW WHAT?

That's why employee leasing and temp agencies exist. You'd have to pay a significantly higher wage by the hour, but the agency takes care of all the payroll taxes and jazz so you don't have to. It's better than risking some ungodly amount of fines and failing multi-state compliance measures.

DOES ALL THIS MEAN THAT GAME DEVELOPERS ARE AT RISK?

Game developers, like software in general, definitely run some risk given those detrimental reliance tests, and the historical use of contractors in the field. It has raised a lot of debate among games industry pros, legal experts, and labor organizers where the line is really drawn for appropriate use of independent contractors and the dynamics of AAA versus indie productions.

With that said, indie developers aren't as ripe for misclassification suits the way that construction, healthcare, and cosmetology companies are where large gray areas appear all the time concerning degrees of control, furnishing of equipment, and whatnot. With the physical elements missing given the ubiquity of computers today, it's really those control aspects that can still slip through the cracks. Even though *Silk* concerned a radically different industry in a different time, it's still precedent that gets cited in misclassification suits: do you retain the RIGHT to control that person's time, even if you're not actually exercising it?

Industry norms get factored into both FLSA and IRS-based misclassification suits. Willfully contracting and building a small business that way was always common in software and game development. While the remote work defense won't hold up in court if you did classify someone incorrectly, lacking a fixed workplace can make the control and timing aspects harder for the authorities to test. Unless you actually asked for timesheets or requested a monitoring program or device be installed in that person's home, how would you know when and how someone is getting work done on the game hundreds of miles away? Or how they were doing it?

Furnishing tools and space is also usually a non-issue for game developers. For the more physical facets of game development like art and audio, the individuals and small businesses offering those services virtually always have their own equipment and supplies, and work with multiple studios.

Unless you're renting an office or private room at a coworking space, you're also unlikely to provide a work space for the rest of your dev team to get their jobs done.

We tend to not have to worry about the financial aspects too much given our propensity to just use the milestone, piecework, and backend royalty methods to pay people rather than fixed weekly or monthly payments. Most people in the indie games space also usually have their own websites and work for multiple studios, even though there's plenty of games industry professionals who'd rather have a job than their own business.

But when it comes down to it, no matter what legislative changes occur on the federal and state levels, don't order someone around as if they're your employee if you don't actually want the cost and liability that comes with the territory. You should be fine and able to keep misclassification fines and suits off your back if you pay close attention to those factors, and the person you work with showing signs that they are dedicated free agents rather than someone looking for a permanent job through you.

*   *   *

If you want to stay a non-employer, it's important to know these distinctions and think about how they've applied to people who've worked on your game or other crucial functions.

You're also going to need to know what an employer-employee relationship really is for the R&D credit but also even for people outside the US. Since many indie studios have team members around the globe, that level's next.

Where in the World Are Your International Dev Team Members?

G AME DEVELOPMENT IS NO longer limited to working with local talent only. So many dev teams are formed by people who found each other on indie game forums, at conventions, and the like. Before COVID caused businesses around the world to pivot to remote operations out of necessity, the first wave of indie developers that sprang up in the shareware and Web 1.0 eras were the pioneers of making games without borders.

Cross-border game studio ownership was a fairly isolated tax law area that is now more common as the world became more interconnected. Having business partners, team members, and investors in other countries isn't just common; at some point in your interactive entertainment career, it's probably inevitable!

In my Himalaya days, my business partner was not a US resident, and neither were a handful of people who worked on our games. Since this gave me a vast amount of tax treaty and nonresident taxation experience, I was always the person called upon for international matters at past tax jobs. Now that digital nomad life and remote teams are simply a fact of life rather than this legal anomaly a handful of indie developers dealt with, I felt this book would not be complete without a chapter that covers both the domestic and foreign sides with cross-border talent or ownership.

DOI: 10.1201/9781003335733-21

Even though laws are slowly catching up to the 21st century, foreign business partners and talent is an area where both US and international law are stubbornly clinging to the 1990s.

Some of these regulations are purposely complicated for both sides to discourage cross-border commerce, and keep jobs and contracts domestic. Companies paying foreigners are frequently met with a lot of confusion, and tend to deal with it by not bothering to file the requisite forms at all. It's such a hassle by design that it makes you want to stick with domestic talent or require that foreign talent have an American tax ID.

But life happens and the most brilliant narrative designer you ever met is from Japan, then you meet your new business partner in your travels who happens to be from Australia, and all of you stumble upon an investor from France who gets you a publishing deal in Sweden.

Not every dev team is necessarily composed of people who even live in the same state as you, much less the same country. Ergo, parts of this chapter are written as if I'm speaking to the nonresident developer dealing with the impacts. It'll be just like those adventure games where you switch playable characters!

I've also largely avoided document numbers and names in most of this book outside of the citation section since, to be frank and obvious, it's boring. More often than not, they mean something to tax professionals rather than the reader. But this chapter will name more of them because foreigners who want to work with American businesses are subject to fairly draconian documentation. Both talent and studios should have an idea of the bureaucracy involved.

Then if you're opening a new studio with a foreigner, the complexity can range from a mild annoyance to brain-crushing deluges of paperwork depending on how you set up the business and how much income it generates. Ironically, it's harder to figure out on both sides when you have someone on contract compared to a foreign employee. Foreigners with self-employment or wage income in the US can be in for one hell of a boss battle.

YOUR RESPONSIBILITIES AS A STUDIO WHEN YOU HAVE FOREIGN TEAM MEMBERS

When you work with a US citizen or green card holder as an independent contractor, you need to get a W-9 (information request form) from them so you know what tax ID to use on their 1099 at the end of the year if they received more than $600. You'll want to collect this *before* the work starts, along with any actual legal contracts.

You don't need to pay or withhold any payroll taxes on their behalf or do any income tax withholding. If that artist or programmer bills you $1,000 you just pay them $1,000 and file a 1099 when the year's up. You need to use Form 1099-NEC for independent contractor payments that are at least $600, Form 1099-MISC for royalty payments that are at least $10.

But if that person is going to be your employee, you need an I-9 form with valid ID (passport or driver's license, plus Social Security card) that proves they're eligible to work in the US. Once that verification is complete, you do have to pay payroll taxes plus withhold them from the employee's pay, along with federal and state or local income taxes.

Foreign employees and independent contractors have a different process that isn't uniformly applied. When you want to work with a foreign contractor, they fill out a form called W8-BEN unless they don't have a valid tax ID like an employer identification number (EIN), Social Security Number (SSN), or International Tax Identification Number (ITIN).

If they have an EIN or ITIN and can be legally considered an independent contractor, you'd issue this person (or their US-based company) Form 1042-S, not 1099-NEC. Foreign employees need authorization to work in the US, which you'll determine by the kind of visa they hold if they're not residents or dual citizens with green cards and SSNs.

You also have to check the totalization agreement (https://www.ssa.gov/international/agreements_overview.html) set by the Social Security Administration to see if you need to take out payroll taxes or if they live in a country that gives them an exemption. Then regardless of whether those taxes are paid or not, they get a W-2 form just like a US citizen would.

We'll focus more on independent contractors from foreign countries, as well as co-owners, because it's what the average indie developer is most likely to deal with. Aside from the obvious reasons why you needed to understand the legal differences between an independent contractor and an employee, they were discussed in depth because you're also going to have to comply with that 20-factor test with foreigners even if they don't live or work stateside.

That's *in addition to* what that person's home country says about their status.

Foreign governments can have different ideas of what constitutes an employee-employer relationship, even if you've made the IRS and

Department of Labor happy. If you hire someone for more than a specific amount of weeks, or simply by virtue of that person providing a service that is considered core to your operations, it can quickly hurl you into a misclassification penalty across the pond even if that person totally satisfied the independent contractor rules in the US. Foreign payroll taxes, overtime, and paid leave regulations can come into play even though you and the person in question never left your respective home countries. Yes. This is live-action *Papers, Please* complete with Jorji handing over a passport made with a crayon.

But if we go with indie norms (the assumption that someone overseas meets both countries' standards for being an independent contractor), you might have to do some withholding from their pay depending on a few factors:

1. What country they live in

2. If a tax treaty exemption for reduced or eliminated withholding applies

3. If you're paying them for services, profit distributions as owners, or game royalties (the withholding rate is usually different for each)

4. If they have an ITIN

We've got another building puzzle, one that's a bit backwards: if someone has an ITIN, then they can claim a tax treaty benefit based on what their home country's treaty offers. If they *don't* have an ITIN, no benefits can be claimed. You have to withhold taxes at the default rate of 30% of whatever you pay them.

So if you pay a composer $2,000 to score your game and they don't have an ITIN, you'd send them $1,400 and $600 to the IRS, and a 1042-S form showing that the $600 was withheld. It's then out of your hands whether or not they file a US tax return to try getting that money back.

This is making that Qi Fruit quest sound fun.

FOREIGN BUSINESS PARTNERS

If you're starting a business with someone who isn't a citizen, you can't do an S corp. You'll have to do a partnership, a multiple-member LLC taxed as one, or a C corp. It's also a good idea to get the ITIN business sorted out as soon as possible, though I'll get into what's involved with applying for one because unfortunately, it's a process that makes little sense.

Partnerships, and LLCs taxed as partnerships, have a rule involving the maximum personal tax rate (37% at the time of writing). If you've got a foreign partner, your studio will have to send 37% of their share of the profits to the IRS. Even if they didn't actually take any cash distributions! Going back to the chapter on business entities, partners are taxed as the profit is earned but the studio doesn't have to withhold any taxes if they're US citizens.

So if your studio has two LLC members with 50% ownership, one US citizen and one foreigner, and you post a $10,000 profit, then both of you are taxed on $5,000 each regardless of whether you take out any cash distributions. The studio won't have to withhold any taxes on your earnings, but you will have to send $1,850 to the IRS on your foreign partner's behalf, even if they didn't actually take any money home. Like the foreign contractors not protected by a tax treaty, they will need to file a tax return to get this money back. And even if a tax treaty is on file, that 37% still needs to be taken out! The only circumstance you're allowed to skirt it is if the studio has a loss for that year.

This makes C corps a little more favorable for indies with foreign business partners. A salary can be paid where the law actually doesn't want officer compensation to be too high, where the problem is usually the opposite with S corps. Then you have the option to classify additional payments as compensation or a dividend, which could result in a far lower withholding rate. If no payments were made to the foreign owner, then assuming their share of studio income was their only US-sourced income, they don't need to file a tax return.

FOR FOREIGNERS: ARE YOU A RESIDENT OR NONRESIDENT ALIEN?

Let's press B and switch. From here on out, you're a foreigner who is getting offers from American studios to come work for them. For simplicity's sake, you're a freelancer/contractor and not an employee or owner. Regardless of which one you are anyhow, you need to know the following distinction.

Aliens aren't referring to The Two Guys from Andromeda. Rather, an alien is merely someone who isn't a citizen. **A nonresident alien (the case for most foreign contractors in the game dev world, as well as some co-owners) is someone who doesn't establish residency in the US, while a**

resident alien is someone who does. Your US taxes are most definitely affected by which category you fall into based on how many days you spend here in the past few years. By default, you're considered a nonresident unless one of the following situations applies:

1. You got a green card for lawful permanent residence at any time in the year (even if you received it on New Year's Eve, you'd be considered a permanent resident for the entire year)

2. You meet the substantial presence test.

Assuming you don't have a green card, the substantial presence test is based on the days you spend in the country over a 3-year period but we got shades of a math puzzle here. Your "substantial presence" has to be 183 days or longer over a 3-year period. This is comprised of at least 31 days during the tax year in question, AND looking at the full year for the present one, ⅓ the year for last year, and ⅙ for two years ago. If you total up 183 days after those phaseouts, you'll be considered a US resident for the year.

Let's say you were in the states for 120 days every year in 2019, 2020, and 2021. You'd count the full 120 days of presence in 2021, 40 days in 2020 (⅓ of 120), and 20 days in 2019 (⅙ of 120). Because the total for the 3-year period is 180 days, you're *not* considered a resident under the substantial presence test for 2021.

You'll need to keep track of how many days you spend in the US to determine whether you're a resident or nonresident. Additionally, if you are indeed a nonresident, you must report how many days you spent in the US on your tax return. Resident aliens need to file the same tax return as citizens, Form 1040, while nonresident aliens file Form 1040NR. We're going to assume that you need the latter in this chapter.

HOW DO I KNOW IF I HAVE TAX TREATY BENEFITS?

Pulling from the citation section of this book, IRS Publication 901 has a full list of the provisions located in each tax treaty currently on file. Tax treaties aren't updated incredibly often, but this publication tends to be updated whenever at least one tax treaty changes. The IRS website should have the most current version available.

Consult Publication 901, and look up your home country to see if you have a lower withholding rate, or a slashed or eliminated tax rate depending on what kind of income it is, plus any other conditions that must be satisfied. Some countries impose time limits or specific work conditions that can bolster or nullify tax benefits.

GLORY TO ARSTOTZKA: DOCUMENTS FOREIGNERS NEED TO GET AN INTERNATIONAL TAX ID NUMBER (ITIN)

In the old days, getting an ITIN was an extremely painful process. You needed to actually be in a position where you must file a tax return, because exceptions were pretty rare. You often had to file a tax return first.

Today, you can submit Form W-7 with your tax return to the foreign taxpayer unit in Austin, Texas (https://www.irs.gov/individuals/how-do-i-apply-for-an-itin). Since you need to submit proof of both identity and foreigner status, and it takes about 14 weeks for the IRS to return official documents, it's best to get certified copies of your foreign passport and other supporting documentation to complete your application. The best way to do this is to find the nearest US embassy in your home country and tell them you need to apply for an ITIN, they can prepare the apostille for you.

Some embassies also function as IRS-authorized certifying acceptance agents (CAAs) which can process your entire application. Foreign accountants that specialize in US tax matters can also take care of this for you for a fee, and without needing to mail in proof of your identity and status. If you plan on being in America at all, you can also make an appointment at IRS centers that process ITINs in person.

If you don't have a passport issued by your home country, check the instructions of Form W-7 to see what other documents are acceptable for proving both foreign status and your identity.

It makes you understand the lovable Jorji so much more.

PAYMENT FOR WORK = EFFECTIVELY-CONNECTED INCOME, ROYALTIES = NOT EFFECTIVELY CONNECTED

After going through the endurance test of getting an ITIN, the next thing you have to worry about is whether or not your income is effectively-connected (ECTI).

In English, effectively-connected means that if you have work or a business in the US, all income connected to it is ECTI plus the business income itself. So if you own a game studio stateside, profits from it would be considered ECTI whether it's a partnership or corp. Whereas you have some unrelated royalties and dividends from an American brokerage account, those would be non-effectively connected income (NECTI).

Having met several people in the adventure game community who typically reside in Europe or Australia, many of them don't want to go through the hassle of obtaining an ITIN, so they instead file for an EIN and just do a sole proprietorship or single-member LLC if they have effectively-connected income through freelancing for American clients. You'll still have to file a 1040NR plus a Schedule C showing your income and expenses. You could also technically do all this without having an ITIN. But it's still considered ECTI.

If you have ECTI, you still have to pay tax on that income after deducting business expenses as well as some allowances similar to what US citizens get. Then you also need to check that totalization agreement once more to wiggle out of paying self-employment tax. If your home country is not covered by the agreement, you have to pay it!

NECTI on the other hand would be items like your royalty income. Thinking of foreign actors and directors who receive royalties for film and TV, it's virtually never considered effectively-connected income for them even though those royalties are a direct result of their work. This is because they don't have a fixed base in the US available for them to work. Film sets can be literally anywhere in the world, and even if the production company shoots on location in the US or has sound stages here, that self-employed actor or director doesn't regularly have an office or set provided to them by any one studio. Ergo, the same could easily be said of a game developer as we tend to lack physical space.

But depending on the conditions that you're receiving royalties, it can easily be considered business income (ECTI). This is because, in most cases, you have to have worked on the game in order to be receiving royalties, and have some kind of fixed and determinable timeframe that you're receiving them. If you get bonus royalties for helping sell the game down the line, that could be construed as ECTI. But if you were going to get that royalty check even if you never made a game again, then you likely don't have to worry as much.

Tax treaty benefits also kick in for copyright royalties, like the ones received for games, that you wouldn't see for contributing your services to an American company. It can include low *tax* rates, not just low withholding rates. Because with ECTI, you still need to pay tax at the ordinary rate.

But regardless of what kind of income it is, rest assured that nonresidents will only have to report their US-sourced income. Whatever you earn in your home country or other countries won't have to be reported on your 1040NR tax return.

POTENTIAL STATE TAX ISSUES FOR FOREIGN OWNERS

Some states will reach into foreign countries and have nasty repercussions for foreign owners, even if they never set foot in that state at all throughout the year. You'll want to be mindful of the state where you set up your studio to make sure that it makes sense for where your business partners reside as well as for you.

Most articles only talk about federal taxes when it comes to foreigners, but having seen lots of businesses get set up in my home state and watching nonresidents get zapped, I figured I'd warn you. New York likes hogging the controller, so to speak.

Be mindful of where you set up the company relative to where all of the owners live. It could be worth sucking up that "foreign corporation doing business" fee in your state by opting for a Delaware or Nevada company so that your foreign business partner will be left alone.

EXPATS: ROOMS THAT DON'T RESET

Press A to go back to tax issues concerning US citizenry. Or rather, someone who still has a Social Security Number and is considered a dual citizen but does not live in the US anymore: an expat.

Expat taxation is incredibly complicated and far beyond the scope of this book, but every time I've taught tax courses for indie developers, I wound up getting questions about it. It has become even more prevalent as digital nomad lifestyles went from a tiny niche to an incredibly common occurrence. So here's the basics.

There are only three countries on the entire planet-- Eritrea, the Philippines, and the United States-- who tax dual citizens. Meaning that even if you leave the country but have dual citizenship, you are taxed based on *citizenship* and not residency. State-level taxes might not be of concern to expats anymore, since you no longer have residency in any US state at all, but you'll still have to file a federal tax return every year.

It's a bit like designing a game with multiple rooms where one room resets after the player leaves it, but then the second room remains static. In terms of nations, the US, the Philippines, and Eritrea are those three nations whose rooms won't reset if you leave them unless you turn in your passport.

If someone on your team is an expat, you generally treat them the same as a US citizen who lives stateside. They need to be issued a W-2, 1099, or K-1 tied to their SSN or EIN. Beyond that, it's on them to properly report the income.

Inversely, if you are an expat receiving income from a company in the US, then you need to report it on your tax return. You have a complete inverse from nonresidents who get some preferential treatment for royalty income: game royalties would be earned income, but there's something called the foreign earned income exclusion, which is adjusted every year for inflation (worth up to $112,000 for 2022).

You have to be a bona fide resident of a foreign country for the year or be present for a majority of the year (330 days). But this income has to be *foreign-sourced*, meaning that it has to come from studios and clients who aren't in the US. If American studios are paying you for your services and/or giving you royalties, you can't opt to exclude it from your income because it wouldn't be foreign-sourced.

But there is a foreign tax credit that you can claim for taxes that you have to pay to the foreign country to prevent double taxation. However, just like with most other personal tax benefits, you can't double dip. And you will also still owe Social Security taxes unless you fall under the protection of that totalization agreement. This includes the dreaded self-employment tax which you also have to pay if you're not protected under the agreement, even if you're taking the foreign earned income exclusion.

* * *

Having foreign talent can have both obvious and hidden costs, but working with foreigners is often inevitable for a lot of digital nomads and indie developers who want to reach diverse audiences and exchange different skills and ideas. While it's fantastic from a game-making perspective, recordkeeping burdens unfortunately increase drastically for all parties involved.

So I saved one of the most important bits for last: how you can find the professionals who are best-suited to help you.

How to Choose and Work with a Tax Professional

CONGRATULATIONS! YOU MADE IT to the end of this book alive and not ready to totally give up and just apply for a studio job instead! (Nothing wrong if that's what you decide, but indie life does mean you need to pay attention to the contents of this book. It's your reality now.)

But yes. I've given you (or at least hope I did) an understanding of the taxation environment of game developers and all its special quirks. Now it's time to figure out how you find a good tax professional if you've never worked with one before or are dissatisfied with who you're currently working with.

WHY SHOULD I WORK WITH A TAX PROFESSIONAL?

I know that the nice tax software salesperson said their program is so easy to use and parses expense reports so smoothly, you won't need an accountant.

Let me tell you as a formerly practicing accountant that this is a bold-faced lie. They're in cahoots with accounting firms and professional societies to drum up business. They WANT you to screw up using that software so that you'll have to hire a professional to fix the mistakes you made.

DOI: 10.1201/9781003335733-22

Unless you have a tax professional in your family who taught you well from an early age or come from a taxation background like I did, you are **definitely** going to have to enlist a professional once you have your own business.

You want a competent professional not just for preparing the actual tax returns, but also for structural aspects that change over time. For state and local tax matters in particular, a tax professional will be more apt to know when you're close to a filing deadline than you are.

When you spend your whole life working for someone else, you usually only have to worry about the ubiquitous April 15th personal tax deadline. Not so when you have your own business.

Even if you've had some simple self-employment forms you've done yourself if you had very few expenses, a tax pro knows exactly what to do with complicated topics like depreciation, buying and selling copyrights, and they can even introduce you to other loopholes that are beyond the scope of this book. Even if you don't have employees, tons of stupid forms sneak up on you like annoying bats in the *Stardew* mines. Late fees can pile up faster than the Twitter ratios of the latest nuclear takes.

A good tax professional can prevent that.

Credentialed tax pros that I'll be describing in more detail later are also mandated to engage in continuing education every year to stay updated on tax laws that constantly change. The tax code is about *1.4 billion* words long. You're a busy game developer crying out for a *Steins;Gate*-style time leap machine, and lamenting having to eat and sleep: is staying up to date on how much the standard meal allowance is for this year and deliberating for hours whether or not you should do a §179 deduction really something you want to spend time on? Didn't think so!

WHAT'S THE DIFFERENCE BETWEEN AN ACCOUNTANT, BOOKKEEPER, AND TAX PREPARER?

You may have heard these three terms used interchangeably, but they actually pertain to totally different aspects of financial management.

Bookkeeping refers to maintaining your chart of accounts then keeping track of your income and expenses, as well as capital contributions and drawings. For large companies that have thousands of transactions per day, they'll usually hire internal bookkeepers while small businesses like ours tend to use a service or individual bookkeeper on contract if you don't do it in-house. The transaction volume is low enough to pull it off.

I personally handle all of my own bookkeeping because I can handle it as a matter of scale and have the proper skillset to take care of it while outsourcing other business functions. If you have no idea how to journalize, adjust, post, and close accounts correctly, and you have so many transactions that you've gone beyond just keeping track of things on an Excel sheet, you'll definitely need a professional bookkeeper. If you don't have many transactions and a spreadsheet or two is sufficient, you probably don't need a bookkeeper just yet.

An **accountant** is someone who looks at what the bookkeeper has kept track of, then prepares financial statements and other documents and calculations, like trial balances, in accordance with U.S. GAAP (generally accepted accounting principles) or IFRS (international financial reporting standards). Accountants also analyze and interpret the financial data given to them, like providing you key ratios based on those statements and how you can improve your bottom line.

So, the bookkeeper keeps track of the data and enters it in the system. The accountant tells you what it means, and creates output in formats that external users are familiar with.

These external users would be banks, investors, and third parties like business intelligence services. Most indie developers won't care about that last one, but if you want to be an iOS developer and/or get certain publisher contracts, you WILL need properly kept books. Apple requires you to make an account with Dun & Bradstreet as part of your draconian trial to become an official iOS developer. You will need financial statements prepared every year, obtain a DUNS number, then hand these statements over to D&B.

Don't want to work with publishers or Apple? That's totally fine. But you'll also need books data for your tax returns once you start making serious dough, because you'll be mandated to do books-to-tax reconciliations. It's also simply a good idea to truly know how your financial performance is, and even if you've been running in the red it's important to know how much of these expenses are allocated to stuff you can pare down or necessary investments in your game, skills, or professional network that were worth the trade-off.

The tax professional that you hire may offer bookkeeping services. If you go with a full-service tax firm, they usually hire bookkeepers just for this reason or possess those skills themselves. This gives them a more up close and personal view of their clients' finances opposed to having to do back-and-forth with external bookkeepers. But not every firm offers this level of service.

A **tax professional** is just what it says on the tin: someone who is a tax expert. A tax preparer may be a full-blown tax professional, or they could be just the tax equivalent of a bookkeeper: someone who knows the basics of filling out forms and simple tax structure, but not intense representation matters and law application.

Now, you know how you hate it when someone on the street says "Oh, you make games? So you make stuff like *Mario*?" and you're facepalming while trying to keep your composure? That's how a lot of accountants and bookkeepers without tax knowledge feel when asked complex questions about taxes.

Just because someone knows accounting doesn't mean they know tax law, and vice versa. Don't assume just because someone knows one area that they know the other. You're going to read more about the professional licenses and designations that dive into this further, but just because someone is a really sharp bookkeeper doesn't mean they know how to apply these transactions to your taxes. Or know how representation and the actual law works.

So while the terms are frequently used interchangeably, accountants, bookkeepers, and tax pros are not one in the same. It doesn't mean you won't find a firm or independent practitioner who does all three, as there are many, but it's important to know that distinction based on your financial priorities. If you'd like to stay small, working with just one professional should be fine. You'll definitely need to know the difference once you're making a lot of money or you'd like to grow.

PRACTICE STANDARDS THAT APPLY TO ACCOUNTANTS AND TAX PROS

With the exception of CPAs and public accountants (a type of accountant rarely seen anymore as most just become CPAs), you don't need a license to call yourself an accountant. Unlicensed accountants usually hold degrees in accounting and/or business, and are more common in the nonprofit and governmental sectors. This is because a lot of business transactions in the private sector usually require a CPA's signature. CPAs are bound by the American Institute of Certified Public Accountants' (AICPA) code of conduct, followed by similar codes instituted by professional associations they voluntarily join. This is also in addition to the standards set by the states they practice in.

Tax pros who aren't CPAs have to adhere to the practice standards outlined by the IRS. The tax code enforces these standards on *enrolled preparers*, which entails CPAs, Enrolled Agents (EAs), and tax attorneys. *Unenrolled preparers* are not licensed, and therefore can't represent you before the IRS and state tax authorities, and aren't held to these rigorous practice standards or representation privileges that enrolled preparers are.

Why do you need to know this total snorefest? First, it's better to work with a professional who is licensed and held to a standard of practice than one who is not. If something goes wrong, you want to go to the right licensing body to swiftly investigate that person. Unenrolled preparers may be good people working in a tax chain or private tax office who are just working on their degrees and getting their feet in the door. They have to start somewhere. But unfortunately a lot of unenrolled preparers also just open up shop and wind up ghosting after tax season and can be harder to trace.

WHY YOU SHOULD BE TERRIFIED OF STATE TAX DEPARTMENTS

Where do you live? Where do you work? Where are the rest of the owners of your studio, if you're not the only one? Your location is definitely going to factor into who your regular tax pro will be. It's cool to work with a bookkeeper across the country who knows the gaming industry, but you'll want someone who knows tax law for where you live and/or set up the studio to do your taxes. Because state tax agencies are scarier than an unmoderated Discord server.

When you piss off a state tax agency or something got misreported to them, you have a hot mess on your hands. They are *really* the ones to be afraid of more than the IRS, contrary to what the media depicts. Thanks to the Internal Revenue Service Restructuring and Reform Act of 1998 (RRA), the IRS can't just swoop into your home unannounced for a shakedown. But your state totally can.

The RRA made the IRS provide you with a due process as well as settlement programs for back taxes. You will receive multiple written notices before they start angling for your money, whereas in New York, you can just get smacked with a levy with only one letter that you barely had time to respond to. Even if you manage to get the levy reversed, you still have to pay this no-recourse $125 "legal fee" for them sending a third-party thieves' guild to raid your bank account in the middle of the night.

States on the other hand don't necessarily have due process. They don't have to provide you with the option to settle back taxes, states' rights issue and all. Over 50% of states even publicly shame you for unpaid taxes! (29 to be exact, according to the *National Journal*.) While unannounced shakedowns are more common with sales tax audits than income tax issues, you could have a state income tax issue or local small business filing that you overlooked, and it could cause a state revenue officer to turn up at your door like some Bumble date gone horrifically wrong.

The latter is especially common in New York. Not the revenue officers turning up like dates who can't take rejection, but forgetting about obscure local small business taxes if you didn't make enough to have to pay them in the past. The MTA and unincorporated business taxes come to mind: you didn't have to pay them before but you do now and it gets overlooked.

Because it can be challenging to find a tax pro who knows the gaming industry, it may seem great to stick with one from an industry hotbed like California or Washington but then you're screwed for your home state if you don't live or set up shop in California or Washington. Even if you live in a state with no income tax, you could still have to deal with state and local taxes to some extent like a horrific sales tax burden or a franchise tax that's more complex than "we're charging this just because you exist."

Why mention that in this chapter? Because you want a tax pro who knows how to fight your local power, not just the IRS. The former has a much stickier and worse yet, closer, hand than you'd think.

WHAT TO LOOK FOR IN A TAX PRO

Obviously, you want someone who you like and have a good rapport with whose knowledge and experience can help your studio as it grows. Still, you can meet one who's very nice and competent but they're just not the right fit. There's other qualities you should also look for, and avoid, in the person you hire to help with your taxes:

1. **Available year-round**. Most credentialed professionals will be unless they're on contract with a firm, in which case availability might be up in the air. Avoid "McTax" chains because you have no guarantee of getting the same preparer every year, and most of those offices only operate seasonally.

2. **Avoid fly-by-night outfits that promise you a bigger refund than the competition.** They're not knowledgeable about actual tax preparation, but know all about selling you refund anticipation loans. The only promise a legit tax pro makes is that they will get your tax bills as low as they legally can.

3. **Second to that, never hire a tax preparer who charges their fee as a percentage of your refund or says they'll take it out of your refund.** A real credentialed tax expert will only charge you based on the complexity or perhaps by form number or amount of pages.

4. **Good tax pros ask lots of (relevant) questions about your life and business to get a thorough assessment of your overall financial situation.** If they just take your documents and don't say much or ask mostly fluff during the interview, you've got a dud.

5. **Technologically literate.** If they can barely turn a computer on and/or are using machines that were dug out of Sumerian ruins, RUN DON'T WALK. You're in a digital profession. You need someone who understands the digital world instead of the accountant who can't comprehend that you don't have a fax machine and uses dated terms like "canned software." Before people from the tax community start hurling 1960s fax machine parts at me, this need not mean they have a new computer every year and top-of-the-line equipment. But if they're barely able to use the technology around them, you should look elsewhere for someone who gets how the digital world operates. Game development isn't a brick-and-mortar business with filing cabinets.

6. **Identify the services you specifically require then go from there.** Do you need a bookkeeper yet? Help with sales tax? International tax forms and law interpretation? Factor these into choosing your tax pro, by asking them about their specialties and services offered.

ETIQUETTE WHEN WORKING WITH A TAX PRO

There are two groups of people in life who you should never mess with: the people who handle your food and the people who handle your money. Your tax pro is someone you want to feel warm fuzzies when they hear from you and not just because you're paying them. Here's how you need to behave when you engage with a tax pro.

1. **This should go without saying since a lot of indie developers work for themselves: but don't balk at a tax pro's fees.** If you're shopping around for one, do that based on how you like them, their specialized knowledge, which accounting cloud services they offer, and other important factors, instead of just going for who will do it the cheapest. Would you want to hear someone whining about how you're too expensive to hire as inflation eats us alive? I think not! Yeah, we know that Phil's Tax Hut down the block, with the guy giving you his used car salesman grin while you gape at the fax machine that's been laying there since Nixon was in office, charges less. If you like his prices better, why aren't you over there?

2. **Be a good recordkeeper, including taking sums of your expenses from your receipts, bank statements, and so on.** You will be loved for this. If you get met with this horror-stricken stare after bringing in a shoebox or a Gmail attachment full of mangled spreadsheets, don't be surprised if you have to pay extra to get them broken down or summarized. Some small firms might postpone your appointment until you do that yourself or outsource it.

3. **If you use a system like Quickbooks, use it correctly.** You will be loved for this even more. I know that the nice instructor said you wouldn't need an accountant once you got used to the program: well, 99% of the time they're lying. If you submit a Quickbooks file that's got income accounts in asset accounts and expenses look suspiciously personal, don't be surprised if you are charged dearly for having a professional fix that mess because the chart of accounts wasn't properly set up in the first place.

4. **Whatever you do, and I mean *whatever* you do, DO NOT tell a licensed tax professional some bull like "My cousin's barber's psychic told me I could write this off!" or even worse yet, "But so-and-so used to let me deduct it."** We hate this more than indie developers hate being asked if we make games like *Mario*, and why won't we get some nice job with a big AAA studio instead of making your own games. Would you tell your doctor "A band-aid on this grievous head injury is fine because a rando on the subway told me so!" I don't think so. Don't tell the professional how to do their job. Now, if you have a citation from an authoritative source like the actual Internal Revenue Code, IRS

publications, the Internal Revenue Manual, or Tax Court cases? Tell them that's where you found what you want to learn more about. Isn't it nifty that I provided those things for you, so your new tax pro doesn't give you endless side-eye? But also, it's not a matter of "letting" you deduct things. Firms that tell people what they want to hear in order to get business will go down soon enough. Or you'll just get a nice letter in your mailbox one day about those penalties and additional taxes you owe.

WHO'S ULTIMATELY RESPONSIBLE?

You. You, you, you.

While you have some protection under the law for having reasonable reliance on a licensed professional, you are still ultimately responsible for what goes on your tax returns, be they business or personal. You have to hold onto at least the last three years' worth of information for your personal taxes, six years for business. All those lovely substantiation rules we went over come into play.

The TurboTax defense also does not hold up in court if you go the self-prepared route. You still have to make sure that your tax returns are done correctly and that everything is accurate. Tax Court says ignorance of the law is no excuse. But if you put yourself in a professional's hands, you'll have a little more protection if something goes south.

It's a tax professional's job to advocate for you rather than play auditors and tax evaders. But if you tell your tax pro that you spent $5,000 on deductible business travel this year, but you really only spent $2,000, you're still ultimately held responsible for that flagrant overstatement.

Accidents happen like misreading or transposing numbers, so if you spot something that you or they tabulated incorrectly by accident, you need to tell your tax pro ASAP so they can amend your return. However, if your tax pro pulls an overstatement or intentional transpose, steals your refund, or any other nasty violations of their duty of care, you can file a grievance with the Office of Return Preparers (oversight division of the IRS) to get that bad egg investigated.

TYPES OF TAX PROFESSIONALS AND A LONGTIME DEBATE

The kinds of tax professionals out there can be dizzying. There's this whole enrolled versus unenrolled preparer dealie and all the different designations. Here are some of the most common ones and how it's significant to you. I wanted to give each one their own section, but something had to be said about the whole CPA vs. Enrolled Agent debate that constantly takes place in tax pro circles. They must be explained together. I know you're probably sharing this with a tax pro, and some of my old peers are also reading this, so here we go.

Certified Public Accountants (CPAs) and Enrolled Agents (EAs)

The most well-known designation, CPAs are licensed by their state's accountancy board and must pass a rigorous four-part exam in all aspects of financial accounting with some tax law thrown in. Most states also require CPAs to have an advanced degree with at minimum a bachelor's degree in accounting, or a business or law degree with 30–36 credits in accounting coursework. Some states also institute a supervised work requirement of at least one or two years before they can get licensed. CPAs must get continuing education every year to stay updated in their practice areas and keep their licenses current. Peer review is also required by some states for certain clients or transactions.

But once again, going back to the "do you make games like *Mario*" thing: not all CPAs concentrate on tax matters. Yet the public is under the impression. It's not necessarily false, but CPAs aren't the only tax experts out there.

Enrolled Agents (EA) expressly focus on taxation. EAs must pass a rigorous three-part exam on nothing but tax law, IRS protocols, and practice standards. An accounting degree isn't required as any education level and major can apply for the license, so long as they pass the exam and background check. Enrolled Agent licensure is federally granted directly by the IRS. There's no supervised work requirement or mandated peer review, but EAs must do at least 24 hours of continuing education every year, including at least two hours in ethics.

Alternatively, if you work for the IRS for at least five years in certain capacities, you can become an Enrolled Agent without having to take the exam once you leave the Service.

I held Enrolled Agent licensure from 2011 to 2020. I didn't renew when I found that the new career I embarked upon just didn't necessitate it anymore. I passed all three parts of the exam on the first try, then eventually worked with the IRS and their government contractor to write EA exam content and determine the minimum competency for EAs. It's rare to find someone outside of the financial industry who actually knows what an

EA is. It was tiresome having to constantly explain it! Even more tiresome than "Do you make games like *Mario*?"

I also got really fed up with all the inane in-fighting like EAs snubbing their noses at CPAs over representation matters and vice versa, and snobbish Big Four CPAs who felt that becoming an EA wasn't a big deal or a legitimate career choice.

I've known experienced CPAs and tax lawyers with multiple degrees who failed the EA exam miserably. Familiarity with tax law requires a mixture of calculations and legal argument as you've probably gathered by now. What's the big difference between CPAs and EAs when it comes to competently helping you with your taxes, aside from the differences outlined earlier?

Marketing. That's all.

AICPA has more marketing pull than EA advocacy groups and tax professional societies for the sheer fact that well...CPAs vastly outnumber EAs. According to Forbes, when this book was first published, there were only about 50,000 EAs admitted to practice compared to 650,000 CPAs. While there's been more concentrated efforts in recent years to raise awareness of the EA designation, more people gravitate to CPAs based on the marketing, plus their wider availability. After all, doesn't "certified" sound more trustworthy than "enrolled"? And wouldn't a studio whose game got 650,000 paid downloads have far more cash to market with than one who sold 50,000 copies?

I've sounded off my cases with many extremely smart and competent CPAs over the years. I've also known CPAs who were brilliant at corporate auditing or financial accounting, but were utterly hopeless with tax law. Then there were the ones who got "creative."

Both EAs and CPAs can represent you in an audit, and handle your tax matters with the authorities so you don't have to. When it comes to representation matters, sometimes EAs are a safer bet than CPAs. Historically speaking, IRS employees have played nicer in the sandbox with EAs because we know the in-house rules by the backs of our hands, and how many directors that agent is under. Despite this, EAs remain the jobbers of the industry (if we have any wrestling fans reading this).

So, when you're trying to figure out what kind of tax expert to regularly work with and are pondering if a CPA is a better choice than an EA, it's not about which group of letters after their name is better. It's merely about the differences in standards and licensing requirements both professionals are held to and that the public is more familiar with.

To conclude this long-winded explanation, both EAs and CPAs will be smart and competent for the most part. The best way to tell which is the right one for you is to prioritize the industrial specialty, as gaming industry experts are hard to find in the professional sector, followed by any additional concerns and needs that you have.

Tax Attorneys

Tax attorneys practice tax law from analytical and interpretation-based standpoints, and can go to bat for you in Tax Court. Like EAs and CPAs, they can also represent you to the IRS and state tax authorities but might be limited to the states in which they are licensed. So they will be your go-to people for legality gray areas and petitioning Tax Court, opposed to the routine preparation of tax returns.

Tax attorneys can also provide structuring advice for when you want to start a new business and are also frequently the go-to people for worker misclassification suits, because many of them are also educated in the relevant labor laws like FLSA.

United States Tax Court Practitioners (USTCPs)

The only non-attorney allowed to represent taxpayers in court. USTCPs are like the EAs of the law field in this regard. They are pretty rare and have a razor-sharp focus on tax law applications and how Tax Court works. If you can find a USTCP who knows the games industry, hold onto them and never let go!

Registered Tax Return Preparer (RTRP) and
Annual Filing Season Program (AFSP)

RTRPs were a short-lived designation that sprang up in the early 2010s as a result of public pressure. For a long time, there were more stringent licensing requirements to cut hair or sell hot dogs than to assist Americans with what's often their biggest financial transaction of the year.

An RTRP had to pass a comparatively less comprehensive exam on individual tax law with a smaller continuing education requirement relative to EAs. However, RTRPs did not have the same representation privileges as EAs, CPAs, and tax attorneys. But there was pushback from the hordes of unlicensed preparers who resented having to get continuing education and pay for a license. In *Loving v. Internal Revenue Service*, an unlicensed tax preparer challenged the Supreme Court, claiming that it was unconstitutional for the IRS to overstep their authority in instituting the RTRP designation. Much to the surprise of the tax professional community, Loving won and struck down the RTRP designation. What was even more baffling was that the IRS appealed, and *lost*.

You might still see some people putting RTRP after their name, even though it no longer exists as of 2014. RTRP was replaced with the voluntary AFSP certification that entails continuing education for unlicensed preparers as a yearly certificate best suited to novice preparers and students.

* * *

And so dear indies, it comes to an end. Thanks for buying this book, and good luck in the tough but rewarding indie developer path! Feel free to connect at sonictoad.com and Taylor & Francis/CRC Press for all of your business education needs.

Now I don't know about you, but I'm ready to actually play something after all this. Even though I've been playing *Heroes of Might and Magic* for over 25 years, and now can't look at it the same...

Index of Citations

H ERE ARE CITATIONS AS WELL AS HELPFUL REFERENCES FOR THE various tax topics addressed in this book. It would be impossible for every single statement to have a citation attached, so it was saved for the more complicated and nebulous explanations particularly in the later chapters. But you have enough to show your tax professional if you have questions or would like to research the matter further yourself.

These statements go in order of chapter then content. No need to jump all over the place!

Publications, forms, notices, Tax Topics, and instructions can be found on irs.gov, unless otherwise noted. Sections (§§) refer to the Internal Revenue Code (Title 26 of the US Code) or Income Tax Regulations, unless a different piece of legislation is being cited and therefore noted.

Note: IRS Publication and instruction links are the HTML versions dynamically updated every year, unless otherwise noted.

Readers also have access to a supplemental webpage that, in addition to posting annual tax law updates, also contains a comprehensive list of helpful resources and all the deep links that did not make it into the ebook version.

Levels 0–1 have no citations.

LEVEL 2: CHAOTIC NEUTRAL MARRIED (FILING STATUSES)

1. Publication 17 (https://www.irs.gov/publications/p17): Your Federal Income Tax

2. Publication 501 (https://www.irs.gov/publications/p501): Exemptions, Standard Deduction, and Filing Information

3. Publication 504 (https://www.irs.gov/publications/p504): Divorced or Separated Individuals

4. Publication 929 (https://www.irs.gov/publications/p929): Tax Rules for Children and Dependents

LEVEL 3: DEDUCTIONS, CREDITS, AND EXCLUSIONS

1. Form 1040 instructions (https://www.irs.gov/instructions/i1040gi)

2. Schedule A instructions (https://www.irs.gov/instructions/i1040sca)

3. Publication 17 (https://www.irs.gov/publications/p17): Your Federal Income Tax

LEVEL 4: SOLID RECORDKEEPING AS AN IMPORTANT FRAMEWORK

1. Publication 583 (https://www.irs.gov/publications/p583): Starting a Business and Keeping Records

LEVEL 5: TAX IMPACTS OF HOW YOUR GAME GETS FUNDED

1. Publication 525 (https://www.irs.gov/publications/p525): Taxable and Nontaxable Income

2. Publication 559 (https://www.irs.gov/publications/p559): Survivors, Executors, and Administrators

3. Publication 970 (https://www.irs.gov/publications/p970): Tax Benefits for Education

4. Corporate grant exceptions: §118

5. Tax-free transfers between corporations: §351

6. §1274(d): Applicable federal rates

7. Federal Register guidance (https://www.govinfo.gov/content/pkg/-FR-2015-03-02/pdf/2015-04213.pdf) for applicable federal rates and family loans (external PDF)

8. IRS Tax Tip 2022-120 (https://www.irs.gov/newsroom/some-things-to-know-about-crowdfunding-and-taxes): Crowdfunding and Taxes

9. FS-2022-20(https://www.irs.gov/newsroom/money-received-through-crowdfunding-may-be-taxable-taxpayers-should-understand-their-obligations-and-the-benefits-of-good-recordkeeping): Clarification on Crowdfunding and Taxes

LEVEL 6: IS GAME DEVELOPMENT YOUR LIVELIHOOD OR JUST A HOBBY?

1. Hobby loss rules defined: §183

2. Reg. §1.183-2(b) the nine-factor test

3. FS-2008-23: Is Your Hobby a For-Profit Endeavor? (https://www.irs.gov/uac/Is-Your-Hobby-a-For-Profit-Endeavor)

4. Publication 535 (https://www.irs.gov/publications/p535): Business Expenses

5. J. Tinnell, 81 TCM 1569, TC Memo 2001-106, Dec. 54,327(M): Court ruled that Tinnell indeed had a business but it was hard to prove since he didn't keep books and records, or any way to evaluate how he did.

6. R.J. McKeever, 80 TCM 358, TC Memo 2000-288, Dec. 54,040(M): Failure to market yourself in some way could constitute failure to operate in a business-like manner.

7. Tony Zidar v. Commissioner: TC Memo 2001-200, 82 TCM 357

8. R.N. Nelson, 81 TCM 1632, TC Memo. 2001-117, Dec. 54,341(M), note 7 for time and effort factor. Nelson needed to keep her job to support her business. Respondent concurred.

9. M.T. Shane v. Commissioner, TC Memo 1995-504: Note 2 for financial status

10. Morton v. United States, 107 A.F.T.R. 2d Par. 2011-1 U.S.T.C.: Morton forms S corp to use private jet for his various businesses. Wins based on profit motive.

11. TC Memo 1999-83, C. Lundquist, 77 TCM 1556, Dec. 53,295(M): Lundquist's horse breeding efforts didn't make sense without the fun parts.

12. L.T. Hoyle v. Commissioner, TC Memo 1994-592: Unlike Lundquist, Hoyle managed to prove the fun he got out of his horsing around was merely incidental.

13. Commissioner v. Groetzinger, 480 U.S. 23 (1987): The current standard for what constitutes a trade or business.

14. Engdahl v. Commissioner, supra at 670: "Given his income, we think it unlikely that petitioner would embark on a hobby costing thousands of dollars and entailing much personal labor without a profit objective."

15. TC Memo 1990-66, Schlafer v. Commissioner: Had a horse racing case very similar to M.T. Shane except the personal pleasure element worked against him.

LEVEL 7: BUSINESS ENTITIES AND FORMALITIES

1. Publication 541 (https://www.irs.gov/publications/p541): Partnerships

2. §705: Partner basis computation

3. Publication 542 (https://www.irs.gov/publications/p542): Corporations

4. Publication 334 (https://www.irs.gov/publications/p334): Tax Guide For Small Businesses

5. Publication 536 (https://www.irs.gov/publications/p536): Net Operating Losses (NOLs) for Individuals, Estates, and Trusts

6. Schedule C instructions (https://www.irs.gov/instructions/i1040sc)

7. Form 1120 instructions (https://www.irs.gov/instructions/i1120)

8. Form 1065 instructions (https://www.irs.gov/instructions/i1065)

9. Form 8832: Entity Classification Election

10. Form 2553: Election By a Small Business Corporation

11. David E. Watson P.C. v. United States, No. 11-1589: Court upholds that Watson did not pay himself a reasonable salary as the sole owner of his S corporation based on median area salary for an accountant with his degree of responsibility.

12. Glass Blocks Unlimited v. Commissioner of Internal Revenue, T.C., Summary Opinion 2013-180: Court sustains that a net operating loss doesn't get you out of paying yourself a salary if you have an S corp, especially if you're the sole owner doing all the work.

LEVEL 8: THE LOAD SCREEN, STARTUP AND ORGANIZATIONAL COSTS

1. Publication 535 (https://www.irs.gov/publications/p535): Business Expenses

2. Publication 334 (https://www.irs.gov/publications/p334): Tax Guide For Small Businesses

3. §248(a): $5,000 expensing election

LEVEL 9: THE MAIN EVENT, BUSINESS EXPENSES

1. §162(a): deduction of business expenses; but only if you have intent to profit

2. Cohan v. Commissioner, 39 F.2d 540, 543-544 (2d Cir. 1930) For the Cohan rule to apply, there must be sufficient evidence in the record to provide a basis for the estimate. See also: Vanicek v. Commissioner, 85 T.C. 731, 743 (1985)

3. Ordinary expense: "Of common or frequent occurrence in the type of business involved." Deputy v. du Pont, 308 US at 495 (1940)

4. Necessary expense: Appropriate and helpful in carrying on trade/-business. Commissioner v. Heininger, 320 U.S. 467, 471 (1943); Heineman v. Commissioner, 82 T.C. 538, 543 (1984)

5. Schedule C taxpayers ultimately bear the burden of proof for their deductions: Rule 142(a); Hradesky v. Commissioner, 65 T.C. 87, 90 (1975), aff'd per curiam, 540 F.2d 821 (5th Cir. 1976)

6. §1.162-5 Income Tax Regs. sets forth the guidelines for determining educational expenses incident to a taxpayer's trade or business that are deductible. See also: TC Summary Opinion 2014-55, Peppers v. Commissioner

7. §1.162-5(a), Income Tax Regs.: Educational expenses are not deductible if they are paid by an individual for education which is part of a program of study that will lead to qualifying the individual for a *new* trade or business.

8. Schwartz v. Commissioner, 69 T.C. 877, 889 (1978): Taxpayer must show sufficient business needs for education expenditures to be conducive to trade or business.

9. Publication 970 (https://www.irs.gov/publications/p970): Tax Benefits for Education

10. Publication 502 (https://www.irs.gov/publications/p502): Medical Expenses

LEVEL 10: LOST LEVELS, NON-DEDUCTIBLE ITEMS

1. Welch v. Helvering (290 US 111, 54 S.Ct. 8, 78 L.Ed. 212): 1933 Supreme Court landmark decision that decided on what was the difference between business and personal expenses and differentiating ordinary business expenses from capital expenditures.

2. §162(f), no deduction for violations of the law

3. §162(e), political and lobbying expenses aren't deductible

4. R.L. Vitale Jr. v. Commissioner, TC Memo 1999-131: Vitale was just starting out as a writer and racked up many expenditures, including several visits to prostitutes and brothels as part of doing research for his book. Court disallowed many of his expenses, because they were not substantiated. However, under the strict substantiation rules of §274(d), he was able to deduct some of his travel to the brothels. Despite this, the Court ruled that the money actually paid to the brothels was so personal in nature that there was no way it could be deductible.

5. Wolters Kluwer Wackiest Tax Cases list (https://www.cch.com/-press/news/2000/20000117t.asp)

6. Publication 536 (https://www.irs.gov/pub/irs-pdf/p536.pdf): Net Operating Losses

7. Extremely brief guidance from the IRS on NOLs (https://www.irs.
gov/newsroom/net-operating-losses)

LEVEL 11: THE BONUS ROUND OF TRAVEL, MEALS, AND ENTERTAINMENT EXPENSES

1. Some expenses cannot be estimated under the Cohan rule per
§274(d); subject to very strict substantiation requirements. §274(-
d)(4) pertains to travel expenses in particular. See also: Sanford v.
Commissioner, 50 T.C. 823, 827-828 (1968), aff'd per curiam, 412
F.2d 201 (2d Cir. 1969) for misuse of the Cohan rule.

2. Publication 463 (https://www.irs.gov/publications/p463): Travel,
Entertainment, Gift, and Car Expenses

3. §1.274-5(j)(2), Income Tax Regs., and §162(a): Deductible business
expenses include the cost of transportation related to business, both
local transportation and the cost of traveling away from home on
overnight trips.

4. §1.274-5(j)(2), Income Tax Regs.: A taxpayer who opts to use the
standard mileage rate is relieved of the obligation to substantiate the
dollar amount of the expense but is *NOT* relieved of the obligation
to substantiate the amount of the *business use* of the car or truck
(the amount of business mileage and how often the car is used for
business purposes), the time of the use of the car or truck, and the
business purpose of the use (driving to a convention, to see a team
member, from equipment rental to event site, etc.)

5. Crawford v. Commissioner, TC Memo 2014-156: Crawford tried to cor-
roborate his testimony of what he used his car for (namely driving to
meetings where he discussed sales of Vemma products, recruitment of
new agents, or both) using a pocket calendar full of handwritten notes
where it had both business and personal remarks on it, and numbers
that may or may not have been miles driven. The Court found that his
calendar was not reliable because it would have a location written on a
date, but his receipts showed he was in another location that day and/or
time. Crawford then admitted that some entries were incorrect. The
notations were also too vague and ambiguous for the Court to know
what to do with them as to determining Crawford's business use of his

vehicle. Crawford also admitted to his employer reimbursing him for many trips and adding personal expenses into his deductions. This case is a good example of business expenses lacking commercial substance. He not only failed to substantiate properly, but also seemed undecided on using actual cost of gas or standard mileage for his travel deductions.

6. §274(n): The cost of business-related meals is a deductible business expense, at least in part. §162(a) declares that payments for meals on business trips away from home are deductible business expenses, but §274(d)(4) clarifies that meal expenses are subject to strict substantiation requirements.

7. Publication 535 (https://www.irs.gov/publications/p535): Business Expenses

8. §1.274-5T(b)(2) Income Tax Regs.: Those four things your overnight travel records must contain. The expenses of travel away from home are subject to the strict substantiation requirements of section §274. §274(d)(1); §1.274-5T(b)(2), Temporary Income Tax Regs., 50 Fed. Reg. 46014 (Nov. 6, 1985). With respect to travel expenses, the taxpayer must show the amount of the expenditure, the date of departure and return for each trip, the number of days away from home spent on business, the destinations or locality of travel, and the business purpose of the travel. As previously stated, each of these elements must be proven by (1) adequate records or (2) other sufficient evidence corroborating the taxpayer's own statement. This also includes who paid: Going back to the 2014 Crawford case (TC Memo 2014-156), it's unclear as to whether Crawford paid those invoices or his employer did. Invoices alone isn't proof you actually paid for these things.

9. Danville Plywood Corp v. United States, 899 F.2d3: President of Danville Plywood invited his customers to the Super Bowl in New Orleans that included a hotel and riverboat cruise. Court declared that the business discussions were only incidental, the Super Bowl was the main attraction so the trip was purely for entertainment. Doesn't pass the "for only" test.

10. Blackshear v. Commissioner, TC Memo 1977-231: Minister Blackshear escorted a group of parishioners to Europe for a tour of

famous religious sites but couldn't demonstrate a profit motive, for himself or his church, for the trip.

11. §1.162-2(b)(1), Income Tax Regs.: If a trip is undertaken for both business and personal reasons, travel expenses are deductible only if the primary purpose of the trip is business.

12. §1.162-2(b)(2), Income Tax Regs.: Whether the primary purpose of the trip is business or personal depends on all the facts and circumstances, and particularly on the amount of time during the trip that the taxpayer devoted to business as compared to the time for personal activities. That second part means that if taking the trip just doesn't make sense without the personal elements, it's not going to be deductible. Just because you have some personal elements in the trip won't jettison your whole deduction, but the main reason you're traveling still needs to be for business.

13. Peppers v. Commissioner, TC Summary Opinion 2014-55: The Court sustains disallowing her travel and meals deductions for the trips she made that were supposedly meant to help her travel agency get reviews. Family members also went with her, which made it harder to prove that trips were for business, especially since reviews weren't published on the site and every trip was made with at least one family member.

14. §1.274-5T(c)(2), Temporary Income Tax Regs., 50 Fed. Reg. 46017 (Nov. 6, 1985): "To meet the adequate records requirements of §274, a taxpayer must maintain some form of records and documentary evidence that in combination are sufficient to establish each element of an expenditure or use." This means that you need something more than just a receipt or bank/charge statement to give your deduction merit. Like if you went to California for GDC, do you have your pass and program? Tweets you sent during that time that prove you were there? If you don't have any of those things, at the very least do you have a confirmation email that you attended? For trips that aren't conventions, what about proof of what you did in these other places such as email and text trails that confirm meetings and plans?

15. McClellan v. Commissioner, TC Memo 2014-257: The couple's company, BCMC, had proof of payment for meals from their bank

statements along with several theater ticket stubs. For the three years they got audited, they spent $19,200, $35,800, and $36,640 on meals and entertainment. The Court declares that the McClellans failed to substantiate whether these meals and entertainment were connected to their travel or to business dinners and entertainment with colleagues: Merely having proof of payment and attendance isn't enough. Thus, the Court slashed their deductible meals and entertainment down to $103, $9,603, and $4,708 respectively for each year. And that's *before* the 50% limit.

16. §1.274-5T(c)(1), Temporary Income Tax Regs., 50 Fed. Reg. 46016-46017 (Nov. 6, 1985): "A contemporaneous log is not required, but corroborative evidence to support a taxpayer's reconstruction of the elements of expenditure or use must have 'a high degree of probative value to elevate such statement' to the Level of credibility of a contemporaneous record." This means that while you need not keep a day-to-day journal with a captain's log of what you did at certain times of the day, it certainly helps. If you don't keep a journal of sorts, then you need other proof that what you were doing on this business trip was well...business. It's not that hard to prove this for expos and conventions, because you'll have PDFs of programs you can download online plus the justification letters on their websites. But it can be a lot harder to prove this for meeting a dev team member, publisher, or other business relationship.

17. Hynes v. Commissioner, 74 T.C. 1266 (1980): Hynes worked as a television news anchor and deducted wardrobe, laundry and dry cleaning, haircuts and makeup. He purchased a particular wardrobe that was restricted in terms of color and pattern that he was able to wear on the air. The Court reasoned that the restriction on his selection of business attire was not significantly different from that applicable to other business professionals who must also limit their selection of clothing to conservative styles and fashions. The Court further reasoned that the fact that Hynes didn't want to wear this wardrobe while away from the station did not signal that the clothing was unsuitable for private and personal wear.

18. Tax Topic 415: Renting Residential and Vacation Property

19. §274(h)(1): If a convention is held outside of North America, you must establish that the meeting is directly related to your trade/-business and that it is as reasonable for it to be held outside of North America.

20. United Title Insurance Co. v. Commissioner, TC Memo 1988-38: The sole owner of North Carolina-based United Title Insurance sponsored out-of-state board meetings every year in major cities far from home. He held meetings in New Orleans, Las Vegas, and Puerto Rico and would invite 11-14 board members, his employees, and several business guests. These guests were North Carolina real estate attorneys, land developers, real estate agents, bankers, lenders, and their spouses and friends. During these meetings, United conducted the annual board meeting then his employees met with the guests to discuss underwriting policies and other topics related to the title business. With the exception of the expenses for the spouses and friends of the business guests, the expenses were deductible. United had to hold the meetings in interesting locales to ensure that the guests would be interested in coming, and the company benefited through the business discussions and strengthening of their business relationships.

21. Private Letter Ruling 8228075: An American medical organization that only had American members held its convention in Paris. Members that attended did not get a deduction. But they would've if their organization had an *international* membership, where surgeons from around the world shared knowledge and techniques. (Private Letter Rulings are IRS rulings for intensely complex transactions and situations where it doesn't escalate to Tax Court. They can be cited in audit defense, appeals, Tax Court, and legal research.)

22. IRS Newsroom: 2022 mileage increases (https://www.irs.gov/-newsroom/irs-increases-mileage-rate-for-remainder-of-2022)

LEVEL 12: TURN-BASED STRATEGY: DEPRECIATION OF BIG-TICKET ITEMS

1. §168: Everything you ever wanted to know about depreciation

2. Publication 551 (https://www.irs.gov/publications/p551): Basis of Assets

3. Publication 946 (https://www.irs.gov/publications/p946): How to Depreciate Property

4. Table 4-1 of Publication 946 (https://www.irs.gov/publications/-p946#en_US_2020_publink100068700) demonstrating depreciation methods

5. §179: Everything you ever wanted to know about expensing big-ticket items

6. Publication 463 (https://www.irs.gov/publications/p463): Travel, Entertainment, Gift, and Car Expenses

7. Car depreciation rates for both actual cost and standard mileage (https://www.irs.gov/publications/p463/ch04.html#en_US_2014_publink1000134864) in Publication 463, look under the header labeled "Maximum Depreciation Deduction for Cars Placed in Service Prior to 2018"

8. §1250: What you recapture upon selling an asset you've already depreciated, referred to as §1250 gain.

9. Publication 544 (https://www.irs.gov/publications/p544): Sales and Other Disposition of Assets

10. Form 4562 Instructions (https://www.irs.gov/instructions/i4562)

LEVEL 13: GONE HOME: THE DEAL WITH HOME OFFICE DEDUCTIONS

1. §280A(c)(1)(A): Your home must be your principal place of business

2. Commissioner v. Soliman, TC Memo 91-998; 506 U.S. 168, 113 S.Ct. 701: Appeal for the landmark case that established management and administrative duties relating to your business can negate the "focal point" test used in determining if a home office is really necessary, providing that none of the places where you work provide you with facilities to do these things.

3. Jackson v. Commissioner, 76 T.C. 696, 700 (1981): In identifying a taxpayer's principal place of business, the Tax Court often seeks to ascertain the "focal point" of their business activities.

4. Proposed Treas. Reg. 1.280A2(b)(3), 45 Fed.Reg. 52399 (1980), as amended, 48 Fed. Reg. 33320 (1983): Salespersons [506 U.S. 168, 172] would be entitled to home office deductions "even though they spend most of their time on the road, as long as they spend "a substantial amount of time on paperwork at home."

5. Baie v. Commissioner, 74 T.C. 105, 109 (1980)

6. Proposed Treas.Reg. 1.280A-2(g)(1), 45 Fed.Reg. 52399, 52404 (1980), as amended, 48 Fed.Reg. 33320, 33324 (1983): A portion of a dwelling unit is used exclusively "only if there is no use of that portion of the unit at any time during the taxable year other than for business purposes."

7. Weightman v. Commissioner, TC Memo 1981-301: The IRS disallowed a home office deduction for a taxpayer who used part of his bedroom as a home office. While it was disallowed based on the exclusive use rule, the Court found that there was actually nothing in the law which supported the idea that a home office must be an entire room in one's home.

8. Huang v. Commissioner, TC Summary Opinion 2002-93: The Court confirmed that they could allow the taxpayer a deduction for 75% of a room that was used exclusively for business, even though the entire room was not used for business purposes.

9. Hughes v. Commissioner, TC Memo 1981-140: The Court ruled that a home office could be located in what would be considered an unconventional place, such as a large walk-in closet, so long as the regular and exclusive rules were met for the space. If the home office occupies only an area of the home opposed to an entire room, it's even more important to segregate all personal activities from it. All relevant furniture and equipment must be confined to the specific home office area, not interspersed among personal items.

10. Publication 587 (https://www.irs.gov/publications/p587): Business Use of Your Home

11. Figuring depreciation of your home using Table A-7 in Publication 946 (https://www.irs.gov/publications/p946)

12. Revenue Procedure 2013-13: Outlines safe harbor rules for home office deduction in lieu of actual expenses

13. Publication 523 (https://www.irs.gov/publications/p523): Selling Your Home

14. §121: Excluded gain on home sale conditions

15. Hamacher v. Commissioner, 94 T.C. 348, 353 (1990): "Accordingly, in order to qualify under section 280A(c), a portion of petitioner's dwelling must be exclusively used on a regular basis as the principal place of business for his trade or business."

16. Williams v. Commissioner, T.C. Memo 1991-567: "The exclusive use test does not require that the portion of a room used for business must be separated physically from the rest of the room by a wall, partition, or other demarcation, but only that the absence of such a physical separation be a factor for the Court to weigh."

LEVEL 14: LATE GAME CONTENT: MINDING YOUR QBI

1. IRS Newsroom: QBI and the 2018 Tax Reform (https://www.irs.gov/-newsroom/qualified-business-income-deduction)

2. Instructions and Forms 8995 (https://www.irs.gov/instructions/i8995) and 8995-A to compute QBI

LEVEL 15: WHY YOUR FISCAL YEAR IS LIKE DINOSAURS LIVING WITH HUMANS

1. Publication 509 (https://www.irs.gov/publications/p509): Tax Calendars

2. §441(g): If you don't keep records, you must use a calendar year.

3. Publication 538 (https://www.irs.gov/publications/p538): Accounting Periods and Methods

4. §451(2)(a): Income is constructively received when an amount is credited to your account or made available to you without restriction. You need not have possession of it. If you authorize someone to be your agent and receive income for you, you are considered to have

received it when your agent receives it. Income is not constructively received if your control of its receipt is subject to substantial restrictions or limitations.

5. Publication 334 (https://www.irs.gov/publications/p334): Tax Guide For Small Businesses

6. §448: Limitations on who can use the cash method

7. Publication 535 (https://www.irs.gov/publications/p535): Business Expenses

8. Burck v. Commissioner, 63 TC 556 (1975) aff'd, 533 F.2d 768 (2d Cir. 1976): Prepayments which are purely tax-motivated may NOT be allowed as a current deduction, even if they meet the 12-month test. See also: McMullan v. United States, 686 F.2d 915 (Ct. Cl. 1982)

9. §461: General rule for tax year of a deduction

10. Revenue Ruling 74-607: Under the "earlier-of test," an accrual basis taxpayer receives income when (1) the required performance occurs, (2) payment therefore is due, or (3) payment therefore is made, whichever happens earliest. Under this test, an accrual basis taxpayer may be treated as a cash basis taxpayer when payment is received before the required performance and before the payment is actually due. (You definitely want to remember this if you're doing a Kickstarter.)

11. Form 3115 Instructions (https://www.irs.gov/instructions/i3115)

12. §166(a)(1): Deduction of bad debts in whole, §166(a)(2) for partial

LEVEL 16: HOW YOU TREAT DEVELOPMENT COSTS AND ALL THE GAMASUTRA CONTENT THAT FILLED YOU WITH FALSE HOPE ABOUT THE R&D CREDIT

1. §174(a) gave you the option to immediately expense all of your R&D expenditures, while §174(b) gave you the option to amortize with a minimum of five years; §174(b) is now the mandate.

2. Revenue Procedure 2000-50: Software development is included in R&D expenditures

3. §280C(c): You cannot take a double benefit for R&D

4. Memorandum from the IRS Chief Counsel on changes to the R&D credit (https://www.irs.gov/pub/irs-lafa/20214101f.pdf) (external PDF)

5. §41: R&D credit basics, the four-part test

6. §41(d)(4)(H): You can't claim the R&D credit for research/-experimentation that has been funded by a third party like a grant program or publisher. This also applies to individuals.

7. Fairchild Industries, Inc. v. United States, 71 F.3d 868: Fairchild tried to defend their stance that in order for their research to not be considered funded by a third party and thus eligible for the R&D credit, that they indeed took a risk and had substantial rights to the research's results. The Court found that Fairchild only got incidental benefits, not substantial rights.

8. §41(b)(2)(D): Types of wages that are allowed for the credit, and wages must be defined by §3401 which simply means there has to be an employee-employer relationship. Contingent labor where you contract someone out and give them a 1099 can't be used at 100% of the cost for the R&D credit.

9. §41(b)(2)(B) and Treasury Regulation §1.41-2(e): Only 65% of contractor pay can be used to calculate the credit

10. Form 6765 instructions (https://www.irs.gov/instructions/i6765)

LEVEL 17: RUBBER CHICKENS WITH PULLEYS IN THE MIDDLE (INVENTORY)

1. Schedule C instructions (https://www.irs.gov/instructions/i1040sc)

2. Publication 535 (https://www.irs.gov/publications/p535): Business Use of Your Home

3. Publication 587 (https://www.irs.gov/publications/p587): Business Use of Your Home

LEVEL 18: SALES TAX: TORMENT

1. Quill Corp. v. North Dakota, 504 U.S. 298 (1992): Landmark case declaring that businesses can't be forced to collect sales tax in states where they don't have presence.

2. South v. Wayfair, Inc. 2017 S.D. 56, 901 N. W. 2d 754, vacated and remanded: Landmark case that overturned Quill, granting state governments the authority to mandate businesses to collect and remit sales tax regardless of physical presence based on number of in-state transactions and/or revenue allocable to in-state customers.

3. National Bellas Hess, Inc. v. Department of Revenue of Illinois, 386 U.S. 753 (1967): held that if your only contact with the state charging sales tax is by mail then there's not enough substance to have nexus in that state.

LEVEL 19: CLASSIFICATION QUEST: DO I ISSUE A W-2 OR 1099?

1. Publication 15 (Circular E) (https://www.irs.gov/publications/p15) Employer's Tax Guide

2. Publication 15-A (https://www.irs.gov/publications/p15a), Employer's Supplementary Tax Guide

3. Publication 1779 (https://www.irs.gov/pub/irs-pdf/p1779.pdf): Independent Contractor or Employee? (external PDF of IRS brochure)

4. Revenue Ruling 87-41: 20-factor test

5. Tieberg v. California Unemployment Insurance Appeals Board 2 Cal.3d 943: Established that the right to control prevails over written and executed independent contractor agreements. See also: SG Borello & Sons Inc. v. Industrial Relations Board 48 Cal.3d 342

6. Employment Tax Regs §31.3401(c)-1(b) defines employer-employee relationship in extreme detail. Primary factor is the right to control and direct not just the results accomplished by the work done, but also HOW they do the work (details and means of finishing the job).

7. Vizcaino v. Microsoft Corp., 120 F.3d 1006 (9th Cir. 1997): When Microsoft had its payroll initially examined there wasn't an appeal that got dragged out to Tax Court. The IRS said the "freelancers" were employees, and Microsoft didn't challenge it. Backdated payroll taxes were paid but Vizcaino later led a class action upon reading the fine print of the generous benefits Microsoft employees were entitled to. District Court threw the case out, but Vizcaino won the appeal.

8. United States v. Silk, 331 U.S. 704 No. 312 (1947): Court upholds that Silk had detrimental reliance on the coal unloaders and retained the right to control how they performed the work even if Silk did not exercise it, and, thus, they were his employees, whereas the transporters had a more significant investment in their own trucks and were not considered a core aspect of Silk's operations.

LEVEL 20: WHERE IN THE WORLD ARE YOUR INTERNATIONAL DEV TEAM MEMBERS?

1. Publication 519 (https://www.irs.gov/publications/p519): US Tax Guide for Aliens

2. Revenue Procedures 80-56 and 84-54: Foreign employees of American businesses who want exemption from payroll taxes under the totalization agreement need to get a certificate of coverage from their home country and give it to the employer. See also: Revenue Ruling 92-9

3. Social Security Administration totalization agreement (https://www.ssa.gov/international/agreements_overview.html): List of countries in the agreement, with some details on how the agreement works

4. §1441: Tax withholding rules for non-resident aliens in general, default rate is 30%

5. §1446: Tax withholding rules for foreign partnerships that have effectively-connected income. §1446(b)(2)(A) says to use the highest personal tax rate in §1 if the foreign partner is not a corporation. For 2022, it is 37%.

6. Publication 515 (https://www.irs.gov/publications/p515): Withholding of Tax on Nonresident Aliens and Foreign Entities

7. Publication 901 (https://www.irs.gov/publications/p901): Tax Treaties

8. Form 1040NR instructions (https://www.irs.gov/instructions/i1040nr)

9. Form W-7 instructions (https://www.irs.gov/instructions/iw7)

10. Income Tax Regs. §1.864-4: Rules for US-sourced income effectively connected with US business. If those game royalties arose because you gave your services to that studio, it's business income, not a royalty. See also: §864(c)

11. Retief Goosen v. Internal Revenue Service, 136 TC 21 (2011): Goosen, a pro golfer and nonresident, had six endorsement contracts. Three of them were with clothing companies that required him to do things like play golf tournaments wearing their clothes and appear at events then in commercials in the same outfits, in addition to using his likeness to promote the clothes. The three other contracts (including one with Electronic Arts!) allowed the companies to use Goosen's likeness and name to promote their products, but they didn't interfere with his tournaments or require him to appear in commercials or otherwise use the products when he played. The Court decided that the clothing company endorsements were business income, but the Electronic Arts and other contracts that didn't involve Goosen going to the golf course were royalties and therefore, not effectively connected income. See also: Cepeda v. Swift & Co., 415 F.2d 1205 (8th Cir. 1969).

12. IRS International Taxpayer Division Information Page: Social Security Tax Consequences of Working Abroad (https://www.irs.gov/individuals/international-taxpayers/social-security-tax-consequences-of-working-abroad)

13. IRS International Taxpayer Division Information Page: Foreign Earned Income Exclusion (https://www.irs.gov/individuals/-international-taxpayers/foreign-earned-income-exclusion)

14. Publication 54 (https://www.irs.gov/publications/p54): Tax Guide for US Citizens and Resident Aliens Abroad

LEVEL 21: HOW TO CHOOSE AND WORK WITH A TAX PROFESSIONAL

1. Circular 230(https://www.irs.gov/pub/irs-pdf/pcir230.pdf): The tax professional's practice standards bible (external PDF)

2. Ellwest Stereo Theatres, Inc. v. Commissioner, TC Memo 1995-610: If you made some bad tax decisions, the IRS will be a little lenient depending on the tax matter, degree of severity, if there's reasonable reliance on a professional. Reasonable reliance applies if a tax advisor has sufficient expertise to justify that reliance (EA, CPA, tax attorney).

3. IRS Newsroom Archive: Loving case outcome (https://www.irs.gov/newsroom/irs-statement-on-court-ruling-related-to-return-preparers)

Index

20-factor test 250, 251, 263
§179 deduction 172–174, 177, 178, 211, 272
199(A) deduction 197
2018 tax reform 1, 20, 24–26, 51, 68, 84, 86, 114, 121–123, 134, 138, 140, 167, 170, 172, 175–177, 181, 196, 197, 221, 232

above the line 23, 24, 28, 29, 112, 113
accountant 2, 4, 10, 32, 40, 41, 80, 84, 92–94, 109, 110, 118, 128, 185, 223, 231, 267, 271, 272–275, 277, 278
accounting method 207, 208, 210, 212, 217, 219
accrual accounting 213–217
accumulated earnings tax 87, 90
actual [car] expenses 130–132, 175, 176
adjusted basis 165, 178
adjusted gross income (AGI) 24, 25, 27–29, 56, 68, 69, 121, 199, 200, 202–204
adjustments 24–26, 193, 199, 200, 204
administrative expenses 105, 107
AFR see applicable federal interest rate (AFR)
AGI see adjusted gross income (AGI)
amortization 95, 96, 98, 99, 164
applicable federal interest rate (AFR) 46–48
articles of incorporation 87
assets 9, 32, 35, 45, 59, 60–61, 77, 95, 110, 114, 164, 165, 167, 170, 171, 174, 177, 200, 201, 223, 226, 229, 237, 238, 278
at-risk limitations 79

bad debts 218
Baie v. Commissioner 185–186
basis 41, 76–79, 103, 104, 111, 158, 165–166, 170, 171, 176–178, 203, 204, 224, 230, 251, 257
basis calculation 77–79
below the line 23, 24, 26, 28, 29, 199
bonus depreciation 117, 134, 140, 213
bookkeeping 170, 172, 186, 238, 272, 273
books and records 32, 57
book value 165, 171
business entities 17, 34, 35, 38, 53, 57, 60, 71–93, 97, 117, 165, 209, 265
business formalities 66, 74, 88, 89–90
business gifts 109–110
business loss 56, 122, 174
business property 175, 178–179, 204
business taxes 11, 14, 19, 26, 37, 68, 88, 106, 211, 276
business travel 111, 118, 132, 139, 142, 143, 148, 150, 158, 161, 279
business vs. hobby 54, 56, 58, 66–67, 69, 120

capital contribution 41, 45, 47, 49, 272
capital expenditures 103, 165
CARES Act 25, 123
carry-back 122–123
carry-forward 122–123
cash accounting 41, 210–212
cash payments 43
C corporation 14, 72, 75, 76, 83, 84–87, 113, 121, 173, 174, 198, 212, 229, 238, 239, 264, 265
Certified Public Accountants (CPAs) 3, 274, 275, 280–282

closely-held corporation 85, 90, 134–135
COGS *see* cost of goods sold (COGS)
Cohan Rule 102–105, 126, 144
Cohan v. Commissioner 103–105
commercial substance 118, 119, 140
Commissioner of the IRS 53
Commissioner v. Groetzinger 56–57
Complete Auto Transit v. Mississippi 244
conference deductions 94, 96, 133, 154,
        155, 159
constructive receipt 210–212
convention deductions 96, 107, 109, 133,
        142, 144–145, 148, 158–161, 165,
        169, 171, 175, 213
conventions 37, 96, 107, 109, 126–128, 133,
        138, 142–145, 147–149, 151, 153,
        161, 165, 166, 168, 169–171, 186,
        213, 236, 237, 242, 246, 252,
        255, 261
corporate income tax 14, 84, 86, 106, 231
corporation 14, 15, 38, 46, 72, 74, 75, 76,
        79–90, 112, 121, 134, 198, 199,
        229, 231, 243, 269
cost of goods sold (COGS) 238–239
cost recovery 94–95
credit cards 33, 35, 37, 38, 48, 94, 105, 150,
        165, 218–219
credits 23–29, 53, 69, 226, 231, 280
crowdfunding 6, 17, 40, 51, 63, 83, 85,
        215–217, 219, 228, 236, 237, 240,
        246, 247

Danville Plywood Corp. vs. United States
        134–135
*David E. Watson, P.C., v. United States of
        America* 80
DBA 88–89
deductions 19, 20, 23–29, 33, 37, 38, 53,
        56, 68, 69, 71, 76, 93, 95–97,
        102–106, 109, 110, 112–115,
        117–121, 123, 125, 126,
        129–134, 136–150, 153–155,
        157, 158, 160, 161, 166, 167–179,
        181–205, 209, 211, 213, 217, 218,
        223, 224, 226, 227, 230–232,
        237–239, 272
default rule 74–76
Department of Defense 147–148

depreciation 98, 130, 163, 164–179,
        191–194, 196, 204, 213, 272
detrimental reliance 63–65, 255, 258
digital download tax 247
digital payment processor 34, 105, 126
direct expenses 190–193
disposal 23, 168, 173, 177
disregarded entity 74
distributions 42, 78–83, 86, 105, 198, 243,
        244, 264, 265
dividends 10, 11, 80, 81, 87, 117, 200, 268
doing business as 88–89
Dormant Commerce Clause 242, 245
double-declining balance (DDB) 170–172,
        174, 177
drawings 41, 73, 77, 78, 231, 272
due process 244, 247, 275, 276
Dutch rule 140, 148

earned income 10, 11, 270
economic reality test 250
educational expenses 17, 112
effectively-connected income 267–269
EIN *see* employer identification number
        (EIN)
employee 3, 11–13, 26, 61, 72, 73, 79, 82,
        83, 85, 91, 97, 104, 112, 120–123,
        134–137, 143, 146, 147, 149, 151,
        154, 181, 201, 224–226, 229, 230,
        244, 249–259, 262, 263, 265,
        272, 281
employer identification number (EIN) 89,
        90–91, 246, 263, 268, 270
Engdahl v. Commissioner 64–65
Enrolled Agent 3, 275, 280
entertainment expenses 33, 125–161
excluded gain 195, 196
exclusion 16, 17, 23–29, 47, 48, 153,
        200, 270
exemption 19, 25, 263, 264
expat taxes 269–270
expense report 37–38, 43, 144, 149, 271
experimental costs 94, 98, 99, 222, 223,
        230, 232

Fair Labor Standards Act (FLSA) 250
family loans 46–47, 48
fictitious business name filing 88–89

finished goods 236
fiscal year 146, 147, 207–219
five-year property 166, 169, 176
flow-through entity 71, 79, 85, 86
FLSA *see* Fair Labor Standards Act (FLSA)
foreign business partner 86–88, 262,
    264–265, 269
foreign employees 262, 263
foreign travel 148
Form 1040 23–25, 27, 266
Form 1065 76, 85
Form 1120 85
Form 2553 75
Form 8995-A 203
Form 8822-B 89
Form 1099-K 270
Form 1099-MISC 42, 250, 263
Form 1099-NEC 250, 263
Form 1042-S 263, 264
Form 1120S 85
Form W-2 12, 14, 81, 113, 122, 204, 226,
    249–259, 263, 270
Form W-7 267
Form W-9 89, 262
for only rule 142, 143
franchise tax 15, 36, 75, 106, 276
freelancers 6, 29, 82, 94, 97, 208, 226, 230,
    249–254, 256, 265
funding 17, 27, 36, 45–51, 53, 61, 62, 66,
    138, 160, 228

GAAP *see* generally accepted accounting
    principles (GAAP)
generally accepted accounting principles
    (GAAP) 40, 273
general partner 78, 79
General Service Administration 146
gifts 16, 17, 28, 46–48, 71, 109, 110, 196,
    198, 238
gift-splitting 47
gift tax 16, 17, 47, 48
Glass Blocks Unlimited v. Commissioner 82
government grants 50, 91
grants 49–50, 66, 86, 210, 228, 232

Hamper v. Commissioner 151
HEALS Act 140
health insurance 24, 25, 27, 111–114

hobby loss 56, 63, 87, 101, 102, 121, 255
home-based business 107, 181
home office deduction 123, 142, 167,
    181–196, 198, 239
Huang v. Commissioner 188
hybrid method 3
Hynes v. Commissioner 151

income tax 9, 10–12, 14, 15, 17, 25, 27, 43,
    71, 76, 84, 86, 102, 106, 118, 231,
    247, 263, 276
incorporation 9, 15, 76, 87, 88, 90, 93,
    95, 96
independent contractor 3, 72, 81, 149–150,
    229, 230, 249–258, 262–264
indirect expenses 190–193
industry code 54, 91–92
Inflation Reduction Act 1, 122
I-9 form 263
insurance 12, 13, 24, 25, 27, 59, 61, 64,
    65, 72, 79, 111, 131, 148, 168,
    190–193, 213, 237, 250, 256
interest 24, 37, 46–48, 57, 58, 76, 77, 80, 94,
    96, 108, 138, 157, 190–193, 195,
    210, 231
Internal Revenue Service Restructuring
    and Reform Act of 1998 275
international conventions 153, 158–161
international tax identification number
    (ITIN) 263, 264, 267, 268
international travel 153–157
inventoriable costs 237
inventory 33, 41, 107, 123, 212, 233,
    235–240
investors 15, 17, 40, 48–51, 62, 76, 78–79,
    83, 85, 94, 136, 138, 228
IRS correspondence 36
itemized deduction 23–25, 68, 112, 113
ITIN *see* international tax identification
    number (ITIN)

limited liability company (LLC) 15, 72,
    73, 74–78, 83, 86, 88, 92, 102,
    113, 122, 173, 199, 202, 256, 264,
    265, 268
limited partner 78–79
listed property 166–168, 174, 175, 177, 178
LLC *see* limited liability company (LLC)

loans 24, 46–48, 94, 165, 228, 277
local travel 126, 142, 143, 161

McAlary LTD v. Commissioner 81
MACRS *see* modified accelerated cost
    recovery system (MACRS)
marketing expenses 107, 108, 217, 226,
    238, 239
meal expenses 118, 133, 138, 139, 150
misclassification 252, 254, 256, 257–259,
    264, 282
modified accelerated cost recovery system
    (MACRS) 163, 169, 170, 171
M.T. Shane v. Commissioner 64–66

NAICS code *see* North American Industry
    Classification System (NAICS
    code)
*National Bellas Hess v. Department of
    Revenue of Illinois* 243
net operating loss (NOL) 51, 83, 86,
    117–123, 173, 190, 192, 193,
    226, 232
networking expenses 108–109, 134, 273
nexus 28, 33–34, 242–246
Nickerson v. Commissioner 64
NOL *see* net operating loss (NOL)
nondeductible items 117–123, 134
non-employer 71–73, 79, 82, 91, 198, 204,
    224–226, 231–232, 256, 259
nonrefundable credit 26, 27, 29
nonresident alien 265–266
North American Industry Classification
    System (NAICS code) 91

office expense 105, 192, 193, 195, 211
Office of Return Preparers 279
operating loss 51, 82, 83, 86, 117–123
ordinary and necessary 102–105, 117, 118
ordinary rate 11, 268
organizational costs 93–99, 164, 208
overnight travel 143–144
owner drawings 41, 78

partnership 74–81, 83, 85, 199, 264,
    265, 268
pass-through entity 71, 85, 87, 121, 232
payment in kind 114

payroll taxes 11–13, 72, 79, 80, 83, 229,
    249, 250, 255–258, 263, 264
Peppers v. Commissioner 118
per diem rates 146–148
per donee exclusion 16, 47, 48
personal income taxes 10, 11, 84
preferential rate 11
prepaid expenses 212–213
professional corporation 80
professional services 110, 200
profits 10, 28, 50, 54–56, 61–66, 68, 73,
    76–87, 101, 107, 108, 113, 121,
    137, 143, 161, 166, 173, 190–193,
    195, 196, 198–200, 202–204, 209,
    210, 212, 228, 238, 239, 253, 264,
    265, 267
Protecting Americans against Tax Hikes
    Act (PATH Act) 224
publication affidavit 88, 96

QBI *see* qualified business income (QBI)
qualified business income (QBI) 26,
    197–205
qualified joint venture 21
Quill Corp v. North Dakota 243–244

raw materials 236
R&D treatment 27, 29, 94, 98, 99, 221–233
reasonable compensation 79–84, 85,
    86, 226
recapture 176–178, 195, 196
receipts 33, 35, 37, 38, 41, 43, 67, 102–105,
    111, 126, 130, 138, 144, 145–150,
    153, 210–212, 244, 278
recordkeeping 2, 19, 31–43, 66, 89,
    104, 118, 167, 170, 172, 209,
    210, 225, 230, 235, 246, 247,
    270, 278
refundable credit 27, 29, 226
rent expenses 107
resale certificate 246
research and experimentation costs 94, 95,
    222, 223, 224
Research and Experimentation Tax
    Credit 224
research expenses 33, 95, 98, 104, 120,
    221, 222

resident alien 265–266
R.L. Vitale Jr. v. Commissioner 120

sales tax 15–16, 25, 33–34, 43, 106, 131,
    152, 236, 239–248, 276, 277
SBA *see* Small Business Administration
    (SBA)
Schedule C 34, 73, 76, 113, 268
Schedule K-1 76, 78, 85
S corporation 14, 79–86, 113, 121, 199,
    226, 230, 264, 265
self-employment tax 13–14, 24, 27, 29, 68,
    69, 73, 77, 79, 80, 82, 83, 85, 87,
    113, 123, 191, 192, 196, 199, 200,
    202, 204, 262, 268, 270, 272
Silk v. United States 254–255
simplified home office deduction 182,
    194–195
Small Business Administration (SBA)
    71, 72
Social Security number 36, 90, 91, 263,
    269, 270
sole proprietorship 73, 75, 77–79, 83, 117,
    191, 199, 202, 268
Soliman v. Commissioner 184–186
specified service trades or businesses
    (SSTBs) 199–203
SSTBs specified service trades or
    businesses (SSTBs)
standard deduction 19, 24–27, 68, 199
standard meals allowance 145–148
standard mileage 129–132, 145, 146,
    148, 176
startup costs 93–99
State Department 148
state tax department 5, 247, 275–276
straight-line depreciation 170–172
supplies expenses 252

tabletop 42, 43, 51, 235, 245
tax bracket 11, 83

Tax Court 2, 7, 9, 33, 53, 56, 57, 59–65, 68,
    81, 86, 102–104, 108, 119, 120,
    125, 134, 150, 182, 184–185, 188,
    216, 279, 282
Tax Cuts and Jobs Act 167
tax ID 66, 262–263
tax professional 2, 4, 6, 7, 20, 26, 31, 32, 41,
    42, 60, 78, 119, 131, 163, 166, 172,
    197, 231, 262, 271–283
tax refund 9
tax return 3, 6, 7, 9, 10, 12–14, 17, 19, 20,
    23, 26–28, 55, 56, 73, 76–78,
    85–87, 89, 96, 104, 106, 112, 113,
    121, 122, 130, 150, 173, 198, 199,
    209–211, 238, 243, 246, 247, 250,
    264–267, 269, 270, 272, 273,
    279, 282
tax treaty 261, 264–268
tax year 11, 47, 51, 77, 78, 95, 98, 123, 132,
    136, 172, 191, 199, 200, 202, 205,
    209, 210, 214, 215, 217, 232,
    250, 266
tentative profit 190–193, 195
totalization agreement 263, 268, 270
transfer tax 16–17
travel expenses 102, 120, 149, 154, 163
TurboTax defense 279

unearned income 10–11

Vizcaino v. Microsoft 254
voluntary settlement program 257

Wayfair v. South Dakota 34
Welch v. Helvering 103
worker misclassification 250, 251, 282
workers compensation 79, 257
work-in-process 236
W-9 verification 89, 262

Zidar v. Commissioner 58

Printed in the United States
by Baker & Taylor Publisher Services

Printed in the United States
by Baker & Taylor Publisher Services